Spinning Wheels

The Politics of Urban School Reform

Frederick M. Hess

BROOKINGS INSTITUTION PRESS

Washington, D.C.

ABOUT BROOKINGS

The Brookings Institution is a private nonprofit organization devoted to research, education, and publication on important issues of domestic and foreign policy. Its principal purpose is to bring knowledge to bear on current and emerging policy problems. The Institution maintains a position of neutrality on issues of public policy. Interpretations or conclusions in Brookings publications should be understood to be solely those of the authors.

Library of Congress Cataloging-in-Publication data

Hess, Frederick M.
    Spinning wheels : the politics of urban school reform / by
Frederick M. Hess.
        p. cm.
Includes bibliographical references.
ISBN 0-8157-3636-3 (cloth : permanent paper)
ISBN 0-8157-3635-5 (pbk. : permanent paper)
1. Education, Urban–United States–Administration–Case studies.
2. Education, Urban–Political aspects–United States–Case studies.
3. Educational change–United States–Case studies. I. Title.
                                                                            98-25373
LC5131 .H44 1998   CIP
370'.9173'2–ddc21

Digital printing

The paper used in this publication meets minimum requirements of the American National Standard for Information Sciences—Permanence of Paper for Printed Library Materials: ANSI Z39.48-1984.

Typeset in Times Roman

Composition by AlphaWebTech
Mechanicsville, Maryland

Preface

It seems so hopeful. The city school board hires a promising, new superintendent, the local papers are filled with accolades and testimonials to his or her acumen, and the new administration announces a wave of exciting initiatives amid bountiful goodwill. The community eagerly awaits active leadership and cutting-edge reforms, interpreting them as evidence that the superintendent is serious about the task. Far too often, however, this exciting beginning comes to naught. Within two to three years the once-revered leader either has disappointed or departed, leaving the task of leadership to a new white knight. Before too long, the dance begins again.

This same sad drama has played out repeatedly in urban school districts in recent years as people of hope and goodwill are repeatedly frustrated in their efforts to help urban youth. In this volume, I suggest that efforts to end this frustrating cycle have been fundamentally misguided. Conventional accounts too often rely on the Goldilocks principle when reviewing past superintendent performance and considering fresh candidates. The refrain tends to be, "This one was too hot, and the one before was too cold, but the next one will be just right." Seeking to explain the inability of one reform wave after another to improve urban schools, academics and policymakers consider curricula and pedagogy, the characteristics of teachers and principals, and various other aspects of educational practice.

However, a fundamental reason that regime after regime fails to produce lasting and significant improvement in urban school systems is the conditions under which urban school administrators operate. Given the constraints they face, the incentives that encourage an emphasis on symbolic leadership, and the nature of their job, it would be surprising if they regularly produced sustained school system improvement. The structure of contemporary urban schooling in the United States has perversely managed to harness high hopes and good intentions in such a way that they produce bad results. I explore this situation in the following pages before considering how new institutional arrangements might modify the frustrating spinning of wheels that characterizes urban education.

I should offer a warning. This book contains no quick, easy solutions to the problems examined. I can offer no magic bullet. In fact, I believe our love affair with miracle remedies has been a serious obstacle to significant school improvement. I hope the reader will consider the proposals discussed in the conclusion in the spirit they are offered, which is to help launch a discussion on how to refocus leadership in urban school systems. And the reader should be aware that every potential remedy I discuss may produce undesirable consequences. I hope this will direct discussion away from arguments about which pedagogy or curriculum is best and toward a consideration of how to make it more likely that any approach will improve schooling.

This book had its genesis in the early 1990s. I trace the basic insights here to my own experiences as a public school teacher in one urban district and a supervisor of student teachers in another during that period. Those ideas were instrumental in helping me make sense of the results that emerged from the mountain of data I collected in 1995 while trying to study the nature of school system agendas. I will leave it to the reader to determine the value of these insights.

Support for the research was generously provided by National Science Foundation grant SBR 95-10489 and by Mellon Foundation Dissertation Research and Dissertation Completion fellowships.

Dozens of people assisted me with various elements of the current project. Particularly important were Paul E. Peterson, Richard F. Elmore, and Gary King, all of whom helped me develop the research and then generously contributed their advice and guidance throughout the course of the project. I would also like to thank Alan A. Altshuler, John Ameer, David W. Brady, Eric Bredo, Nancy E. Burns, Michael Casserly, Terry N. Clark, Matthew Dickinson, Morris Fiorina, Michael G. Hagen, Walter Heinecke, Amy Kantrowitz, David L. Leal, Tom Loveless, Bob McNergney, Kay Merseth, Gary Orfield, Bradley Palmquist, H. Douglas Price, Diane Ravitch, Theda Skocpol, Kevin Smith, Clarence N. Stone, Sarah Turner, Sidney Verba, and several anonymous reviewers for their assistance, advice, and suggestions at various points in my research. Thanks also go to Cheri Grand for her marketing advice. For support of a different kind, I thank Todd Anderman, Loren Baron, Mandy Magallanes, Scott Orenstein, David Romano, Dave Walsh, and Eric Yanco. I would like to offer a special thanks to Stephanie Timmons and Phyllis Palmore for their invaluable organizational and research skills.

Nancy Davidson at Brookings was tremendously supportive as editor. Barbara de Boinville edited the manuscript, Joanne Lockard and Mariah Seagle proofread the pages, and Susan Fels compiled the index. Of course, all opinions expressed are mine alone and any errors are attributable solely to me.

To my mom and dad,
for all their love and support through the years

Contents

Figures

PART ONE
The Politics

1

The Politics of
Urban School Reform

True leadership takes time. A desert thunderstorm strikes with
a flash and a roar, releasing all its water and energy at once.
But the flashes quickly fade, and the water is mostly lost in
runoff. Effective leadership takes the time to allow efforts and
skills the chance to sink in, as opposed to the flash-flood phenomenon of high-visibility attempts at quick fixes.

TOM KEAN, *former governor of New Jersey*[1]

ONE OF THE FEW POINTS of unanimity in contemporary American politics is the belief that urban
schooling is in dramatic need of improvement. In recent decades this belief
has helped to promote the waves of reform that have swept American education and then dissipated without producing sustained change. Why have
such widely endorsed reform efforts proved so ephemeral? Why has so
much experimentation produced so little significant change?

The problem is not with the individual reforms, but with the nature of
the reform enterprise itself.[2] In most cases "reform" efforts are not the solution to problems in urban schooling and are only incidentally about im-

1. See his introduction to Bacharach (1990, xiv).

2. In this book, "education reform" is defined as efforts planned to change schools in order to
correct perceived educational problems. The particular reforms discussed are the district-oriented
Third Wave reforms proposed in the early 1990s. This definition of reform is derived from the
work of Tyack and Cuban (1995, 4), who define educational reforms as "planned efforts to change
schools in order to correct perceived social and educational problems." Because this book focuses
on efforts to improve school performance and not to reshape schooling, Tyack and Cuban's "social
problems" dimension is excluded. The reforms examined in this book are primarily what Rich
(1996, 7) has termed "procedural reforms," emphasizing "the introduction of new and different
pedagogical processes."

3

proving education at all. In fact, fascination with reform is a distraction that does not add substantive value and may have negative consequences. The frenetic embrace of new approaches is not productive, largely because the very institutional incentives that drive reform activity also make likely the failure of individual reforms. Policymakers are driven by professional and community pressures to initiate a great deal of activity, because it demonstrates leadership and steers the local education agenda onto politically and professionally comfortable ground.

Of course, schooling is rarely discussed in these terms. This book is based upon a recent study of fifty-seven school districts. The study was originally designed to trace the diffusion and rhythms of Third Wave school reform, rather than to critique the very premise of reform.[3] However, interviews with more than 300 highly placed observers strongly suggested an underlying political dynamic. Although very few respondents cited reform efforts as consciously political, one after another described behavior that fit a pattern of symbolic activity. It is precisely because school reform is not seen as political that it is symbolically effective. If reform were merely seen as political posturing, it would no longer convey the hopeful message that "things will get better soon."

Although previous research has suggested that urban school systems are largely insulated from electoral politics, urban school system policymakers are highly sensitive to community and professional pressures.[4] The conse-

3. Since 1983 American schools have experienced three distinct waves of school reform. The first began immediately before publication of *A Nation at Risk*, the 1983 government report on the condition of American schools. State governors and legislators sought to remedy perceived shortcomings in their schools with formal, top-down measures: more rigorous academic standards for students and higher professional standards for teachers. The First Wave did not assume that education needed to be fundamentally changed, but sought to improve the existing delivery system through a more rigorous curriculum, longer school days, more highly qualified teachers, and more homework. See Passow (1990).

The Second Wave of reform emerged in the late 1980s and focused on school-level changes: new forms of accountability, school restructuring, site-based management, and teacher empowerment and professionalism. It emphasized the need to remake schools from the ground up, one building at a time. See Kirst (1990).

The Third Wave of reform was premised on the notion that the first two waves had failed because American education needed to be restructured at the school district level. Beginning in the early 1990s, the Third Wave was interwoven with the advent of research calling for "systemic school reform." District leaders tried to alter teaching practice by decentralizing power within school districts, increasing time for teacher planning and preparation, changing the classroom role of the teacher from that of lecturer to that of guide, emphasizing problem-solving skills, using alternative assessments to measure student learning, grouping students in new ways, integrating more small group and tutorial instructional sessions into the school day, and clustering teachers into teams. See Olson and Rothman (1993).

4. See Cibulka and Olsen (1993), Wirt and Kirst (1972), and Zeigler and Jennings (1974) for a discussion of the insulation of schools from traditional electoral politics. Political scientists such as

quence is that reform efforts are more heavily influenced by political pressures than by educational considerations.[5] District policymakers constantly embrace politically attractive changes, producing prodigious amounts of reform at a pace inimical to effective implementation. As a result, these reforms do not significantly alter the nature of schooling, but they do manage to frustrate, confuse, and finally alienate faculty.[6] In fact, a state of constant reform is the status quo in urban school systems.

Recent statistics point out the magnitude of the problem: "America's troubled urban schools are particularly worrisome because their performance conspires to keep a vast army of disadvantaged students from ever having a chance to develop their gifts. During the 1993–94 school year, central city public schools enrolled more than twelve million children, representing more than 29 percent of the nation's students."[7]

Reform Is the Status Quo

Reform essentially becomes a tool that legitimizes the performance of urban school districts.[8] By embracing reform, policymakers recognize public dissatisfaction with urban school performance and promise that improvement is around the corner. Not only are districts pursuing an immense number of reforms, they recycle initiatives, constantly modify previous initiatives, and adopt innovative reform A to replace practice B even as another district is adopting B as an innovative reform to replace practice A.

The collective exercise of reform has become a spinning of wheels. More and more energy is expended in an effort that goes nowhere. Like a car stuck on a muddy road, urban school districts have not benefited from simply spinning the wheels more and more rapidly. Getting urban schools

---

Meier and Stewart (1991) have discussed the responsiveness of schools to community pressures, while education scholars such as Kowalski (1995) have discussed the susceptibility of school leaders to professional pressures.

5. Many educators express a desire to "leave the schools out of politics." Although reformers have long thought that "cleaning streets, running schools, and collecting garbage ought to be no more controversial, and therefore no more political, than selling groceries . . . politics, like sex, cannot be abolished." Public school administrators and policymakers spend public money, are hired by political figures, and deal with issues in the public realm. Public schools are political, whether or not decisions are made on partisan grounds and regardless of whether the decision-makers think of themselves as politicians. See Banfield and Wilson (1963, 1, 20).

6. Hill, Pierce, and Guthrie (1997, 48) have observed that "the succession of conflicting initiatives has made school staffs cynical about the motives and competence of their superiors and tentative in the implementation of any particular reform."

7. U.S. Department of Education (1996, 70).

8. Meyer and Rowan (1991, 57) have noted that one way in which organizations attempt to maintain legitimacy when unable to rely on demonstrated outcomes is by promising reform: "People may picture the present as unworkable but the future as filled with promising reforms of both structure and activity."

unstuck requires a shift in emphasis—away from the pursuit of the curricular or pedagogical "silver bullet" that will *really* work—and toward an understanding of why urban school systems engage in reform and why nearly every reform produces disappointing results.[9] Insufficient attention to the larger framework within which school reform is pursued has crippled efforts to understand the failure of school reform.

Urban school systems are governed by a superintendent who drives district policy. Influential and visible, the superintendent becomes the lightning rod for all things, good and bad. Meanwhile, school districts are overseen by amateur school boards that are responsible for policy. Board members are held accountable for the sustained mediocre performance of urban schools, but they have little power to generate short-term solutions. As a result, they rely on the professional school personnel, placing superintendents "under tremendous pressure to produce short-term results. Many feel they must undertake everything all at once in every school in order to prove their worth."[10] Crucially, these efforts at reform rarely challenge the "grammar" of teaching and learning, largely because of political obstacles and potential conflicts.[11]

Alexis de Tocqueville once wrote, "America is a land of wonders in which everything is in constant motion and every change seems an improvement." School reform is premised on the belief that the troubled state of urban education is from current practice and that dramatic changes are needed, a belief that has fed the professional education community's inclination to innovate. Active administrators enhance their professional reputation and community stature. The belief that innovation will eventually bring improvement is not unique to education. Researchers generally presume that more innovation is the mark of a good organization.[12] The problem is that quick fixes and short-term leadership have distracted attention

---

9. An editorial in the Baton Rouge, Louisiana, daily newspaper expressed the popular frustration with school reform: "And so it goes: Another superintendent, another 'reform' School Board, and yet another generation of East Baton Rouge Parish public school children will exit the schools only marginally prepared to compete." See *The Advocate* (1997, 6B). A similar editorial in a Cleveland paper noted, "The job of superintendent in an urban district is a meat grinder. . . . But there's no doubt changing captains every few years at the Cleveland schools has led to an errant ship of state that badly suffers from a lack of continuity and clear direction. . . . It's unfair to expect the superintendent to keep too many plates spinning in the air at the same time." See *Crains Cleveland Business* (1995, 10).

10. Wagner (1994, 79).

11. See Tyack and Tobin (1994).

12. See Elmore (1991a).

from improving instruction, constructing positive school cultures, and encouraging and rewarding professional competence.

This churning of reform distracts faculty from the core functions of teaching and learning. Evidence on the performance of parochial schools and high-performing schools suggests that the best schools are able to develop expertise in specific approaches.[13] School improvement requires time, focus, and the commitment of core personnel. To succeed, the leadership must focus on selected reforms and then nurture those efforts in the schools. The very good schools "often aren't very innovative; indeed, their main strength often seems to be that they persist in, and develop increasingly deep understandings of, well-developed theories of teaching and learning."[14] Churning through a series of short-term initiatives does not necessarily cause urban school districts to perform poorly, and the present research cannot quantify the impact that policy churn has on school performance. However, a wealth of research on school reform suggests that reforms fail because of inadequate implementation, planning, and coordination, precisely the problems that result from policy churn.[15]

"American education is awash in faddish innovations that sweep through the profession," notes Chester E. Finn, the former assistant secretary of education. "Because of this faddishness, American education often appears to be in the throes of ceaseless change. Yet few of these innovations endure. Fewer yield improved results. And nearly all of them are made within the boundaries of the old design."[16]

The stop and start nature of reform activity particularly damages school culture by discouraging cooperation and reducing motivation among teachers who "have watched wave after wave of educational 'reform'" come and go.[17] Teachers' behavior is shaped by their experiences, their relationships with fellow teachers and administrators, the institutional de-

13. See research by Bryk, Lee, and Holland (1993) and Lee (1997) on parochial schools. See Chubb and Moe (1990); Lightfoot (1983); and Purkey and Smith (1985) on high-performing schools.

14. See Elmore (1991a, 38).

15. Some research has even suggested that schools that engage in too many reforms hurt student outcomes. See Bryk and others (1993); Kyle (1993); and Lee and Smith (1994). This evidence is not yet well established, and these school-level results say little about district-level effects, but the findings are entirely consistent with the present argument. See chapter 7 for a more detailed discussion of the effects of policy churn.

16. Finn (1997, 229).

17. Mohrman and Lawler (1996, 117).

mands of their role, and the culture of their school.[18] As policy churn increases the stress and uncertainty of teaching, teachers learn to view school reform efforts with a skeptical eye. As a result, teachers have discouraging personal experiences with reform and learn to view reform efforts as an institutional imposition. Veteran teachers then help to foster a cynical school culture in which teachers will disregard new reforms once they are safely behind the closed doors of their classrooms.

Recent large-scale data on teaching practice help to illustrate this problem. The Third International Mathematics and Science Study, conducted during the 1995 school year, was hailed by the U.S. Department of Education as the "largest, most comprehensive, and most rigorous international comparison ever undertaken." U.S. students, according to the study, performed poorly in math and science compared with their peers in other nations. More significantly, for our purposes, the study included the first large-scale observational study of U.S. teaching ever undertaken. Several elements of teaching practice in the United States compared unfavorably with practice in higher performing German and Japanese schools. Most U.S. math teachers "report familiarity with reform recommendations," but "only a few apply the key points in their classrooms." The report also suggests that "U.S. teachers do not receive as much practical training and daily support as their German and Japanese colleagues." The reported failure of U.S. teachers to utilize recommended practices or to receive adequate training and daily support is precisely the problem we anticipate.[19]

The problem is not that districts do a number of things. In fact, advocates of systemic reform sometimes suggest that reform will be most effective if advanced by a multifaceted, integrated approach.[20] The problem is that urban districts appear to do a number of things in a stop-and-start, chaotic fashion that is not part of any clear strategy to improve specific elements of school performance. Consequently, the evidence presented in this book requires attention to the context and nature of reform efforts. The amount of reform is problematic because of the way in which reform is pursued.

The churning of reform is not a problem that solely plagues urban school districts. It troubles many kinds of school districts and bureaucracies in general. However, it is a much more virulent and pressing problem in urban districts because of the way they are configured and governed. Urban districts have a far greater need to use all of their resources efficiently in order to improve students' abysmal performance. While the present

18. For instance, see Blase and Anderson (1995) or Schempp, Sparkes, and Templin (1993).
19. U.S. Department of Education (1998, 1, 3, 4).
20. See O'Day (1996).

work focuses upon urban districts, this should not minimize the wider applicability of the lessons learned.

Research on school leadership has concentrated on explaining the various ways in which leaders behave.[21] By focusing on the internal organizational process of schools, it has deepened our understanding of school administration. However, because this research focuses on the styles of individual school leaders, it has been unable to address the larger external forces that constrain the choices made by any leader—regardless of personal style or inclinations. The existing work does not account for institutional influences and therefore may overstate how leadership styles affect school reform.

This chapter and the next explore how organizational constraints and professional incentives encourage district policymakers to treat reform as a political exercise. Subsequent chapters more fully develop and test the implications of a political understanding of urban school reform. They demonstrate that the amount of reform proposed, the types of reforms proposed, the places where reforms are proposed, and the effects of high rates of reform activity are all consistent with a political explanation of urban school reform.

Critiques of Urban Schooling

Critiques of urban schooling almost invariably begin with the presumption that urban public school systems are in a state of crisis.[22] They usually end with clarion calls for change and an accelerated search for "solutions." These critiques have dominated the discourse and leant urgency to calls for reform. After the much-publicized 1983 report *A Nation at Risk* lambasted the nation's schools, school reform accelerated to an unprecedented pace. The reforms of the 1980s have been called "probably the most sustained period of educational reform since the progressive era" and "the most widespread, intense, public, comprehensive, and sustained [reform] effort in our history."[23] One account found "an estimated 3,000 separate school-reform measures enacted" during the 1980s.[24] By 1984 there were 275 state-level task forces evaluating education and recommending new policies, a number that had increased by 1990.[25] By 1995 at least a dozen

21. See, for example, Anderson and Shirley (1995); Deal and Patterson (1994); and Reitzug and Reeves (1992).

22. Tyack and Cuban (1995, 35–37), however, argue that schools are not getting worse. Berliner and Biddle (1995) and Hill (1995) argue that schools are more effective than is generally understood.

23. Elmore (1991b, 2) and Murphy (1991, viii).

24. Toch (1991, 36).

25. Glasman and Glasman (1990) and Orlich (1989).

major networks promoted school reform and funded a stew of reform models and initiatives.[26] In fact, a 1995 press release by the California Department of Education bragged that 1,883 schools in California alone were engaged in reform as part of the Goals 2000 national reform effort.

Nonetheless, a cacophony of reform efforts marketed as solutions to unsatisfactory school performance has produced little substantive change in urban schooling: "While education is awash in innovation, most innovations have little impact on the 'core technology' of the enterprise—processes of teaching and learning in classrooms and schools." [27] The lack of change has traditionally been traced to the complexity of teaching, the inertia of public school bureaucracies, or the poor design of reforms. While these analyses all have merit, they say little about why planning has been poor or why reformers have been unable to alter the teaching and learning core.

The consistent failure of reforms to deliver promised improvement has done little to cool the ardor of reformers. The presumption that more reform, or different kinds of reform, will improve schooling is a constant in the research on school reform. The Institute for Educational Leadership noted that three major reports published in 1992 and 1993 were all "strong testimonials to the need for change."[28]

Advocates of school reform have a simple explanation for continued mediocrity: the right solutions have not yet been used. They argue that there has not been enough reform, that the correct reforms have not been used, that reforms were not given a fair trial, or all of the above. For instance, they say state mandated efforts in the 1980s were ineffective because the states erred in promoting reform packages that lacked coherence. Other critics have argued that districts often manage large-scale reform efforts in ways that produce failure. These critiques are valid; districts do not select the optimal reforms, nor do they nurture or properly implement reforms. On the other hand, the consistent failure of nearly every large-scale reform suggests that a more fundamental problem exists.

Disappointing Fruits of School Reform

The dismal results of these extensive reform efforts prompted the RAND Corporation's 1995 report on Reinventing Public Education to begin with the question "Why has a decade of work on school reform pro-

26. Tittle (1995).
27. Elmore (1991a, 4). See also Plank (1988).
28. Danzberger, Kirst, and Usdan (1992, xii).

duced so little?"[29] Without entering into the long-running debates on the quality or productivity of America's urban schools, it can be safely stated that the school reform efforts of the 1980s and 1990s have not improved urban schooling. There is widespread agreement on this point.[30] After thirty years of reforms, "the benefits have not equaled the costs, and all too often the situation has seemed to worsen."[31] While this study assesses whether the problems of reform have remained constant or grown worse over time, the shortcomings of reform efforts were recognized as early as the mid-1960s. In 1964 one observer noted that innovations such as team teaching, programmed instruction, or ungraded schools were ultimately rejected or resulted in unanticipated problems. By 1970 the Center for Urban Education had evaluated more than sixty projects and documented "a series of earnest attempts" that "invite an impression of cumulative failure."[32]

Problems with reform are symptomatic of the institutional problems underlying school district governance. Institutional incentives encourage urban policymakers to concentrate on proposing change, rather than on improving teaching and learning. Reform is not necessarily about producing results, because the visible or verbal adoption of innovations may suffice to meet the needs of the policymakers. In fact, the demands of political leadership and professional behavior generally make it more politically profitable to innovate without risking the costs of real change. As a result, policymakers face strong incentives to use reform as a tactic to ease political tension and address political demands.[33]

The politics of school reform is not a new phenomenon. Consider the failed reform movement in Philadelphia in the late 1960s. A new board of education rapidly doubled its school budget and "recruited a new, dynamic

29. Hill (1995, ix). A recent high-profile reform push has enjoyed similarly discouraging reviews. In the early 1990s billionaire Walter Annenberg gave $500 million to public schooling, with most of the money earmarked for schools in the nation's largest cities. Four years after this record-setting gift the *Washington Post* reported "growing fears that the gift has become so tangled in the politics of big-city school systems, or divided among so many groups for so many purposes, that overall the benefits may be marginal. To some, the uncertain fate of Annenberg's charity offers another stark illustration of how difficult it is, even armed with a half-billion dollars, to make progress in the tumultuous world of urban public education." See Sanchez (1997, A1).

30. Anyon (1997); Bourisaw and Berry (1996); Clark and Astuto (1994); Cuban (1984, 1995); Elmore (1997); Firestone, Fuhrman, and Kirst (1991); Ladd (1996); Lewis (1996); Mirel (1994); Muncey and McQuillan (1993); Orlich (1989); Rothman (1993); Sarason (1996); Sizer (1996b); and Wehlage, Smith, and Lipman (1992). See also *Washington Post* (1995, A26) and *Chicago Tribune* (1997, 16) editorials on the "failure" of school reform.

31. Fullan (1991, xi).

32. Wayland (1964, 588) and Meranto (1970, 125).

33. See discussions by Cuban (1984); Fullan (1991); and Pincus (1974).

superintendent" to launch "a wide range of innovating programs." Despite all the activity, the school system remained "essentially the same institution it was before the new regime," while the experience increased "community cynicism toward the system."[34] Nonetheless, more than twenty years later the hiring of a new reform-minded superintendent again stirred hope. In 1995 a Philadelphia respondent in the present study excitedly announced:

> I would think of the greatest success as being the hiring of our new superintendent, who comes with an agenda to really revamp the school district. And, I think it's difficult to say that it's been the greatest success yet, because it still needs to be proved. But it's the greatest success, if for no other reason, than that the district has finally understood it needs to have radical change.

Policymakers' emphasis on the politically attractive aspects of reform has produced inattention to the details of implementing reform. As a consequence, "policies and reforms often fall apart when they encounter the realities of daily life in the classrooms."[35]

Why do local policymakers call attention to themselves by taking dramatic and visible action, when conventional accounts suggest that they are motivated more by the desire to avoid blame than to seek credit?[36] It is because the best way to avoid blame is to appear proactive. For superintendents, doing too much is far safer than doing too little.[37] Inaction is the worst possible sin for a public official facing a crisis. George Gallup noted in 1962, "Any sharp drop in popularity is likely to come from the President's inaction in the face of an important event. Inaction hurts a President more than anything else. A President can take some action, even a wrong

34. Meranto (1970, 148–49).

35. Pauly (1991, 115). Pauly reports that "it is now routine for teachers to admit their failure to comply with official school district policies" (122). One study of high school teachers in Philadelphia found that the "vast majority" ignored curriculum mandates or adapted them to their classrooms. See Rothman (1988). Powell, Farrar, and Cohen (1985, 302) note that courses added in reforms are often ineffective because they are "taught by the same old overworked and frequently undereducated teachers."

36. Weaver (1986) suggests that penalties for attracting blame are clearer and more immediate than are the rewards for earning credit, encouraging an emphasis on blame avoidance.

37. See Firestone, Fuhrman, and Kirst (1991) and Hill, Foster, and Gendler (1990) for a discussion of the sense of crisis during the initiation of Third Wave reforms in the early 1990s. Carter and Cunningham (1997, 99) have observed that school boards will "forgive a superintendent for trying too hard, [but] very few accept halfhearted effort." In districts where the schools are not thought to be in crisis, such as many suburban systems or one-school private "systems," the rewards for proactivity are smaller and the penalties for reflexive action much greater.

one, and not lose his popularity."[38] For example, when American hostages were seized in Lebanon in 1985, the Reagan administration felt compelled to act: "A cautious policy of 'wait and see' and 'put the hostages' safety first' might have been the better part of wisdom, but, as one news reporter commented, with the media down their backs, administration officials 'cannot be seen as doing nothing even if they want to do nothing.'"[39]

The Dominant Superintendent

The superintendent is the dominant actor in local school systems, particularly in urban districts. Big-city superintendents determine the shape of the school board's agenda and the amount of information that board members receive. Power has been centralized in the superintendent's hands at the behest of the school board because the superintendent is a full-time, professional expert who has a staff and is able to speak for the entire administration. As professionals supervised by amateur boards, superintendents have a virtual monopoly on educational expertise and other detailed information. The pressures they face are similar to those that have politicized the role of the city manager:

> It is normally "good politics" for councilmen to maneuver the manager into taking, or seeming to take, responsibility for risky or controversial measures. Being elected at large on a nonpartisan ballot, they are much more likely to be turned out of office by a vote against them than by one for their opponents. . . . If all goes well, they can take credit later with the electorate. If not, they can blame [the city manager] and perhaps even make "political capital" by firing him.[40]

Historical, community, and organizational contexts shape the nature of superintendent leadership. In *Leading to Change*, Susan Moore Johnson studied superintendents in twelve school districts. She found that conventional expectations of heroic leadership are unrealistic and greatly exceed the real power of contemporary superintendents.[41] Johnson suggests that the notion of heroic leadership misconstrues the real nature of the superintendency and increases the burden that superintendents must shoulder. Superintendents are constricted by limited positional power and organiza-

---

38. In Edelman (1972, 78).
39. Stone (1988, 115).
40. Banfield and Wilson (1963, 175).
41. Cohen and March (1986, 2) have made a similar argument about college presidents. Compared with heroic expectations of what the president can accomplish, the president has modest control over the events of college life.

tional complexity, but those who learn to work effectively within their role are the pivotal players in improving the performance of a school system. The key to effectively leading districts toward educational improvement is to first construct a "capacity for change" in the district through political and managerial leadership. The most important structural problem implied by Johnson's analysis is that few superintendents ever have the opportunity to construct this capacity.[42]

Urban superintendents are particularly hampered by their short tenure, because they are rarely in one place long enough to make a significant difference. The typical tenure for an urban superintendent is three years or less.[43] As educational scholar Theodore Kowalski has argued, "The idea that one individual can successfully transform a complex organization by imposing his or her vision in a relatively short period of time is simply myopic."[44]

The superintendent's tendency to focus on initiating—rather than implementing—reform is reinforced both by the brevity of tenure and by school board expectations. Boards use the superintendent as a convenient scapegoat, not out of malice, but because the political incentives to do so are nearly irresistible. School boards delegate issues of educational substance to the administration, thus insulating the board from dissatisfaction with the schools while permitting the board to replace a disappointing superintendent with one who inspires confidence in the community.

Like the hiring of a new college president, the hiring of a superintendent is an important institutional ritual.[45] Indeed, "the dismissal of an ineffective superintendent is thought to mark the end of bad times; the appointment of a new superintendent is heralded as the beginning of a new age."[46] One respondent in the current study noted the ritual embrace of change: "School board elections were held last year and a new superintendent was appointed. The board felt it was time to change administrators, to put in new blood and change things around." Board members who fail to use the superintendent as the point man or woman for reform court political risk and increase the likelihood that they will eventually be replaced by members

42. Johnson (1996).

43. See Carter and Cunningham (1997) and Council of Great City Schools (1992). This trend has become part of the popular wisdom for educators. Michael Casserly, the executive director of the Council of Great City Schools, has noted that many big-city superintendents measure their time as school leaders in "'dog years,' because they generally have tenures lasting no more than two years." See Fagan (1997, F-1).

44. Kowalski (1995, 152).

45. See McLaughlin and Riesman (1990).

46. Johnson (1996, xi).

who will. In return for serving as lightning rods for criticism, superintendents are accorded a great deal of leeway and disproportionate credit when their tenure is perceived as successful.[47]

Institutional Incentives for Reform

This work is not an attempt to assess the real performance of urban school systems. The significant fact is the conventional perception of a crisis in urban schooling. Regardless of the "real" performance of urban schools, this book explores why reform has not seemed to noticeably improve matters, and why reform nonetheless continues to command attention. It does not argue that reform is disappointing or seek to explain the school-level reasons for disappointments. It accepts as a starting point the long and distinguished literature on these topics.[48] I do examine why the same problems recur with reform time after time and why the lessons of the 1980s have not seemed to make the Third Wave reforms of the 1990s more effective.

This study uses comparative empirical analysis to document much that has been suggested or hinted at in previous case studies and historiographies. Using data on reform collected at a higher level of aggregation and for a broader sample than has been attempted previously, this analysis proceeds to work out more explicitly explanations that are implicit but undeveloped in previous considerations of school reform. In order to gain the breadth of vision necessary to this project, it was essential to trade some depth of context and refrain from attempting to connect district-level behaviors to activity at the school or classroom level. As a consequence, the analysis laid out in this book, although unconventional and controversial, is actually more limited in its scope than many analyses of contemporary education. This book does not seek to determine how well America's urban schools are performing, the reasons for unsatisfactory performance,

47. The urban school board–superintendent relationship is like the relationship between treasurer's offices at corporations and the active money managers they hire to invest pension fund assets. Rather than use unmanaged stock market indexes, corporations hire pension fund managers, even though these managers have consistently underperformed the market. Why would corporations continue to use managers who appear to "subtract rather than to add value"? Corporations persist in using managers who subtract value for many of the same reasons that urban school boards continually hire and fire superintendents. Treasurers' offices "delegate money management in order to reduce responsibility for potentially poor performance." They "can always replace a poorly performing money manager" and thereby free themselves from blame and appear vigilant. See Lakonishok, Shleifer, and Vishny (1992, 341–43).

48. Excellent works on this topic include Barth (1991); Chubb and Moe (1990); Cuban (1988, 1990); Elmore (1996); Orlich (1989); Sarason (1991); and Wagner (1994).

or what measures will solve any existing troubles. What is new here is a political and institutional explanation of why urban school reform has frequently disappointed, and why those disappointments have not led to significant changes in the practice of reform. The message of this book is akin
to the physician's credo to "first do no harm." The argument that institutional incentives produce symbolic behavior and policy churn does not
suggest that moderating these behaviors will "fix" urban schooling. However, these behaviors do generate a plethora of reforms that waste resources and promote a cynical school culture, undermining substantive efforts to improve teaching and learning.

The evidence in this volume does not forge an unbroken chain linking
policy churn to implementation to school-level performance. Rather, my
purpose is to suggest how the institutional circumstances of urban schooling conspire to negatively shape policy generation and implementation.

The high rates of reform activity explained by policy churn impede implementation, and a wealth of previous research has documented that full
and effective implementation is the key to sustained improvement in the
schools. This work offers a broader political explanation of why those
problems persist.

Structures do not make results inevitable, but they do shape incentives
and encourage certain behaviors over others. Because formal and informal
structures are susceptible to change, behavioral patterns are not set in
stone. Institutional structures may be altered formally, and actors can reshape the informal structure through their actions and decisions. Consequently, the model of urban schooling that drives this analysis is not presumed to be inevitable or omnipresent. Districts that seek to structure their
systems differently, or that have seen policymakers rework the informal institutional arrangements to shape expectations and assessment, are able to
establish patterns of behavior different from those described here. In these
alternative systems, different patterns of leadership on reform can exist and
flourish. However, rather than lionizing the leaders in these systems, we
would do better to look at the complex of factors that characterize these
school districts.

Because this analysis reflects poorly on the present management of urban school systems, because it questions the value of the multi-
million-dollar reform industry, and because it may be mistakenly interpreted as questioning the motives of policymakers and reform advocates, it
is likely to be challenged by many of the traditional authorities on school
reform and urban education. I welcome the research and discussion
prompted by this volume, as my intention is to promote discussion of is-

sues that have been inadequately addressed. In fact, my hope is that this book will convince readers that the discussion of urban school reform has focused on the wrong questions. I contend that the rarely addressed issue of institutional constraints ought to be a topic of keen interest to educators and policymakers, and that the pedagogical and leadership practices that receive so much attention ought to be issues of lesser concern.

Previous Research on the Politics of School Reform

Most analyses of school reform are framed in a rather general fashion. Useful insights are implicit in the various analytic frameworks, but the theories are not spelled out at a specific level. The present work attempts to unify insights from these previous analyses and to spell out and then empirically examine some of the arguments implicit in the literature.

Prompted by the continued failure of reform to achieve its promised goals, several authors have recently studied the phenomenon of policy churn and explored its causes. In *A Geology of School Reform*, Liane Brouillette traces the two-year experience of restructuring in one school district, paying particular attention to previous reform efforts and to district history that shaped the fate of the current restructuring. Brouillette describes the community and school-based conflicts that impede reforms and explores the roots of these conflicts, emphasizing the philosophic disagreements that frustrate efforts to improve schools across the United States. Brouillette found that efforts at significant restructuring in a small district were hampered by conflicting beliefs within the community and concludes that more open and vigorous dialogue is necessary if school reform is to succeed. This careful historiography, while depicting a district very different from most of those studied here, emphasizes the importance of disagreement regarding the purpose of schooling. Building upon Brouillette's analysis, I attempt to locate the cultural disagreement about the purpose and nature of education within a larger institutional framework and explore in a more comparative fashion the implications of this framework for school reform.[49]

Diana Tittle tells a similar story from a journalistic perspective in *Welcome to Heights High*. She traces the fate of school reform in one high school in order to lay bare "the destructive organizational, political, social, and racial tensions . . . that stand in the way of successful school restructuring." Whereas Brouillette emphasizes community-based conflicts and the ways in which they frustrate reform efforts, Tittle focuses on a school-based "culture of inertia" that stymies change. Tittle's careful case study

49. Brouillette (1996).

demonstrates how institutional and cultural constraints frustrate reform efforts at the school level. While the institutional milieu of a school is very
different from that of a school district, Tittle highlights several elements of
single-school governance that are also problematic for district policymakers: the "revolving-door" nature of administrative leadership, centralization of school management, the passive-conservative sociology of the
teaching profession, lack of institutional memory, the political underpin-
nings of school boards, and the role of limited resources. The current work
can be viewed as a comparative and more systematic exploration of the
points that emerge in Tittle's case study.[50]

In *Tinkering Towards Utopia*, David Tyack and Larry Cuban observe
the recurrent pursuit of utopian ideals and the failure of reforms to change
the ways that schools look and act. Noting that "Americans celebrate innovation," the authors explore the paradox that educators have been attacked
for being "moss-backs who resist change" and suckers for "foolish notions
[that] circulate through the system at high velocity." Blending political and
institutional analysis, they argue that reforms are devised, promoted, and
adopted as a consequence of group politics. The actual implementation of
reform in schools is shaped by operational regularities that "have imprinted
themselves on students, educators, and the public as the essential features
of a 'real school.'" Notions of "real school" are protected by popular conceptions of schooling and by the routines of teacher practice. Tyack and
Cuban conclude that it is hardest to achieve change "where it counts the
most—in the daily interaction of teachers and students." This change is
possible, they believe, with commitment, resources, and an accurate understanding of schools as institutions. The argument made here is entirely consistent with their thesis, while refining their political and institutional
discussion. It empirically examines some of the implications of a political
understanding of school reform by exploring the activity of urban districts
during a specific period of time.[51]

Wilbur Rich's *Black Mayors and School Politics* proffers explicitly political explanations for the failure of urban school reform in Newark, Detroit, and Gary. Rich argues that "school cartels" of "professional school
administrators, school activists, and union leaders" control school policy
and resist "substantive reforms," those entailing changes in "governance,
institutional structures, and personnel." Instead, the cartel favors "procedural reforms" that introduce "new and different pedagogical processes."

---

50. Tittle (1995, x, 263).
51. Tyack and Cuban (1995, 4, 7, 10).

The cartel defines procedural reforms as representing real reform and then hires superintendents "with the promise that they will change things." Opposition groups, particularly those that favor substantive reforms, are discredited or coopted by the cartel. Rich's valuable discussion explores the tendency of urban districts to engage in symbolic reform. Because of his case study approach, his focus on the cartel's resistance to substantive reform, and his overriding interest in racial politics, Rich is unable to address the comparative nature of pedagogical reform with much precision. Furthermore, Rich does not attempt to say much about the structural incentives that shape the behavior of cartel members. My work specifies how the institutional structure interacts with the local political environment to influence the way that administrators and policymakers manage reform.[52]

In *Ghetto Schooling*, Jean Anyon argues that the problems with America's urban schools are largely a product of economic devastation, racial stigmatization, and political isolation. She attributes the problems Newark encountered with school reform in the 1990s in large part to the "gradual ghettoization and stigmatization over time of the city's minority poor," the "twentieth century economic devastation of the city," and "nearly a century of isolation of urban leaders from federal and state power." As a result, Anyon believes successful education reform is "dependent on improvements in the lives and opportunities of inner city residents." Focusing on factors external to urban districts like economic constraints, federalism, and urban isolation, Anyon describes the larger universe that frames the local pursuit of school reform. Her conclusion that political and economic stresses are responsible for urban school districts' unsatisfactory performance and for the persistent failure of reform is largely consistent with the argument made here. However, while Anyon is primarily concerned with using the historical record to explain why urban school districts face the constraints that they do, I am more concerned with exploring just how those constraints shape political behavior.[53]

Alternative Explanations of School Reform

The symbolic reform analysis presented in this volume is not the only explanation of the disappointing performance of school reform. Four alternative analyses are presented here: the union critique, the public sector critique, the monopoly critique, and the micromanagement critique. These analyses are primarily concerned with the ambitious task of explaining

52. Rich (1996, 5–7).
53. Anyon (1997, xv, 168).

school performance, paying less attention to the reform process. However, these explanations do have implications for school reform. All of these theories can coexist quite easily with the present argument since they explain suboptimal school performance, while this volume concentrates on examining the fate of reform. Further, each analysis contributes useful insights. In terms of explaining the politics of reform, however, the evidence in this study appears to be most consistent with the implications of a symbolic understanding of reform.

The Union Critique

Unions, which are particularly strong in the same urban districts with an inordinate number of low-performing schools, have been blamed for reducing the productivity of schooling. Economist Caroline Hoxby has argued that "teachers' unions are primarily rent seeking [organizations], raising school budgets and school inputs but lowering student achievement by decreasing the productivity of inputs."[54] Other researchers have concluded that unionized districts, because of collective bargaining, appear to work less well for students who are below average. This suggests that collective bargaining could be a particular problem in the nation's impoverished urban districts. In fact, some union critics argue that the stringent provisions of union contracts and the political strength of teachers' unions make it difficult for policymakers or administrators to impose accountability mechanisms or to make these mechanisms function effectively. For instance, one account documents the role that teachers' concerns about contracts, personal security, and salaries played in the failure of an elaborate reform effort in Bensenville, Illinois.[55]

While the union critique may help to explain school performance, it tells us little about the fate of school reform or the incidence of reform. Critics argue that the conditions demanded by teachers' unions are so stringent that districts are unable to improve performance and that union opposition impedes the ability of schools to concentrate on the business of improving educational performance. The union critique does not specifically address the question of school reform, though it implies that unions impede the ability of districts to make desirable changes in behavior.

This critique can be interpreted to suggest either that districts will not be able to push through reforms or that reforms will be enacted only after be-

54. Hoxby (1996, 711).
55. See Eberts and Stone (1984) or Lieberman (1997) for an elaboration of the union critique and Mirel (1994) for an account of the Bensenville difficulties.

ing defanged by the unions. There is some support for the second argument. Unions do not necessarily impede the massive amount of school reform taking place, but they certainly help to ensure that it does not threaten established school procedures. The evidence presented in chapter 3, however, challenges the argument that unions are responsible for choking off school improvement. Neither union strength nor union affiliation appears to have a significant effect on the extent of reform activity. Most significantly, the union critique does not help to explain the immense rate of reform activity or its appeal for superintendents and school boards.

The Public Sector Critique

Political scientists John Chubb and Terry Moe have suggested that public sector schools are crippled by overbureaucratization, which is largely attributable to political conflict. The warring factions in the body politic, each conscious that it could lose its majority, try to make their preferences permanent by writing them into legislation. The result is an increasing proliferation of rules and regulations, all of which undermine school autonomy and thereby impede school performance. Chubb and Moe suggest that all of the highly touted reforms of the 1980s were actually nothing more than efforts to tinker with existing arrangements; the reforms had all been "cut from the same institutional mold" and did not have the potential to dramatically improve education.[56] This is a somewhat different argument from my less sweeping claim that reforms have not helped because of the manner in which they have been pursued. The two analyses are complementary but distinct.

As the evidence in chapters 3 and 4 demonstrates, there is a great deal of consensus on school reform and the plethora of reform activity. This evidence does not support the partisan conflict and bureaucratic regulation explanation, which suggests that excessive rigidity and rule-based decisionmaking stifle reform activity. In fact, interest groups and political interests play a small role in local school policymaking. School reform is not a hotly contested process characterized by conflicting factions, but a nonconflictual policy area guided by professional administrators.

The Monopoly Critique

Critics of the public school monopoly argue that market-driven competition will stimulate the development and improvement of schools.[57] A

56. Chubb and Moe (1990, 11).
57. See Friedman (1982).

market critique of education has suggested that performance is suboptimal because public schools are free from the pressures of competition. Because their clients have nowhere else to turn, public school personnel presumably have lacked the incentive to improve their performance or to utilize resources more efficiently. Insulation from competitive pressures has made school organizations bloated entities with little reason to change the status quo. Critiques of the public school monopoly also tend to emphasize the bureaucratization of urban school governance.[58] Other critics have noted the consolidation of school districts and the growth of urban populations. As a result, the typical school board member must attempt to represent huge constituencies, "making representation an absolute sham in many urban districts."[59]

The monopoly analysis may explain the performance of schools, but it does not explain the incidence or nature of reform. Chapters 5 and 6 provide evidence that district policymakers consider the political appeal of reforms and are responsive to community pressure. These findings contradict the monopolistic notion that red tape, regulations, and bureaucratic bloat create an unresponsive school leadership and stifle any attempts at change. The monopolistic position of urban public schools is not responsible for policy churn or for its negative effects on reform activity.

The Micromanagement Critique

School boards have long been critiqued for the manner in which they govern school districts. Critics have suggested that school boards fail to respect the limits of their competence, inadvertently causing difficulties in their efforts to micromanage school affairs. Research by the Institute for Educational Leadership has found that boards spend too much time on administrative trivia, impeding the performance of system administrators, and too little time on substantive policy issues.[60] School boards were also faulted for not making policy in a collective fashion, spending insufficient time framing and considering the larger questions of education policy, being isolated from other community sectors and government entities, and generally behaving in a reactive rather than a proactive fashion. The amateur makeup, minimal training, and sparse resources of school boards contribute to troubled and invasive system leadership that inhibits the performance of professional educators. The micromanagement critique is more an explanation of the performance of school leadership in general than an

---

58. See Ravitch and Viteritti (1997) and Tyack (1974).
59. Iannaccone and Lutz (1995, 45).
60. See Danzberger and Usdan (1992) and Institute for Educational Leadership (1986).

attempt to understand school performance or school reform in particular, but it does have implications for the nature and extent of school reform.

An analysis of reform rooted in the micromanagement critique may overstate the culpability of board members for policy churn. As the evidence in chapter 3 suggests, boards tend to allow system administrators to take the lead in proposing reforms, and board members usually support whatever reforms are presented. Additionally, the micromanagement explanation suffers from an inability to explain just why board members engage in micromanagement. The symbolic reform explanation, that board members have institutional incentives to support proposals drafted by the professional administrators, is consistent with the micromanagement critique while helping to more fully explain the observed behavior.

Data Collection for This Study

How much reform takes place in urban school systems and why does it occur? These questions guided the data collection for this study, which examines the nature of school reform and school politics in a stratified random sample of fifty-seven urban U.S. school districts during the 1992–95 period. This approach was designed as a compromise between an intensive study of a few districts and a cursory examination of a broad sample. Data were primarily collected through 325 structured telephone interviews conducted with fixed-position respondents in the fifty-seven districts. The research design targeted six fixed-position respondents in each district, for a total of 342. Consequently, the 325 interviews represented a success rate of 95 percent.[61]

The fifty-seven sample districts included a cross-section of urban school districts in the United States. Districts are not necessarily coterminous with the local city, so the predominant school district in each city was studied. For simplicity of presentation, specific districts are referred to by the local city's name, rather than by the name of the school district.[62] Over four-fifths of sample districts were at least 99 percent urban, and just five were less than 90 percent urban. Despite being highly urbanized, the districts varied greatly in population: fifteen districts had 50,000 to 100,000 residents in 1990, and fourteen had more than 500,000 residents. The sample districts, all of which enrolled at least 5,000 students, were among the largest 10 percent of the nation's school districts in 1990–91.[63] The mean

61. The research methodology is discussed in appendix A.
62. The actual school districts used are identified in appendix B.
63. Norton and others (1996, 113).

district in the sample had seventy-three public schools.[64] The sample was also geographically representative, with the fifty-seven districts located in twenty-four different states and evenly dispersed by geographic region.[65]

The interview instrument utilized closed-ended and open-ended questions, permitting both quantitative analysis of the results and narrative discussion of findings. I scheduled and conducted all interviews over a nine-month period in 1995. The mean interview lasted about forty minutes, during which time interviewees were asked three sets of questions. The first were open-ended questions about local education during the 1992–95 period. The second concerned each district's experience from 1992 to 1995 with five different types of Third Wave reform: day and time measures, curriculum, evaluation, professional development, and site-based management. These questions were primarily closed-ended. Questions on each type of reform began by asking about the visibility and controversiality of that reform locally. Respondents then were asked whether a "significant" reform of that type had been made, about the details of the proposal, the reactions of local interests, and the fate of the proposal. This sequence was repeated for each reform type. Each of the five reforms was examined for each district. The third series of questions concerned school board behavior, the role of community groups, and the local institutional context.

The six types of individuals selected in each district were chosen because they were likely to be informed observers of the local education scene and to ensure a variety of perspectives on school affairs from inside and outside the school system. The first interview was conducted with the local education reporter for the leading circulation newspaper in the district. Inhabitants of the positions targeted for subsequent interviews were obtained from the journalist. The five interviewees, in addition to the journalist, were the head of the teachers' union, the "most knowledgeable" senior school administrator, the head of the local Chamber of Commerce or the most influential local business group, the head of the most influential local minority organization, and the "most knowledgeable" school board member. The board member was selected according to the consensus of prior interviewees in the district. If a targeted respondent suggested that someone else within the organization was actually a more appropriate person to interview, the suggestion was accepted.[66]

64. The large average number of schools per district is not a product of a few exceptionally large districts. The sample did not include New York, Chicago, or Los Angeles.

65. Because of the diversity of urban districts in the sample, the patterns of observed behavior are particularly noteworthy.

66. Summary information on the six types of respondents is presented in appendix D.

Respondents were utilized as privileged observers who could report accurately and in some detail about local schooling. Because formal policy pronouncements in local school affairs can be misleading, and because district policy is often the sum of unrecorded administrative actions, the accounts of informed local observers may be a more accurate measure than the formal record.[67] Individual responses were gathered as a means of understanding the process of urban school reform. Because the primary unit of analysis in this study is the district—not the individual—the multiple responses in each district were averaged into composite values for the purpose of analysis. Combining responses from across the community into composite indexes for each district minimized problems caused by the biases or incomplete knowledge of any one respondent.

The Five Reform Categories

Five categories of reform formed the policy core of Third Wave school reforms in the 1990s. The five reforms were selected because they comprised the programmatic elements of an eight-part series on school reform that *Education Week*, the education community's newspaper of record, ran in early 1993. Their prominence in *Education Week* during the 1992–95 period of interest provided assurance that these reforms were of practical interest to educational practitioners and scholars. Because the Third Wave reforms were just gathering steam in the early 1990s, much of the action on these reforms conveniently took place during the 1992–95 period. The five kinds of reform studied are summarized below.

DAY AND TIME MEASURES.   Efforts to reform the school day and the use of time in schools generally focus on either adding more classroom time or on rearranging the school day so as to permit time to be used in different ways. Measures that add a fixed amount of time to the school day, add days to the school year, or require a minimum number of classroom hours are examples of reforms that seek to increase the amount of time students spend learning. Adjusting the length of classes to encourage new kinds of instruction or juggling the school week to create opportunities for professional development are efforts that seek to use time adjustments to alter teaching practice. Of the five types of reform, changes in time were the most likely to be handled at the school site level, rather than through districtwide policy.

67. The extent of knowledge and experience possessed by local observers of politics and policy is often not appreciated. For instance, seventeen years was the mean response to the question "How long have you been following local educational affairs?"

School day and calendar reforms normally attracted very little attention, because they were mundane and were often handled at the school sites. Despite this low public profile, significant changes in the school day or calendar can disturb the daily lives of teachers and families, and thus carry a high risk of instigating conflict. The most common scheduling reforms, accounting for more than a third of all measures cited by respondents, were proposals to extend the school day or to move to a year-round schedule at selected district schools.

CURRICULUM.   Curricular reforms encompass a wide range of proposals dealing with what and how students learn. This category included attempts to strengthen promotion or graduation requirements, to introduce multicultural approaches, to revise reading lists, and to increase experiential ("hands-on") learning. The most frequently proposed measures were some form of heightened graduation requirement and multicultural or inclusive curricula, but more than a dozen different kinds of measures were cited.

EVALUATION.   Evaluation reforms address the ways in which students' performance is measured. Proposals to reform evaluation include shifting from one kind of assessment to another, increasing the frequency of testing, and using test results in new ways. Third Wave reforms, in general, have been trumpeted as emphasizing a closer connection between what tests measure and what students are actually taught. Reformers have particularly advocated portfolio assessment (collections of student work) and outcome-based measures in lieu of traditional standardized tests. Ironically, while the experts were touting authentic assessment, some rank and file were promoting traditional assessment. More than a quarter of the reform efforts cited by respondents involved districts shifting toward more standardized testing. For instance, a South Bend, Indiana, respondent explained that the district had "raised standards for student performance and added a graduation test that's administered in the tenth grade. We raised the percentage scores required and the range of skills needed." A Santa Monica, California, respondent described the opposite change: "We have moved away from certain kinds of assessment tests, such as multiple choice and essay questions, to more authentic assessment and to portfolios and that sort of primary performance documentation." Both kinds of change were hailed as reform and considered to be progress, even though respondents and reformers viewed the two approaches as largely contradictory.

PROFESSIONAL DEVELOPMENT.   Professional development reforms are intended to improve the effectiveness of teachers by enhancing their instructional skills. Professional development reforms ranged from minimal changes, like instituting once-a-month after-school workshops for teachers, to creating local academies that would work with sets of teachers for six or eight weeks at a stretch. Other measures included mandated training in areas such as racial sensitivity or bilingual education, providing time for teams of teachers to meet, or revising teacher evaluation.

Professional development generally attracted little attention and proved relatively uncontroversial. The reason for the low level of controversy is that generally only measures acceptable to the union were proposed, with the most common reforms simply giving teachers more time for professional development or modifying the emphasis of existing programs. Of the five reforms studied, the union was reported to exert the most influence on behalf of, and to be most favorably disposed toward, professional development proposals. Respondents described professional development reform as offering little reason for teachers to oppose it. A Bloomington, Indiana, respondent said of the "most significant" local proposal, "I'm not sure you can even call it a proposal. It was offering more workshops for teachers and time off for teachers to do these kinds of things." In Boston, the district and union negotiated a contract that created a center for leadership development to provide "professional development opportunities for teachers, parents, and administrators."

SITE-BASED MANAGEMENT.   Site-based management (SBM) is the attempt to shift the control of schools from the central administration to the school sites. There are many possible ways to handle SBM, depending on which functions the system attempts to devolve, how completely the functions are turned over to school sites, and who is given control at the school site. Respondents were often unsure about what SBM entailed locally, and they described the nature of site control as varying from one site to another. SBM was the most popular of the five reforms studied, largely because it was a symbolically attractive reform that was visible and provoked relatively little controversy. As one school board member, who had just stepped down as president, said, "[Site-based management] was basically a political move. The association is very supportive of it. . . . [The school board] will go along with it, but we're not going to go out on the streets and die on this one."

MEASURING REFORM ACTIVITY.   For purposes of analysis, the five kinds of reform were combined into an index measuring the amount of reform activity taking place in each district. For each of the five types of school reform studied, each respondent was asked whether each of the five kinds of reform had been proposed locally. The percentage of respondents reporting a given proposal in a given district was then determined and used as the measure of local activity on that reform. For instance, if four out of six respondents said a reform had been proposed, its value was coded as 0.67. This system was used because it ensured that districts in which all respondents did or did not report a measure would be treated differently from districts in which local observers disagreed about reform activity. The number of total reforms proposed in each district was produced by adding up the number of areas in which a reform had been proposed.

The number of different initiatives cited in each district for each kind of reform made it impossible to compare specific initiatives within each type of reform. For instance, within a given district, respondents would disagree about what curriculum reform entailed, about the most significant initiative, and about the fate of that initiative. This study cast a wide net, in studying an unprecedented number of reforms on an unprecedented scale, but the cost of that broad scope was an unavoidable imprecision in the measures of reform.

Problems with Studying School Reform

Studying public policy is a difficult and murky process.[68] Policy is intimately shaped by bureaucratic practice, issues of implementation, institutional behavior, and other opaque elements. Comparative efforts to study policymaking at the state or local level are particularly handicapped by the lack of public resources, formal records, extensive paperwork, and attentive organized interests that make it possible to assemble relatively reliable analyses of policymaking at the national level.

These problems are all too evident when it comes to studying education policy. U.S. schools are managed by more than 15,000 independent school districts. School district budgets are set by the school system administration, with minimal attention devoted to clarifying expenditures or line items. School board meetings are preserved only in sketchy board minutes, which can be difficult to access and difficult to interpret unless one is fully versed in district affairs.[69] Partly because gathering data on urban school

---

68. See the excellent discussion of this issue by Sabatier (1991).
69. Even for local newspaper reporters, "one of the toughest assignments for a new reporter is to accurately cover a school board or board of trustees meeting. Topics discussed and the proce-

reform is onerous and because the data tend to be imprecise, scholars have concentrated on a more rewarding and easily addressed question: which reforms will produce the "best" results? The nature of disciplinary scholarship also discourages comparative research on school district policy. Most students of education policy are education specialists primarily interested in the efficacy of specific initiatives or pedagogies, while political scientists and policy scholars have little interest in rooting through the diffuse and inaccessible mass of local activity.

Conclusion

The following chapters use data collected in this study to examine the causes, extent, and consequences of policy churn. Chapter 2 describes the many incentives, personal and organizational, to reform schools. Chapter 3 explores the political role of the school board, arguing that conventional accounts understate its role in Third Wave reform while overstating the role of state governments and teachers' unions. Chapters 4 through 7 argue that the amount of reform activity, the reforms that were utilized most widely, the districts where activity took place, and the relative performance of reforms in high-activity and low-activity districts in the 1992–95 period were consistent with the expectations of a political explanation of school reform. Chapter 8 summarizes the findings in the study and offers some thoughts on how to address the problem of policy churn.

To be sure, individual reform initiatives are not necessarily bad ideas, and school policymakers have entirely honorable intentions when proposing them. It is entirely possible that any given reform will enhance school performance if properly implemented. The cruel paradox is that the same impulses that drive education policymakers to adopt reform ensure that they will do so in conditions that make large-scale success highly unlikely. Problems with urban school reform are symptoms of the institutional structure of urban school districts. Until those larger constraints are addressed, attempts to improve schooling through any reform—no matter how well designed—are likely to prove futile and waste resources.

---

dural nature of these meetings may be unfamiliar and confusing." Hennessey and Kowalski (1996, 213–14).

2

Organizational and Personal Incentives for Reform

S OME RESEARCHERS have described schools as organized anarchies characterized by ambiguous goals,
unclear technology, and fluid participation. Others have noted that school
systems are "loosely coupled" systems, in which there are loose connec-
tions between administrators and teachers, and among teachers and
school-level administrators. Both analyses imply an organization without
clear accountability or control. Decisionmaking in these diffi-
cult-to-manage organizations approximates a "garbage can" model, in
which problems, solutions, and choice opportunities interact to produce decisions. Trapped in this morass, school system policymakers try to gain
control of their organizations and maintain legitimacy by emphasizing
manageable issues rather than by focusing on the thorny core processes of
teaching and learning. Organizational analyses that build on this work have
provided valuable insights, but they have not led to sustained empirical research. In particular, researchers have not systematically examined how
policymakers seek to control their organizations and maintain legitimacy.[1]

Drawing on previous work in organizational theory, education policy,
and political science, a general framework exploring how organizations approach innovation is presented here. Though applied specifically to urban
school reform, this framework can help to explain why certain kinds of organizations engage in continual bouts of reform, while others are much less
inclined to do so.

---

1. Aldrich and Marsden (1988) and Willower (1992). See Cohen and March (1986) and
March and Olsen (1987) for a general discussion of decisionmaking in organizations. See Weick
(1976) on the "loose coupling" of school systems. For the seminal discussion of how policymakers
maintain legitimacy, see Meyer and Rowan (1991).

Organizational Incentives for Symbolic Reform

Three dimensions of an organization's institutional structure and environment may encourage its leaders to emphasize the symbolic value of reform: the accountability of the organization, the ease with which its leaders can change the organization's technical core, and the visibility and centrality of the organization in the public's mind. Leaders of organizations with agreed-upon outcome measures, easily modified technical cores, and shelter from heavy public scrutiny are more likely to promote substantive change than symbolic change. This is because leaders who are judged on actual output, who control output quality, and who receive less frenzied scrutiny find that productivity strongly influences their perceived performance—thus making a focus on organizational outcomes an attractive investment of time and energy.

In organizations with little accountability, difficult-to-control technical cores, and intense public scrutiny, the perceived performance of organizational leaders will bear little relationship to their actual effectiveness. In organizations of this second type, there are strong incentives for leaders to focus on symbolic activity. Urban school districts with weak accountability mechanisms, opaque technical cores, and a visible public role encourage politically motivated change. Consequently, policymakers face strong incentives to launch and promote new initiatives.

Lack of Accountability for Performance

In urban school districts there is "an inability to define and measure true educational quality—the bottom line. . . . While the profit margin determines how well a company is doing, there is no reliable way to measure a school's success."[2] This lack of effective accountability makes it difficult to judge leaders on performance. As Chester Finn, the former assistant secretary of education, has noted, "Without clear standards and reliable indicators of performance in relation to precise objectives, it is impossible to hold anyone—student, teacher, principal, school system, or state—accountable for success or failure."[3]

Instead, policymakers tend to be judged on proxies for district quality. The most notable proxy is input—visible efforts to improve the schools.

2. Wagner (1994, 245).
3. Finn (1997, 241).

These kinds of accountability concerns are present in many organizations, particularly in the public sector. Hugh Heclo has observed, "Knowing when a business has increased its market penetration from 40 percent to 42 percent is not like knowing when people have decent housing or proper health care."[4] Lacking confidence that perceived organization output will reflect their efforts, leaders have little incentive to focus on productivity.

Difficulties assessing the value added by schooling are not immutable. They can be overcome, particularly if an "objective" assessment is accepted as a measure of students' performance. For instance, Western European nations and Japan use national exams. A consensus instrument reduces the problems of measuring output and makes outcome goals more concrete. Concrete goals, in turn, discourage emphasis on leadership input and symbolic behavior.[5] Regardless of the validity of the Western European and Japanese tests, they offer clear standards by which school employees will be judged. The existence of the tests subsumes concerns about what schooling should be about. Nations that use test scores to sort students into different schools and tracks also reduce conflict about the purpose of education (because expectations are no longer universal) and simplify the comparison of student performance (because groupings of students are more homogeneous). In rejecting this kind of system, the United States has been forced to use a complex of vague and sometimes conflicting measures to evaluate heterogeneous groups of students.

Five factors currently make it extraordinarily difficult to hold urban schools accountable using concrete outcomes: heterogeneous student groupings and the lack of common and universal tests, disagreement over the purpose of schooling, rapid leadership turnover, the massive problems in urban areas, and limited firsthand community experience of school performance.[6]

UNCLEAR OUTCOMES.   Because the quality of the students entering large public school systems and the value added by the systems cannot be determined with precision, the "criteria for school effectiveness remain un-

4. Heclo (1977, 202). See also Lynn (1981) and Peterson, Rabe, and Wong (1991) for elaboration.

5. Edelman (1972).

6. Many large public programs, particularly in urban areas, suffer similar difficulties. For instance, attempts to evaluate the effects of urban enterprise zones have been plagued by the long-term nature of the programs, weak experimental controls and baselines, and the need for more analysis of political and institutional factors. See Gunn (1993).

clear or in dispute."[7] Assessing the "value added" by school systems is difficult due to validity concerns about test instruments and the uneven quality of students across districts. Because districts face unequal challenges, school district performance cannot be easily assessed by simply comparing across districts. Accurately assessing how much students improve and how much value is added by schools in urban school districts is a sophisticated exercise that is difficult and rarely done.

Concerns about the fairness and efficacy of testing instruments have led scholars to doubt the utility or accuracy of current assessment tools. Finn has argued, "Most of the [educational] data we need, we cannot get. Much of what we get, we cannot trust. Of that which we can trust, far too much is obsolete, unintelligible to laymen, or unsuited to crucial analyses and comparisons."[8] A 1987 study reported that if the states were to be believed, "no state was below average at the elementary level on any of the six major nationally normed, commercially available tests." Further, 90 percent of local school districts claimed their average scores exceeded the national average.[9] Indeed, school districts systematically and artificially inflate test scores in numerous ways.[10] Even such seemingly universal and comparative tests as the Scholastic Aptitude Test (SAT) and the American College Test (ACT) provide poor measures of district performance, because they are taken by a self-selected population and because local scores are largely a function of the percentage of total students choosing to be tested.[11]

Testing lends itself to manipulation, particularly by school policymakers who stand to reap professional rewards if their leadership is deemed effective. For instance, in the early 1980s Atlanta's reformist superintendent, Alonzo Crim, garnered national accolades for rapidly increasing district test scores to national norms. However, subsequent statewide testing found that the district actually had the lowest scores in the state, worse even than those in comparable urban districts. The district had inflated its scores using deceptive practices that included a less competitive base test, artificially low comparative scores, and manipulation of the test-taking population.[12] The dubious quality of educational assessment,

7. Newmann (1991, 59).

8. Finn (1991, 263). The problem is aggravated because "the closer one gets to individual schools, teachers, and pupils, the fuzzier those 'standards' get and the more obscure the data about performance."

9. Cannell (1987, 1–2).

10. Clotfelter and Ladd (1996) and Lieberman (1993).

11. Powell and Steelman (1996).

made less reliable by administrative chicanery, means "objective" scores can provide an unreliable measure of system performance.

Concerns about validity and comparability are even greater for more "authentic" assessment approaches. After three years of experimentation, Vermont's authentic assessment reform was hailed for producing clear performance standards. Trial runs, however, found that inter-rater reliability on the assessment instrument was not high enough to permit the comparison of students, schools, or districts.[13] In sum, there is a lack of good data on whether student performance in urban schools is improving, forcing observers to turn elsewhere for cues.

DISAGREEMENT ON THE MISSION OF PUBLIC EDUCATION.   There is confusion not only over how to measure school system performance, but over what desirable performance entails. "Most people agree, at least in a general way, about what constitutes good health. Agreement on what constitutes a 'good' education is harder to come by," notes one scholar.[14] Educators are expected to satisfy a variety of demands, the relative significance of which is shifting and subject to change.

Particularly given the religious, ethnic, geographical, racial, and cultural heterogeneity of the United States, there is no widespread agreement about what an education should include.[15] There is not even agreement that a student who knows more factual material is necessarily a better educated student. Various educators argue that the schools should help students become active learners, democratic citizens, reflective members of a multicultural society, activists for social reconstruction, or self-directed ethical citizens. Others believe the schools should simply do a better job of teaching material and analytic skills. The widespread disagreement on the mission of public education is aggravated by the universal nature of U.S. education: students with very different needs and abilities are all served by a formally undifferentiated system. This leads to multiple goals and subsequent demands that schools be evaluated by numerous criteria. Policymakers must negotiate the question of what they *should* be doing before focusing on how to do it. Varied demands make it difficult to tell when a district has

12. The story is told in some detail by Orfield and Ashkinaze (1991, 118–23).

13. See Clarke and Agne (1997, 304).

14. Brouillette (1996, 2). See Bierlein (1993); Lezotte (1992); Stout, Tallerico, and Scribner (1995); and Powell, Farrar, and Cohen (1985) for further discussion of this issue.

15. For different conceptions of the appropriate goals of schooling, see Freire (1970); Gutmann (1987); Hirsch (1987); Nieto (1992); and Sizer (1996a).

performed adequately, since almost any district is satisfying some demands and failing to satisfy others.

EXECUTIVE TURNOVER.   Because most urban superintendents hold office for about three years, "it is virtually impossible to accurately determine the value of their contributions."[16] By comparison, the CEOs in corporate America during the 1980s and 1990s—a period popularly viewed as marked by instability and dramatic change—had an average tenure of eight to nine years.[17] It is difficult to hold short-tenure leaders accountable for multiyear trends. Educational improvement, a cumulative and long-term process, may show up only faintly at first. Students generally attend primary and secondary schools for thirteen years, while most school policymakers are in office a fraction of that time. Consequently, policymakers are only fractionally responsible for a cohort's performance. Urban superintendents simply are not around long enough to be held accountable for changes in performance. Superintendents are often evaluated based on perceived changes in district outcomes caused by their predecessor's performance, random factors, or the local environment.

ENVIRONMENTAL OBSTACLES.   The troubled environment of urban schools masks and inhibits their performance. Separating system performance from the surrounding ills becomes problematic in urban areas where the student population is buffeted by crime, drugs, teenage pregnancy, unstable families, poverty, and violence.[18] The massive effects of community and home environment on student performance have been widely recognized at least since the issuance of the Coleman report in 1966.[19] Many impediments to student performance are only minimally tractable to school-based remedies. This makes it more difficult to assess the impact of particular educational policies on school outcomes.

CONSUMERS' LIMITED DIRECT EXPERIENCE WITH PRODUCT.   Finally, the people who pay for schools do not actually use the good that they purchase. Education is purchased for someone else, making the quality of edu-

16. Kowalski (1995, 64).
17. See Smart (1997).
18. Sizer (1968, 320) long ago noted that "schooling is but a minor influence on many children." More recent research demonstrates that student achievement continues to be the product of many factors, only some of them school related. See U.S. Department of Education (1998).
19. Coleman and others (1966).

cation more difficult for the buyer to judge.[20] It is easier to evaluate the quality of a good by using it than by observing the satisfaction of a third party. While some tangible products that are purchased for a third party, like baby food and children's clothes, can be observed firsthand and physically compared, such comparisons are much more difficult for services. At best, a parent gains direct experience of a school through their child's homework assignments, communications from the child's teacher, PTA newsletters, and parent-teacher conferences. The cues enjoyed by residents without children in the public schools are even scantier.

The large number of schools in urban school districts aggravates these problems. In small districts of a half-dozen schools, community members are likely to feel comfortable extrapolating system performance from their perception of one or two schools. In a district of seventy-three schools (the sample mean), however, residents are unlikely to feel they can evaluate the system's overall performance based on firsthand information.[21] Concrete improvement in system performance may have only a weak effect on public opinion of system leadership in large districts.

Individuals without firsthand evidence about politics or policy rely heavily on the cues provided by local activists, community leaders, and the media.[22] The result is that media coverage has a bigger impact in large districts than in small districts. The community's reliance on local leaders and the media for cues about a district's performance reduces district leaders' ability to directly shape perceptions of system quality. This situation encourages the school leadership to emphasize visible and dramatic initiatives that will translate well to the general public.

Core Ambiguity

Policymakers find it very difficult to produce real change in schooling. They are restricted by contracts and civil service rules, while the opaqueness

20. The difficulty in evaluating schools is illustrated by decades of polling that shows most people view their children's school and their local school system positively, but the U.S. school system as a whole very negatively. See Elam, Rose, and Gallup (1994) and *The Public Perspective* (1993). Although people have grave concerns about the quality of the nation's schools, they have difficulty determining whether a given school or school system has problems.

21. Take a hypothetical couple with one child in elementary school and a second in high school. Through their children's activities, the parents might be in contact with the parents of children at one or two other elementary schools. In a small district of five schools, the couple is acquainted with families in over half of the district schools. In a district of seventy-three schools, the same couple will be acquainted with families in less than 5 percent of the district's schools.

22. See Carmines and Stimson (1989); Stimson (1990); and Popkin (1991).

of the teaching and learning core makes it difficult for administrators to know what effect changes will have.[23] In fields like the environment and agriculture, policymakers can utilize measures that produce unambiguous results. This is not the case in education, where "an enormous volume of educational research has turned up no curriculum, teaching technique, or special school program that consistently improves students' school performance."[24] Because there is no body of solutions with consistent effects, educators are unable to rely upon a set of time-tested remedies to set matters right.

Disagreement as to what good pedagogy entails makes it hard to control the quality of faculty. Evidence refutes the conventional wisdom that good teaching is obvious. The *Encyclopedia of Educational Research* has reported on the problems supervisors have evaluating the effectiveness of teachers: "It is so difficult to judge teacher effectiveness by observing teacher performance that hardly anyone can do it." Furthermore, the methods of assessing teachers' performance all have demonstrated flaws: "None of the three principal strategies available for evaluating teachers [competency tests, rating scales, measuring effectiveness] works satisfactorily." If evaluators cannot agree on what good teaching practice entails or how to measure it, administrators will have trouble directing classroom improvement.[25]

LACK OF TOOLS.   Not only do policymakers lack a clear sense of what constitutes good practice, but the tools at their disposal to improve teaching and learning are limited. Administrators have little formal authority to control teachers and classrooms. They "cannot monitor intensively enough to verify teachers' compliance, and . . . they can do little to reward or punish teachers. They cannot, for example, give or withhold raises, promote or demote, or substantially change assignments or working conditions as an incentive."[26] Improving teaching is particularly difficult for urban administrators overseeing faculties burdened by safety concerns, inadequate facilities, bureaucracy, unstable student populations, and a lack of classroom resources. Ossified urban bureaucracies tend to blunt the effectiveness of those tools that administrators may have at their disposal.

23. A report by the Organization for Economic Cooperation and Development concluded that "the search for the 'educational production function' that began in the 1960s ha[s] proven futile." See OECD (1996, 23).
24. Pauly (1991, 2).
25. Medley (1992, 1345, 1348).
26. Walker (1992, 285).

LOOSELY COUPLED ORGANIZATION OF LARGE URBAN SYSTEMS. School systems are "loosely coupled" organizations in which schools within a district and the classrooms within a school maintain a great deal of independence.[27] The "egg-crate" construction of classrooms gives teachers little sustained contact with one another, making it difficult to force reform into classroom practice. Isolated in this way, teachers cannot be easily supervised and are able to buffer themselves from the school around them by simply closing the classroom door.[28] In this context, lasting change in teaching and learning practice requires that reforms be delivered into each classroom separately and then infused into the school culture by sustained administrative effort.

The problems of loose coupling are accentuated in urban systems. The administrative team must supervise practice in dozens of schools and thousands of classrooms, and must do it through layers of management that increasingly distance the superintendent from students and their teachers.[29] While leaders in a small district may minimize the problems of loose coupling through a sustained personal presence in the schools and by careful hiring, these strategies are less effective in a system of fifty or one hundred schools with multiple layers of administrators and coordinators.

LACK OF TIME.   Finally, rapid executive turnover impedes the superintendent's ability to produce real organizational improvement. Although urban school observers like to imagine that each new superintendent brings the promise of an immediate turnaround, this is unrealistic: "Given the time needed to implement reforms, the long duration of schooling, and the cumulative nature of achievement, it is clearly unreasonable to expect the reforms to have large effects on test scores almost immediately after they [are] formally adopted."[30]

The textbook approach to education reform gives superintendents a long list of tasks: form committees to involve key stakeholders, give the committees an extended period to launch planning, have the participants agree

27. Weick (1976).
28. See Barth (1980) or Darling-Hammond (1996) for a discussion of how teachers' isolation affects reform efforts. Sizer (1996a, 65) has observed that "system reform, even if exquisitely designed, can founder on the unwillingness or incompetence of teachers. Top-down plans are easy to sabotage: teachers can close their doors and do what they want. . . . The people doing the job have to believe in it."
29. See Rogers and Chung (1983); Tyack (1974); and Ravitch and Viteritti (1997).
30. Koretz (1990, 385).

on priority objectives, generate plans from these guidelines, and initiate implementation with care to garner feedback and tend to the organizational culture. Transforming schools requires that administrators have "enough time to create change, make the necessary reforms, and measure the reforms. Such a process requires approximately two to five years."[31] Other researchers have suggested that the time necessary to fully implement changes in teaching practice is more like five to ten years.[32] In short, most urban school systems are too big, program effects occur too far downstream, and system outcomes are too ambiguous for superintendents to have a significant impact in just three or four years.

High Visibility

Schooling and education occupy a central place in the national consciousness.[33] Deemed essential to national well-being, schools are the most visible service provided by local government. Locally elected school boards deal with two of the leading concerns in any community: children and tax dollars. Schools are a source of community pride and have a direct impact upon local economic prospects and property values. Schools are also uniquely moral institutions that have long been viewed as "the cardinal organization of civic education and socialization."[34] Socializing children who are required by law to attend, schools are freighted with great normative significance.

With so much at stake, urban school policymakers cannot toil in anonymity. If school systems attracted little notice, the inability of policymakers to demonstrate improvement or to produce rapid changes in teaching and learning would be less significant. However, because schools are in the public eye, policymakers are pressed—not simply to run the schools well—but to convince the community that the schools are being run well.

The effects of high visibility are compounded because the media are not equipped to evaluate school system leadership based on actual performance. The pace of news reporting and the press's emphasis on the unique

31. Gallegos (1996, 27).

32. See David (1989) and Murphy (1991).

33. For instance, a 1996 NBC News/*Wall Street Journal* poll asked respondents to rate, on a scale of one to ten, how important to them each of sixteen issues was in deciding their vote for president in 1996. Respondents most frequently rated "dealing with education" as "most important." See *The Public Perspective* (1996, 42).

34. Iannaccone and Lutz (1995, 43). See also Greenfield (1995).

rather than the typical mean that school issues tend to be covered sporadically and superficially.[35] Urban school district policymakers are visible and vulnerable, and they are judged by media and local leaders who lack the means to evaluate their performance in a thorough and unbiased manner.

Input as the Barometer of Success

Since the community has difficulty judging superintendents, administrators, and board members on the actual improvements they produce, it judges them on their input—how innovative and hard-working they appear to be in pursuit of school improvement.[36] James Q. Wilson has observed that many public sector executives face similar incentives to emphasize activity rather than administration, "because they tend to be judged not by whether their agency is well-run but by whether the policies with which they are identified seem to succeed or fail."[37]

Reform is an ideal input measure because it is a visible promise of improvement. Indeed, "a certain magic surrounds the word change . . . that word seems to tap a well of hope—that events, conditions, and people will somehow be better than they are now."[38] Solving problems is less important to the political and professional health of school administrators than appearing to tackle them. None of this means that administrators do not want to solve problems, just that appearances become crucial. The support of the professional education community on reform becomes particularly important when appearances matter, because the professional pedigree protects the reformer from charges of malfeasance if the reform is perceived as unsuccessful.

Since superintendents have immense difficulty changing academic results, they benefit from this emphasis on effort. District visibility and the media's inability to objectively assess system performance intensify the focus on short-term public relations considerations. The media particularly tends to focus on dramatic and easily understood stories like test scores, violent incidents, lawsuits, awards, and reforms. The latter are the most ame-

---

35. See Ansolabehere, Behr, and Iyengar (1993); Banfield and Wilson (1963); and Patterson (1994) for a discussion of the media and the role it plays.

36. Carter and Cunningham (1997, 99) note, "Effort is probably the single most important factor in a board's assessment of a superintendent's performance."

37. Wilson (1989, 217).

38. Hanson (1996, 281).

nable to administrative control and the most certain to generate positive publicity.[39] One business community respondent in this study bluntly noted: "The superintendent put [curriculum reform] out there, but nothing seemed to happen with it. It was about control, not education reform. It was just doing something to keep your job from going away." Another respondent observed, "I don't think the newspapers challenge the school system to prove what it is that they're doing. . . . The administrators make all kinds of flowery statements about their success, but are never pushed by the media to prove where it is happening." In a turn rich with irony, the community support inspired by reform is then cited by policymakers as a success in its own right. One respondent noted that the district cited enhanced business community support as a success: "They've been able to draw in private companies and individuals to help fund some of the needs of the schools [and] they tout that quite a bit."

Proactivity also provides superintendents with certain benefits. It places them in a posture of control and allows them to shape the district agenda in a positive fashion. An active superintendent appears to know what the problems are and how to solve them. This dynamic not only encourages the pursuit of visible "solutions," but also the depiction of complex problems as simple ones that can be solved in a straightforward fashion. Because community residents and leaders "desire to believe that things are under control, that someone is responsible," policymakers strive to "create the illusion of control."[40]

Personal Incentives for Proactivity

The incentives encouraging superintendents to appear proactive are not malicious. Effective leadership requires that a superintendent retain his or her position, enjoy public confidence, and rally fiscal and volunteer support from the local community—all of which are aided by a superinten-

---

39. Urban school policymakers may not necessarily embrace reform, but it is one of the few reliable tools they possess. Similarly, city government policymakers seeking to bolster their reputations sometimes use tax breaks for companies to reassure the public "that something is being done about economic problems," while giving politicians "a chance to take credit for positive investment trends in the city." What makes tax abatement so attractive? Like school reform, it is available: "Like drowning sailors, politicians in declining economic areas grasp at anything thrown their way that could be a lifesaver. . . . The lack of alternatives is the key to understanding the attractiveness of tax abatement." See Swanstrom (1985, 147).

40. Stone (1988, 115). Also see Stone (1989) for a discussion of how problems get defined.

dent's reputation as competent and proactive.[41] The motivations compelling urban superintendents to indulge in the politics of school reform are rooted in the requirements of professional success and in the need to gain the support of the local community.

Professional Reputation

Those reformers perceived as successful are offered increasingly prestigious positions atop larger and larger districts, and find doors into government, consulting, and academia opened to them.[42] Proactive reformers are sought after by more prestigious districts, increasing their influence and visibility, while modeling a path to success that is replicated through self-selection and emulation. Less active superintendents are selected out. This Darwinian process operates regardless of whether superintendents use reform strategically, and it ensures that proactive superintendents dominate the profession.

A ware of their short expected tenure, superintendents learn to think of their present position as a short-term posting and to keep an eye on the job market. Superintendents need to rapidly establish their reputations, which they do by emphasizing input at the expense of careful program design, oversight, and implementation. Carrying on a predecessor's innovations is a caretaker role that does little to establish a strong reputation, so new superintendents fare better by launching their own reforms. Even successful oversight and implementation are often professionally self-defeating, because program successes are attributed to the program's initiator. On the other hand, the current superintendent who retains a predecessor's disappointing program will be blamed for not having "fixed" it.

Urban superintendents are faced with a dilemma. They can assume the role of manager and concentrate on refining specific initiatives; this en-

41. This point is similar to the observation by Mayhew (1974) that a member of Congress must first be reelected in order to pursue any other goal, however ennobling that larger goal may be.

42. Examples of this phenomenon abound. Deborah McGriff, a Detroit superintendent who pushed an aggressive school choice reform agenda, left to become an executive with the Edison Project. Thomas Payzant, the young superintendent of San Diego schools, moved first to a position in the U.S. Department of Education and then to the superintendency in Boston. Joseph Fernandez, who initiated an extensive site-based management program in Dade County, Florida, was made chancellor of the New York City school system. Robert Peterkin, whose tenure at the Milwaukee Public Schools featured a number of ambitious reform efforts, left to run the Urban Superintendents Program at Harvard University.

hances the likelihood of bringing about significant change but is politically dangerous. Or they can assume the role of reformer, initiating a great deal of activity and letting others worry about the results; this puts them in a position to take credit for successes—even while making significant change unlikely.

The unreliability of district-level outcome measures means that outcomes are largely perceptual. In this environment superintendents thrive by having visible programs that can plausibly be credited for apparent improvements. If the system is perceived as improving, the superintendent who proposes dramatic new initiatives can reap the credit. On the other hand, superintendents stand to gain no credit if they work to improve the system without changing existing policy. Any visible improvement will likely be credited to the predecessor who initiated the policy.

If the system is not thought to be improving, a superintendent without a visible agenda will be attacked as a "do-nothing" and replaced by a more promising successor. An activist superintendent is still in severe trouble if the system is not perceived as improving, but he or she may win a reprieve, either because "time is needed to make the program work" or because "he is battling hard to turn the schools around." Whether or not the schools are viewed as improving, proactive superintendents fare better professionally.[43] Superintendents do not have to be acting consciously or strategically for this dynamic to hold, because the institutional politics will weed out less-active administrators in favor of proactive ones.

This institutional dynamic reinforces the natural tendency of superintendents to overindulge in innovation. Like professionals of all stripes, superintendents want to do exciting new things that utilize their training and skills.[44] Superintendents have entered administration in order to improve school systems and their academic preparation has trained them to do this with innovative approaches.[45] Ambitious and highly trained executives desire to leave their mark and try new ideas. As one journalist observed of the

43. Former New York City Commissioner William Bratton provides an excellent example of how an active reform agenda can advance an executive's career. After Bratton became police commissioner in 1994, serious crimes there declined by 40 percent over a two-year period. Bratton attributed the drop to "his own aggressive management techniques." However, some criminologists credited the drop more to "a decline in the number of crime-prone juveniles, the introduction of longer jail sentences, and a shift from crack to heroin." Regardless of the empirical reasons for the drop in crime, Bratton was rewarded with international news coverage and a six-figure book contract. See Kaplan (1996, 3).

44. Mohr (1969); Ogawa (1994); and Wilson (1989).

45. Cuban (1976).

local superintendent, "She's a big proponent of school reform; she likes trying new ideas and strategies."

Professional pressures to be proactive are reinforced by the foundation members, researchers, professors, policymakers, and administrators who make up the educational policy community. Members of this community gain stature and resources by hunting for solutions, by getting programs in motion, and by seeing their ideas popularized.[46] Those reformers whose proposals are adopted gain stature, funding, and career advancement. Hot reforms "are featured in stories in the media [and] leading proponents are often able to secure funds from foundations or government agencies to mount demonstration projects."[47] Not unique to education, this phenomenon reflects the general perception that pursuing new solutions is what talented professionals do.[48] Senator Daniel Moynihan, a former Harvard professor and White House adviser, has noted that advisers to professional policymakers tend "to measure their success by the number of things they got started."[49] For members of the reform industry, it is less important that a proposal actually be new or significant than that it appear to be. The frequent result is that "new" innovations are actually recycled from previous waves of innovation.

The professional education community is insulated from the day-to-day routines of schooling and the messy details of reform efforts.[50] Consequently, it is quite easy for the reform advocates, academics, consultants, and state and national policymakers to slip into the habit of encouraging superintendents to move quickly and to show quick results. Foundations and government agencies find reform activity particularly well suited to their needs and are highly supportive of reform. Reforms are visible, promise obvious social value, only require funding for a specific purpose and a limited duration, permit the funder to point to a specific and promising contribution, and avoid entangling the funder in open-ended relationships. The need of the foundations and government agencies that fund and promote education reforms to generate visible, short-term results increases the pressure on reformers to move quickly and to oversell the results of each reform. One union respondent commented on how an influx of funding from the Pew Foundation encouraged a rosy appraisal of reform:

46. Brint and Karabel (1991); Heclo (1978); Magat (1995); and Rogers (1962).
47. Walker (1992, 282).
48. See Altshuler (1997) and Orlich (1989).
49. Quoted in Boyd (1978, 590–91).
50. See Silberman (1970) for a discussion.

I need to explain the role of the Pew Foundation, which has given money to the school board to push some of these reforms. The managers for Pew, in an effort to protect their reputation, manipulated an inaccurate study of what they had done. . . . If Pew gives you fifteen million dollars, then the reputation of the guy who gave you the money is affected. . . . [In the school system] there was an admission that [the program] didn't work. But they keep pretending that it did. And, if the union mentions it, then it's just, "There goes the union again."

There is little incentive for members of the reform community to spend time or energy questioning the value of a given "silver bullet," except when they are advancing an alternative solution. The result is an outpouring of remedies, with little dispassionate analysis. For instance, an extensive literature review in 1990 on site-based management found thirty-seven articles advocating SBM but just two directly contested its desirability or feasibility.[51]

The professional education community enjoys a mutually advantageous accommodation with district policymakers, who use the support of the reform community to win favorable press, professional recognition, and community support. The shared community of educational reformers and practitioners is a small one in which the "leaders . . . know one another (by name, if not personally), attend many of the same meetings, follow many of the same sources of news and opinion, and generally keep in touch."[52] In this context being affiliated with a hot, new idea is a ticket to professional stature and recognition. Superintendents who attempt dramatic innovations garner grants and professional rewards that are then used as proxies for performance. One Memphis respondent explained that the district's greatest recent achievement was being named a New American Schools Development Corporation district, even though there had been no substantive impact, because it meant that "Memphis is a progressive system." Superintendents who do not attempt innovations risk being perceived as laggards by their peers and the broader policy community. Because the perception of a superintendent's competence is crucial, status in the professional education community and the backing of reformers who validate a reform are tremendous resources.

51. See Malen, Ogawa, and Kranz (1990).
52. Walker (1992, 282).

Wanting to produce rapid improvement, or at least wanting to demonstrate commitment to rapid improvement, school boards seek superintendents identified with professionally endorsed remedies. Rather than hiring superintendents with the expectation that they will study the school system and then gradually develop a strategy to improve the school organization, boards often hire superintendents on the basis of a predetermined reform agenda. As one journalist noted, the current superintendent, "a former national education consultant," was recruited to come in "and put his agenda into action."

In 1971 Louis Smith and Pat Keith reported the advent of the "traveling salesperson" who spreads educational fads by shoring up friendly superintendents in the effort to gain adherents. They described the "out-of-town speaker who trades glowing epithets with the superintendent" and who "laud[s] the superintendent and the bright spots of Milford," and the superintendent who "introduce[s] the speaker as an educational statesman of 'ideas and integrity.'" The authors observed: "These characters need something new and different to talk about as they journey around. They reach so many people that a 'new' idea can spread rapidly. Superintendents and others looking for fame can grab hold and offer their school a case in point."[53] One union respondent in this study described the reform industry as a salesperson's scheme: "There's evidence that a lot of this stuff doesn't work as advertised. The experts are salespeople, they sell ideas and then hire each other at enormous salaries."

Community Prestige

In addition to professional reputation, a second, highly ironic, motivation spurs reform. Community support, regardless of the superintendent's professional aspirations, is crucial to any urban district's ability to improve its schools. District policymakers have a much better chance to produce substantial improvement if they enjoy business support, parental cooperation, the active participation of community organizations, and the backing of municipal officials. One respondent credited most of the district's recent successes to business, corporate, and civic support: "We have a tremendous education foundation. It probably leads the nation as far as corporate business. The district leaders are responsible. . . . [W]e have a Doorways program, where the community is sponsoring individual children for college scholarships and they are given mentors through school. It has been

53. Smith and Keith (1971, 118–19).

tremendously successful." The surest way for a school leader to earn this kind of support is to cultivate a reputation as a promising innovator. Superintendents who initiate reform efforts are feted in the local media, praised by the mayor and local business community, and offered a honeymoon in which to reshape troubled school systems.

Even those superintendents whose professional status is fairly secure are propelled into proactivity—if only as a tactic to rally resources and support. Because community members and school system participants are often unwilling to wait for results, superintendents who focus on the long term and fail to propose quick fixes will be handicapped by a lack of support and resources. Superintendents who proceed in a controlled, deliberate, incremental fashion will find their effectiveness hobbled by a lack of community prestige. In short, pursuing significant change in a responsible manner undermines the superintendent's ability to secure the resources and community trust necessary to enact significant change.

Community impatience with long-term solutions is understandable. It is considered perverse to explicitly suggest that a district "write off" the educational prospects of children over a certain age, simply because education is a long-term process. Diane Ravitch, a former assistant secretary of education, has noted that parents consider the suggestion that they wait for reforms to take hold "an outrageous proposition, for our own children live this day, in the here and now, and they cannot wait around to see whether the school will get better in five or ten years."[54] At some basic level communities want to believe that all children in the school district will have a chance to receive an adequate education before they graduate. Policymakers who talk about incremental progress are implicitly suggesting that the district will not improve rapidly enough to help many students. Seeking rapid improvement, communities rally behind those superintendents who promise to deliver just that. One respondent noted that the community was impatient because the superintendent had been in office two years without turning around the test scores: "The superintendent that they have now they've had for over two years, but his contract was up for renewal and they didn't renew it . . . due to the low early warning test scores."

The reputation of being a superintendent who gets things done enhances a superintendent's ability to actually get things done. One San Francisco respondent discussed the immense positive impact that the superintendency of Ray Cortines had on local support for the public schools:

54. Ravitch (1997, 253).

The move from thinking that "public schools are all bad" to "there's real leadership there" was initiated and really started rolling in Ray Cortines's time. So a lot of our success, particularly with people in leadership roles in the city, with businesspeople, politicians, state representatives thinking the school system isn't terrible, but is a shining light among districts, was under him. The present superintendent, the present board members, all benefit from that.

Even a superintendent who would prefer to proceed incrementally needs to enter with a proactive stance, simply to buy the time and support necessary to be effective.

A Commitment to Change

Easily blamed for unimaginative leadership, incrementalist superintendents tend to lose out in the Darwinian process of selection and promotion. Consequently, superintendents are encouraged to churn out reform with one hand, while seeking to manage and maintain the district with the other. These hectic reform efforts can produce chaos and do grave damage to a district's management and morale. One administrator discussed at length the damage a "boy wonder" superintendent with a hyperactive reform agenda had wrought after being hired on the strength of his professional reputation:

> We had the bad news [superintendent] for ... 51 weeks. He was an organization wrecker. It was unbelievable how a good organization was dismantled. If I'd have taken notes, I could have written a book. ... We found him in [another state], a search committee found him. He had a reputation as a boy wonder. Anybody in [this district] will tell you how he wrecked a good organization.

The administrator continued, describing the long-term harm done:

> The organization did not heal rapidly. The current superintendent has worked five years to try to rebuild the organization, and he's still working on it. The [former] superintendent poisoned the relationship with the teachers and the administration. ... [H]e made changes without input from staff members or the district. ... He came in, and his first thing was, "I'm not going to change anything." That lasted

10 days. For the next 50 days, and I counted this, a major change was made every day. I'm not kidding.

Focusing his energies on producing change, the superintendent was an ineffective manager. The administrator continued,

"I didn't want to get associated with him. I'll tell you how bad it was, we had to add a number of teachers to get in compliance with the [law mandating student-teacher ratios in the elementary schools]. Well, he just got the board to approve hiring those people at one board meeting. He ate up all the tax increase we can get under law with that one thing. [He left] no room [in the budget] for growth, inflation, salary [raises], the middle school concept, or any of the things he wanted to do. I got drafted to tell him this. And his reaction was, "Omigosh." He hit himself in the head. He hadn't thought it through, he hadn't thought about it. And the next board meeting he had them rescind [the hiring decision] because he couldn't afford it. As bright and as quick as he was, he was so impulsive it was unbelievable. He didn't think about culture or what people do. He just came in and knocked around.

The superintendent finally wore out his welcome and was driven out by the board: "Only one board member wanted to keep him when he left. He had come in with 7-0 board support, and his one supporter at the end was crazy. There was no board turnover in the interim. The board president said to the administrators at the end, 'Why didn't you all come to us and tell us how bad the guy was?'" A record as an "organization wrecker" has not kept this superintendent from steady employment. In fact, based on his reputation as a dynamic reformer, the superintendent has moved on from one district to the next: "he's the comeback kid. . . . He's got the ability to get a job, but not to keep a job."

SUPERINTENDENTS ARE HIRED FROM OUTSIDE.   The revolving door to the big-city superintendent's office and the need to quickly make a mark deter long-range planning or attention to managing for long-term improvement. A short expected tenure—the mean superintendent in this study had been in place 3.8 years—means that superintendents have only a short time to establish a track record. In fact, 40 percent of the superintendents in the sample districts had been in office for two years or less, and only one in five had been in place more than five years.[55]

Seventy-percent of the fifty-three districts had at least two superintendents between 1991 and 1995, and 30 percent had three or more superintendents in that five-year span. One school board president aptly summed up the expected rate of superintendent turnover, "The new superintendent is in his third year. . . . Usually, in an urban district, two or three years is it." One superintendent has observed that many superintendents leave on their own because "they want to move just like the Methodist ministers—to bigger school districts."[56] The fact that superintendents cannot expect to be around when their policies come to fruition discourages a focus on long-term improvement and encourages an emphasis on short-term crises and projecting a reassuring image of progress.

This short-term emphasis is aggravated because urban boards, in a blame-deflecting embrace of reform, tend to hire new superintendents from outside the system. As one respondent commented, "We did hire a new superintendent [an outsider] a year ago, and he promised to reform the system and change it from top to bottom." It is common for outsider superintendents to enter districts with a mission to "shake up the system," thus alleviating any obligation to build upon previous initiatives. Not unusual was the district where "the newly elected board brought in a superintendent to reorganize the district in 1990. He stayed two years, which was all he wanted, and then he declared success and left."

Hiring an outsider ensures that the superintendent will have no commitment to existent policies. The knowledge that one's successor will likely be an outsider discourages both initiatives that require sustained support and attempts to groom successors to carry on one's policies. Just 11 percent of the sample districts hired their current and their previous superintendents from within the district, while nearly 40 percent had hired both their current and their previous superintendents from outside of the district. Sixty percent of districts had hired their current superintendent from outside the district.

TURNOVER ACCELERATES THE PACE OF REFORM.   Superintendents rush into reform initiatives early in their tenure, when they are least knowl-

---

55. These statistics are based on the 53 districts for which superintendent data were collected.
56. Kowalski (1995, 37).

edgeable about the district and its needs, because they are able to rely upon broad public support and little opposition during an initial "honeymoon" period.[57] This is a crucial opportunity for superintendents to enact favored solutions, build popular support, and establish a proactive record, because they will gradually alienate some supporters over time. As one superintendent described the beginning of his tenure, "I just did what I wanted to do. You know, you have a period of time when you have a honeymoon. For me, it lasted about a year."

The effect of turnover on district activity was examined by comparing how many kinds of reform were initiated in districts with rapid superintendent turnover as opposed to those with stable leadership. Those districts that hired three or more superintendents in the 1991–95 period proposed 13 percent more reform than districts that had only one superintendent throughout the period. The sixteen districts with just one superintendent proposed reforms in 3.1 of the five Third Wave reform areas, while the sixteen with three or more superintendents proposed reform in 3.5 areas. Similarly, districts with superintendents in office for two years or less were much more active than districts with veteran superintendents, despite the logistical problems a new superintendent confronts in simply getting new proposals under way. The twenty-one districts where superintendents had been in office for two years or less proposed reforms in an average of 3.4 reform areas—a 30 percent increase from the 2.6 kinds of reform proposed in the six districts where the superintendents had been in place for seven or more years. Because of the high rate of turnover, only a handful of long-term superintendents were available for comparison. While new superintendents pursued reform much more aggressively than did veterans, even superintendents with extremely long tenure initiated large amounts of reform.

The evidence suggests that superintendents do not analyze district needs, select the appropriate reforms, and then focus on implementation. Rather, each successive superintendent quickly launches new programs, often with widespread support. One board member spoke approvingly of the multiple measures that a series of superintendents in a high-turnover district had initiated but not completed: "[S]ince there's been quite a bit of turnover . . . each [superintendent] has played a role to move [the district]

---

57. See Light (1983); Brody (1991); and Neustadt (1990) for a discussion of executive honeymoons in national politics.

forward. . . . No one superintendent took it from the planning stage to implementation. There have been changes along the way."

ALL SUPERINTENDENTS IN SAMPLE SUPPORT ALL REFORMS.   All superintendents, but especially new superintendents, propose and support reform. For each of the five kinds of reform (time and school day, curriculum, evaluation of students, professional development, and site-based management) in every single district, the respondents rated the superintendent as supportive of proposed reforms.[58] These dramatic figures are consistent with a previous finding that superintendents get their way 99 percent of the time when dealing with school boards.[59]

Politically successful superintendents learn to help the school board forge a consensus on reform efforts. One union respondent observed that the superintendent "won't take a vote unless he has a consensus. He's very careful about not bringing votes to the public unless he's done his homework on it." By defusing board members' concerns and earning their broad support for reform, the superintendent meets the expectations of both the professional and local communities.

The Churning of School Reform

Each successive superintendent is hired to implement a reform agenda. Each has incentives that encourage more emphasis on program initiation than on follow-through. The short expected tenure of superintendents means that few are in place long enough to oversee the full life-cycle of a reform, and incoming superintendents are not rewarded for implementing a predecessor's program. The result is "policy churn"—an endless stream of new initiatives, with the schools and teachers never having time to become comfortable with any given change. For example, faced with poor educa-

58. Each time a respondent said that a given type of reform had been proposed, the respondent was asked whether the superintendent had supported, not taken a position on, or opposed the reform. Each district was scored according to the mean local response. Only those districts where a reform was reported by at least one respondent were included. That is why reforms were sometimes reported for fewer than fifty-seven districts. Fifty districts were reported for time and school day measures, fifty-one districts for evaluation measures, and fifty-six districts for professional development measures.

59. See Zeigler, Kehoe, and Reisman (1985).

tional results, the Milwaukee public schools "launched initiative after initiative in the name of educational reform." Not only have these efforts "not produced improved academic achievement. . . . In some cases, the ink is barely dry on one project before the next is begun."[60] This churning helps to explain why education innovations seem to have a very short half-life. The same kinds of measures reappear with different packaging and different names. In fact, while some districts in the sample were busily working to reform practice A to practice B, other districts were "reforming" from B to A.

Faced with this endless stream of half-measures, veteran teachers turn cynical about the process of reform and do not invest much energy in conforming with reforms that will likely soon be gone. As education scholar Susan Moore Johnson has observed:

> Rapid turnover, particularly in urban districts, leaves teachers and principals even more skeptical about superintendents' proposals. Knowing that superintendents must make their mark quickly if they are to keep their jobs or find better ones, teachers and principals often resent becoming agents of someone else's career advancement. Fearing that rapid and visible change imposed by a new superintendent may lead to inchoate programs and wasted energy, teachers and others often become cynical and resist superintendents' enthusiastic plans to reform them and their schools.[61]

School districts engage in a number of reform initiatives, with one generation of reforms following another, while never fully implementing any given reform. Reform can actually be a hindrance, consuming time, money, and energy, while distracting school personnel from becoming more proficient at specific teaching and learning tasks.

Any given method of schooling or teaching is likely to prove more effective with practice and refinement. However, the time and energy consumed by cycles of reform make it more difficult for urban school boards, educators, and parents to focus on improving particular approaches to teaching and learning. The result is that education innovation "is both a

60. Mitchell (1994, 13–14).
61. Johnson (1996, 92).

story about periodic cycles of policy innovation around relatively predict-able themes and a story about a 'cottage industry' of innovations in instruc-tional practice, neither of which seem to have much sustained effect on the enterprise as a whole."[62]

A frenetic search for quick solutions is precisely the kind of leadership unlikely to produce long-term improvement. Good management practice requires leaders to become knowledgeable of their organization's behav-ior, institutions, problems, and culture before proposing changes and to support changes with careful planning, training, and implementation.[63] Or-ganization members need time to absorb the new expectations and adjust their behavior. A management consulting executive has suggested, "Change requires close attention to all aspects of people-management. New internal cultures demand new behaviors, new selection processes. . . . But, what we all-too-often see in these key areas is an unconnected and sometimes ill-timed series of changes."[64]

Meaningful change requires time, and it is time that is in short supply for urban superintendents. Urban districts that are desperately in need of delib-erate, effective improvement are guided by unstable leaders in a short-term environment. The result is that urban policymakers pursue reform with in-sufficient planning and fragmented organizational support.

The contradiction between the imperatives of reform practice and the tenets of management practice is so strong that some ardent reformers have attempted to argue that planning is superfluous or harmful. Given the con-straints education policymakers face, it is not surprising that some have tended to give implementation short shrift. Most full-length books advo-cating specific "silver bullet" reforms offer no more than a handful of vague banalities regarding implementation or the public policy process. Attempting to make policy churn into a virtue, ardent reformers maintain that districts need to practice "fluid" change: "More than a few educational researchers believe planning makes little contribution to serious school im-provement. . . . [S]ome studies suggest that 'top-down, technological plan-ning' planning should give way to a more fluid model, in which 'a thou-sand flowers bloom.'"[65] Other reformers have called for an unstructured

62. Elmore (1991a, 5).

63. See Donnelly, Gibson, and Ivancevich (1981) and Hersey and Blanchard (1977) for a gen-eral discussion of managing change. See Doll (1996) and Ornstein and Hunkins (1993) for a dis-cussion of managing educational change.

64. Hay Group (1996).

65. Louis and Miles (1991, 95).

process of "continuous change," which avoids the "ossification" of standards or predetermined goals.[66] This belief that planning stifles reform has enshrined innovation as an end in itself and has caused "reformers [to lose] sight of the supposed central questions of the purpose of change."[67] The desire to have "a thousand flowers bloom" opens the floodgates to a thousand slapdash reforms.

Hull: A Study in School Reform Politics

In 1987 a rookie superintendent took the helm of Hull, Massachusetts, a small urban school district, when the old superintendent retired in 1987. After the successive defeats of a tax increase, the school board sought a reformer in order to bolster community support. A board member explained that "after two failed efforts to override Proposition Two-and-a-Half in town, we needed someone who would be proactive, dynamic, strong in community relations, and an innovator. We needed someone to keep kids from abandoning ship and going to private schools, to establish a campaign that this was a good school system to send kids to." [68]

The new superintendent's first priority was to build community confidence in the school system. Claire Scheff, the new superintendent, told district faculty that her first goals were "to restore public confidence in the Hull Schools, to establish trust and credibility with the community; and, through the first two goals, to secure enough financial support to operate the schools." Scheff came into office inclined to pursue change, noting, "I want to feel I am making a difference." Scheff began by launching a barrage of reforms in her first eighteen months. Her efforts "in 1989 alone reflect[ed] more change than many superintendents attempt in a decade." The flurry of reform generated positive public attention and increased community support for the schools. Meanwhile, Scheff won career-enhancing plaudits for her energetic leadership:

In 1989–90, the town voted to increase both the superintendent's salary and the school budget for the first time in a number of years. . . . That year, [Scheff] became the first rookie superintendent to be honored with the President's Award of the Massachusetts Associations

66. Clarke and Agne (1997, 350).
67. Fullan (1991, 23).
68. See chapter 1 in Wagner (1994).

of School Superintendents. Area newspapers began to run very positive, upbeat stories about changes in the school system. By 1990,
headlines like "The Sky's the Limit" . . . were commonplace in the
local papers.[69]

Scheff earned accolades from her peers and the community, but not from
Hull's teachers. The faculty worried "about all the changes, which they felt
were being imposed upon them by a young, upstart superintendent" who
"continued to move forward in 1990 with far-reaching plans." After nearly
two years of "dynamic leadership and bold plans for systemic change" little progress was evident, while "students and teachers alike seem disen-
gaged and deeply demoralized."

Why did Scheff's motivated leadership fail to win faculty support? In
fact, the teachers were not demoralized despite Scheff's dynamic leadership, but were overwhelmed by the amount of activity:

> Trying to undertake too many changes at once was [a problem]. . . .
> When asked what had been hardest about the year, one teacher said,
> "Everything's been too fragmented. There have been too many
> things initiated. . . . It would have been far better to have devoted
> time and energy to a few things, instead of trying to do so much."

These comments were echoed by many teachers. Their difficulty resulted in part "from their inexperience with teaching techniques new to
them. . . . They wanted to see teachers successfully doing some of the
things they were being asked to try. They wanted models for change and
more training." Given the pace of change, these resources were not available. Reform also soaked up teachers' time. One teacher commented, "I've
never worked so hard in my life as I have this year. What's been so hard is
that we had no models. We had to start from scratch." Time was only part
of the problem, however. Time and resources alone "would not necessarily
have produced clear goals."

Slightly over three years into Scheff's administration, "most Hull teachers . . . seemed to be sitting on the sidelines—perhaps waiting for what they
saw as the latest school reform fad to blow over, or waiting for a new superintendent." Within two more years, Scheff declared victory and left

69. All the quotes in this section are from Wagner (1994, 21–24, 47–51, and 78).

Hull for a more prestigious job as superintendent of a larger system, leaving a slew of unfinished initiatives and a resentful faculty. Scheff entered the system with an unfocused and demanding set of reforms that required teachers to invest substantial time and energy. The visible presence of these reforms effectively addressed public relations concerns, but the initial moves were not accompanied by attention to training faculty, convincing teachers to accept the reforms as integral and permanent, by a focused commitment, or by adequate resources. The result was that the faculty did not cooperate with the initiatives and, despite positive public response, little real change occurred in the schools. In the end after the district had churned through one more cynicism-enhancing wave of reform, the superintendent rode an enhanced reputation to a better job.

Conclusion

The experience of the urban school district in Hull is not unique. Theodore Sizer, the chairman of the Coalition for Essential Schools and former dean of the Harvard Graduate School of Education, believes the system of public school governance

is fundamentally flawed. . . . I've watched too many good people in too many districts come in as the new superintendent—the answer to the prayer, the man on the white horse. Three years later they're out on their ear and the next one is brought in. Now this one is going to get it right. And then the next one, and then the next one.[70]

The pressures of "professional reputation" and "community prestige" compel superintendents' political use of school reform.[71] The effects of the two are intertwined, and this study leaves the task of disaggregating their influence to future research. The combined effect, however, is unmistakable: waves of symbolic rather than substantive reform.

Superintendents, like all organizational leaders, are likely to focus on outcomes when they know that accurate assessments of the outcomes they produce are available; they can substantially affect the outcomes; and those judging their performance use the assessments in a manner that emphasizes

70. Sizer (1996b, 4).
71. Richard Neustadt's notion of presidential "public prestige" and "professional reputation" is somewhat reworked in this context. See Neustadt (1990).

substantive performance. Unfortunately, none of these conditions exists in urban schools.

Efforts to change urban schools are handicapped by the very nature of schooling. Hemmed in by contracts, civil service rules, and few means to reward or sanction employees, superintendents have very limited influence on urban school organizations. Educators also lack proven and reliable methods with which to produce better teaching and learning. Confusion over how to improve teaching and learning is compounded by the loosely coupled nature and large size of urban school systems, which make it difficult for policymakers to change what happens in the classroom. Frustration with mediocre school performance aggravates this situation because the residents in urban districts are not willing to wait several years for slow-developing improvements to take shape.[72] Educators respond by promising quick results, thereby forcing themselves to tackle a painstaking and uncertain job in a slipshod fashion.

72. After declaring that improving Boston's schools would be his top priority, Mayor Tom Menino hired former San Diego superintendent and renowned reformer Thomas Payzant as superintendent in 1995 and charged him with turning around the floundering system. Payzant instituted a new test in the spring of 1996 in order to take stock of the system's difficulties. On the new test, fewer than one in four eleventh graders scored at grade level on math or reading skills. Despite this miserable performance, the executive director of the Citywide Parents Council said, "I expect to see a big improvement next year, *at least for all grades to be at the basic level.*" See Avenoso (1996, 1 [emphasis added]).

3

The Supporting Players in Urban School Reform

THERE IS LITTLE empirical research assessing the roles of school boards, unions, and states in district-level reform activity. Conventional accounts have underestimated the importance of school boards while emphasizing the influence of state governments and teachers' unions. Understanding of school reform has been particularly impeded by misconceptions about the nature of urban school boards. They are usually portrayed in the press as conflictual, ideologically driven, and resistant to reform.[1] To the contrary, school boards tend to be politically moderate, and they have cooperated on Third Wave reforms endorsed by professional administrators. Together boards and administrators have supported a churning cycle of largely symbolic activity.

To manage an enormous organization with meager resources, urban school boards seek superintendents who can bolster the board's collective stature. A visible reform agenda permits superintendents, and indirectly board members, to claim credit for promoting school improvement while reducing public controversy. Urban boards cooperated on Third Wave reforms, even as they battled over particularistic and politically rewarding issues like salaries and school closings. Eager to promote an image of progress and promise, amateur board members leave it to the experienced

---

1. Danzberger (1994, 370) has suggested that "overt dysfunctional conflict is too often in evidence in the public meetings of the majority of urban school boards." Duchensne (1998, 39a) gives another account of a conflictual board: "Midway through the school year, teachers are teaching, the students are learning, and the Dallas school board is bickering." A *Plain Dealer* article reported that the Citizens' League of Greater Cleveland had called Cleveland's school board "too broken to fix" (Stephens 1995a, 1B).

administrators to take the lead on reform and forge proposals that enjoy broad board support.

Teachers' unions are often characterized as ardent opponents of school reform.[2] This study challenges that interpretation, at least for the kinds of reforms prominent in the Third Wave. Teachers' contract language limits the nature and scope of permissible reforms, and their unions are more receptive to reforms that do not challenge contract parameters.[3] Because they had a great deal of input through the contract and through negotiations with the administration, unions during 1992 to 1995 were generally supportive of the proposed reforms. However, the need to win union acquiescence discourages local policymakers from emphasizing reforms that require significant change from teachers.

State mandates help to shape school reform, but the real impact of state reform efforts is largely determined by local capacity and conditions.[4] Studied from the district level, state mandates are hazier and less influential than they appear from a state-centered perspective. Local respondents considered the state's role in school policy to be more financial than reform oriented. The states encouraged high rates of reform activity but were not the primary engines of Third Wave reform. Respondents clearly viewed superintendents and school boards as the dominant actors in local school policy (see figure 3-1).

School Boards: Eager to Please

Urban school boards are loosely structured bodies characterized by limited resources, an imperfect grasp of the school system, and a nonpartisan environment. These traits make it easy for boards to appear rudderless. In fact, urban boards demonstrated remarkable cohesion in their support of reform.

Local school boards have been wrongly "cast in a passive role as weak reactors or even deterrents, rather than as partners in shaping educational improvement."[5] In fact, they tend to cohesively endorse reform proposals.

---

2. Popular accounts depict teachers' unions as a powerful force in schooling and assail the unions for resisting reform. "In the 34 years since the signing of the first teacher collective-bargaining contract in New York City, teacher unions have become the single most influential force in public education. . . . [T]he intransigence of the unions has slowed the pace of school reforms, eroding public confidence in the schools" (Toch and others 1996, 62). See also Chase (1996, 24); Gergen (1997, 100); and Slackman (1997, A3).

3. Bierlein (1993); Magat (1995); and Rury (1993).

4. Chrispeels (1997); Driscoll (1996); and Kirp and Driver (1995).

5. Wirt and Kirst (1989, 163).

Figure 3-1. Most Influential Actors in the Making of Local School Policy, 1992–95

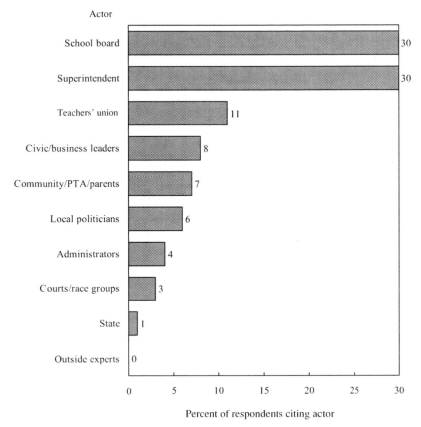

Source: Author's data.

Boards engaged in extended open conflict risk being brought up sharply by the local voters. As one board member noted, "Even though [the board] cover[s] all income levels and races and ethnicities in the city, we've collaborated quite effectively [on reform]. We don't have a lot of the pettiness and infighting." When urban school boards address reform, the respondents reported relatively little controversy. The popular perception that urban boards are conflictual can be largely attributed to the fights that erupt over zero-sum issues like contracts, salaries, and school closings.[6]

---

6. As one NAACP director said of school policy in his district, "It's all about economics, jobs and contracts, rather than educating the students."

Urban board management of school reform is distinct from its management of other issues. In his classic study of the Chicago school board, Paul Peterson has noted that the board addressed some issues in a "pluralist" fashion and others in a "unitary" fashion. Pluralist bargaining involves the competition among various groups seeking to protect their class, race, neighborhood, or ideological interests. Unitary bargaining is more likely when board members agree on certain objectives and steer their decisions according to these objectives.[7] Although most of the allocative and distributive issues that come before urban boards prompt them to behave in a pluralist fashion, the nature of reform makes it easy to consider reform in a unitary fashion.

To compensate for pluralist conflicts, urban boards cooperate when addressing reform because they need to convey the impression that they are advancing the public interest. Board members are concerned with maintaining their community stature for at least three reasons. First, most members will face reelection challenges and some entertain thoughts of running for higher office. Second, members can rely on neither geographical distance nor the prestige of high office to buffer them from community dissatisfaction. Third, the community support attracted by respected leadership is viewed by board members as crucial for financial support and improved school performance. "One of the key questions is whether we have the level of community interest to make it to the finish line," said one board member about a local reform. In urban districts, where a frustrated public generally views school performance as poor, boards badly need to demonstrate their competence.

Without the guideposts of party or ideology, board members have great difficulty stirring and mobilizing the party faithful. This is particularly true because the public is generally apathetic about school governance. When running for reelection or higher office, members rely on their stature, the board's reputation, and narrow neighborhood or community constituencies. Because community members have little detailed knowledge of school affairs, a board member gets little credit for arguing about reform. Such a stance can even make the board member appear cavalier about school improvement. A board member is more likely to take a controversial position on neighborhood or values-laden issues that promise electoral support from a specific bloc of local constituents.

In South Bend, Indiana, a respondent reported that community attention to education focused on the building of a new high school and the closing

7. Peterson (1976).

of other schools. Community divisions became apparent. "Some people are putting a racial tone on it," the respondent explained. "They don't want the new school in the inner city, but moved to suburban areas."

The Political Value of School Reform

Conflicts over resource distribution, ideology, morality, and ethnic tension are inevitable. The extent of discord is aggravated, however, by the amateurism and informal structure of urban boards. Reform can help boards compensate for their handicaps in attempting to resolve or manage these conflicts. Boards cede the job of managing the district to the administrative staff, under the direction of the superintendent, then encourage the superintendent to promote reform as a means of improving the school system. Finally, the board quietly reaches consensus on reform under the direction of the superintendent, who has the resources to initiate and direct reform efforts.

Boards that lack the credibility that reform helps to augment can find themselves the target of a community uprising when distributive or ideological conflicts become too prominent. One respondent described community frustration with a board that "didn't believe in compromise, and had a lot of conflict in school board meetings." The result was a housecleaning: "Community dissatisfaction produced voter input that changed the board. . . . Two new board members were elected within the last year, and five within the last three years." When confronted with community displeasure, a board either cultivates its reputation or risks being purged and governed by a new majority that will do so.

Amateurism

Urban school boards lack a strong formal organization, operate in a largely nonpartisan political environment, conduct all formal votes in the public eye, and lack the time or resources necessary for disciplined legislating.[8] Members are elected in sparsely attended elections; the central issues are often undefined and the candidates' positions unclear. Said one minority organization respondent:

> In a school board election, there are twelve people up and it's like throwing six darts at a board, and the six people hit win the election.

8. Wirt and Kirst (1989).

It's a hard thing to grasp what the real issues are. . . . Some get elected because they seem like gutsy fighters and not because they're going to reduce taxes. But sometimes voter turnout is so small that it doesn't really represent the community.

Three-quarters of the sample school boards had at least seven members, and a third had nine or more members.[9] Problems coordinating and controlling the behavior of seven or nine part-time amateurs were aggravated because 80 percent of the sample school boards meet no more than two times a month. Part-time status further restricts the ability of board members to attend to school system issues. In only two or three of the sample districts did board salaries approach those of full-time legislators. The mean salary for board members in the sample districts was $4,280 a year. Even for members in the twenty-six districts with 250,000 or more residents, the mean annual salary was only $6,160.

Limited resources aggravate the demands placed on school board members. Eighty-nine percent of the sample districts provided board members with neither personal staff nor personal office space. In fact, just one district supplied board members with personal staff. The part-time members who populate boards are left largely to their own devices. A board member in a district with more than 48,000 students described board facilities this way: "We can find a desk somewhere. Someone will move over for a board member." This informal arrangement was fairly typical. Another board member described "a cubbyhole in the district offices that we all use." Probably the most typical setup was the functional but minimalist arrangement in Pittsburgh, where the board shared "group office space and two secretaries for all nine board members. There is also a board office with a desk and a computer that all nine members share."

Boards have few politically seasoned members to guide them. On fewer than one in three boards had even one member previously run for another political office, and fewer than 5 percent of boards had multiple members who had done so. School boards are a place where novices begin their political career, and frequently where individuals have their first in-depth involvement in educational affairs.

9. The following statistics on school board makeup include fifty-six of the fifty-seven sample districts.

Boards endure a great deal of membership turnover, which impedes institutional memory and coordinated governance.[10] Nearly three out of four boards had a membership that included at least 25 percent first-term members. A respondent explained that the amateur status of board members narrowed the board's base of experience and vision: "Board members are volunteers with limited power, so oftentimes they're dealing with a fairly limited perspective. I don't want to say they're handmaidens of the administration, but a lot of times their time is spent more on personnel issues and negotiating contracts." Ninety-five percent of the sample school boards were selected in a staggered fashion. This further complicates governance by preventing cohesive majorities from taking control of a board in a single election.

A substantial majority (57 percent) of school board members in the sample districts were elected at-large, with most of the rest elected in district elections. Fewer than 10 percent of board members in the sample districts were appointed to office. At-large election makes it difficult for board members to rely upon constituency service and neighborhood representation to build support, forcing members to worry more about the community's perception of the board as a whole.

Nonpartisan and Moderate School Boards

School boards operate in a nonpartisan environment, in which board members lack the guidance of party and have no convenient way to assess constituent sentiment. Of the fifty-one sample districts in which boards were elected, 94 percent were selected in nonpartisan elections; the five appointed boards were all selected in a nonpartisan manner featuring a screening committee of community leaders. When respondents were asked to rank the influence of community groups on school board decisions, they cited the local Democratic and Republican parties as exerting the least influence of the nine groups named. Traditional political parties play a minimal role in school affairs, and the resulting nonpartisanship encourages

10. See Arnold (1990) for a discussion of this point in the context of the U.S. Congress. On school boards the high rate of turnover is not due to exceptionally long terms, which would ensure that board members might acquire extensive experience in a single term. In the sample districts more than 70 percent of board terms ran for four years, while just 12 percent of terms ran longer than that.

"candidates to avoid controversial questions . . . because the situation requires them to try to appeal to the whole electorate."[11]

On some hot-button issues board members can obey the dictates of ideology, neighborhood, or race. One board respondent reported that his board clashed only on racial issues: "The only bloc voting you see is on something that's a racial issue." On questions of reform, however, ideology and community rarely provide useful cues. In this ambiguous environment board divisions are rare and tend to have little to do with partisan politics or liberal-conservative ideology.

Consistent with the evidence on nonpartisanship, most of the boards in the sample were described as politically moderate. Contrary to some reports, there was no evidence that conservative or religious groups exerted much influence on the boards studied. Fewer than 5 percent of them were described as either "very conservative" or "very liberal" by local respondents. Member coalitions shifted on different issues. "If it's a financial issue, there's one bloc; if it's an educational issue it's a different bloc," explained one Duluth, Minnesota, respondent. A respondent in Minneapolis observed, "Blocs are divided sometimes by color lines, other times by financial lines. Other times it's just due to personal understandings." Board divisions appear to owe as much to personality as to ideology. One board member said of her board's voting blocs, "God only knows what differentiates the blocs. I guess it's who you know."

Surprisingly Ambitious Members

School board members across the broad range of districts have been depicted as lacking political ambition.[12] Political inexperience, however, is not the same as a lack of political interest. Rather, a former urban superintendent has argued that contemporary school board members are "pure politicians"—"concerned primarily with reelection or higher political office and paying assiduous attention to serving political constituents."[13] One respondent scathingly said, "For instance, in Oakland, everybody's given up on the schools, so board members feel okay about using the school board

11. Banfield and Wilson (1963, 165).
12. Wirt and Kirst (1989). Other research, however, has argued that board members are indeed "concerned with political constituents and with getting reelected" (Carter and Cunningham 1997, 103). The president of the Center for Leadership in School Reform has suggested that most urban school board members view themselves as political figures (Holland 1994, 2B).
13. Bennett (1991, 23).

for personal advancement." In fact, urban school boards provide something of a political training ground. One administrator observed:

> The school committee is the initial political vehicle for one moving up politically. The first thing you do if you're interested in being a political player in [the city] is to run for the school committee. That becomes a stepping stone for running for city council, which becomes a stepping stone for running for the state house. So there's a lot of interest in the school committee. . . . It's a feeding chain.

In an urban district it is not unusual for an incumbent board member to be defeated or for a sitting board member to pursue higher office. Over half of the sample districts had an incumbent board member defeated in a re-election bid between 1992 and 1995. These figures are more impressive if one recognizes that merely knowing someone who had a close election, or hearing stories about close calls, can cause legislators to run scared.[14] Over half of all school board members had seen at least one fellow board member recently defeated, and most board members had witnessed at least one serious challenge in the past three years. When asked about the frequency of "serious" school board challenges, respondents in every district reported that incumbent board members are seriously challenged at least "sometimes," and 58 percent of districts reported that incumbents "usually" or "always" face a "serious challenger." On no school board is the possibility of being challenged and defeated an irrelevant consideration.

School boards are a starting point for those entering community politics. Most boards had members aspiring to higher office, and just under half of the districts had a board member run for higher office in the 1992–95 period. Just as the knowledge of another's near-defeat may instill fear in a board member, the knowledge that others have launched a political career from the board may inspire others with similar ambitions.[15]

A majority of boards in the sample were described as "mostly" composed of members ambitious for higher office. No board was viewed as entirely apolitical. The political nature of boards is heightened because some board members initially ran for office due to neighborhood concerns, but get bitten by the political bug once in office. As one self-professed amateur

14. Mayhew (1974).
15. Superintendents interviewed by Kowalski (1995, 50) considered board members to be politically ambitious.

board member said, "When anyone asks me about [city council], I tell them that of course I think about that."

Harsh Consequences for Controversial Boards

Members of school boards seen as irresponsible can face harsh political consequences. Consequently, board members use reform to demonstrate their unity and competence, and this perception of unity helps to protect the reputations and political prospects of board members.

Unified boards were substantially less likely to see incumbent board members seriously challenged or defeated during 1992 to 1995 than were divided boards. There was a negative 0.40 correlation between district board unity (measured on a zero-to-ten scale where zero meant "no agreement" and ten meant "board unanimity") and the frequency with which incumbent board members were "seriously challenged" for reelection. Between 1992 and 1995, incumbent members of unified boards were also less likely to be defeated. Incumbent board members fared better in districts with unified boards. While it is difficult to determine definitively whether board unity aided incumbents or whether more stable boards become more unified over time, the reduced number of serious challengers in unified districts strongly suggests that members of unified boards benefit politically from board cohesion.

The hazardous consequences of untamed conflict were most clear in sample districts where the community lost faith in the board and purged the membership. Respondents described community purges between 1988 and 1995 in several districts. Local organizations, often with the business community playing a prominent role, backed slates of candidates pledging to refocus the board on improving the school system. St. Louis and Atlanta offer excellent illustrations of how insufficient attention to the board's reputation crippled its members' reputations, political ambitions, and policy goals.

PRESERVING THE CIVIC REPUTATION IN ST. LOUIS.   The St. Louis school board was purged in the early 1990s after years of recurring conflict had led to the formation of a citywide reform coalition called Civic Progress. Supported by the business community, Civic Progress assumed leadership in the school fight.

The controversial school board had taken shape in the late 1980s, a period marked by concerns over racial issues and the condition of facilities. The community had "withheld any bond approval from 1962 to 1990, as a result of the problems they felt with the racial mix." Community apathy and frustration with this state of affairs led in 1988 to a "white citizens' council," which captured six of the twelve seats on the at-large school board. Because "the white group voted in a bloc," the district went "about three years with overwhelmingly 6-6 votes, so we never got anything done." Money was also in short supply. The district finally passed a bond in 1990, but it was immediately challenged and later thrown out on a technicality.

The white rights group's agenda, and the ensuing paralysis on the school board, created anxiety among the community leaders and the downtown business community. The white citizens' council was seen as divisive and blamed for the problems. One respondent remembered that concern with the board "had a lot to do with the image of the city as a whole, and the big-time business people didn't want us to be painted as a racist southern city." Another respondent described the white citizens' council as an organization that "infiltrated" the board and then "went about the business of destroying the St. Louis public schools." The respondent explained:

> [The district] had a black superintendent at the time, and the white citizens' council group were hell-bent on destroying or trying to destroy any cooperativeness in the community. They wouldn't even visit the north side schools, which are predominantly minority, and anything related to the minority population they had nothing to do with. This was all done under the guise of stopping busing. They felt the only way to do this was to stop minority hiring and stop anything that smacked of fairness or equity.

By 1992 the community had been mobilized. "People were energized by . . . the fact that the judge threw out the hard-fought bond issue . . . [and by] the head-on clash of two slates, the white rights group and a progressive slate." The effort to purge the board was spearheaded by black community leaders: "There had been a coalition of progressive and interracial leaders offering and financing a slate. The black leadership roundtable generated the impetus for the coalition, and the business community is in that coalition." From that impetus emerged Civic Progress, the community-wide coalition.

Community leaders organized a cooperative organization to funnel assistance to the Civic Progress slate and to remove the embarrassing board members.[16] The PTA, the Chamber of Commerce, the NAACP, and civic associations supported the progressive slate. "Nobody tiptoed around the issue. It was full steam ahead," recalled one respondent. Another respondent remembered the behind-the-scenes maneuvering:

> We were able to get rid of the white supremacists . . . [and] it was accomplished sub rosa. Our school board is elected at large, so we set up sort of a funnel organization that screened candidates and that offered backing for those candidates that most adequately seemed to reflect good policies for the school system. The assistance was a little bit of everything, some financial, some working of the press, some public relations assistance for the slate we thought was most adequate. There was no formal endorsement.

Fearing that the city's reputation would sustain long-term damage, business community leaders and wealthy suburban residents worked together to oust the white citizens' council. Initially it was viewed as an economic conservative group "and then that mask came away and people saw they were really a separatist group," explained another respondent. "And once people understood what was going on, the vote was tremendous in terms of turnout and support of the progressive slate."

Members of the white citizens' council "were either defeated or chose not to run again." One respondent in 1995 noted that "seven or eight out of the twelve members on the current board were supported by Civic Progress, though Civic Progress doesn't support them openly."

The broad-based membership of Civic Progress was unusual in St. Louis politics, usually characterized by tensions between its urban and suburban residents. One respondent described the status quo: "Most of the people on the Civic Progress board are well off financially . . . nominally live in the county, and generally send their kids to private schools. So they try to keep a low profile because [they] don't want it to look to city resi-

---

16. When business and civic leaders get involved in school affairs, they frequently do so through ad hoc or umbrella organizations. There are at least two reasons for this. First, community leaders primarily become active in school affairs in response to a perceived crisis, in which unifying, broad-based organizations help to rally the community. Second, business leaders may be hesitant about being too visible in civic affairs. This reliance on broad-based organizations also can increase the pressure that business and civic leaders bring to bear on the board. Because the "ad hoc association" is "brought into being for a particular purpose and is expected to pass out of existence when that purpose has been accomplished, [it] . . . lacks the permanent association's motive to avoid controversy. Its membership and leadership, moreover, are recruited with its particular purpose in mind, and they are therefore relatively cohesive and highly motivated" (Banfield and Wilson 1963, 257).

dents like the rich county sons-of-bitches are telling us in the city how to run our schools."

The St. Louis board was purged for embarrassing the city. Civic leaders were galvanized by the fear that St. Louis would be marked as racist. Vocal black leaders, responding to financial problems as well as racial concerns, stirred to action a once apathetic community. Concern for the city's reputation united civic leaders from the urban and suburban communities and prompted business leaders to get involved.

CLOSING DOWN THE CIRCUS IN ATLANTA.   Independent of the city government after the city charter was revised in the 1970s, Atlanta's nine-member board did not receive much public attention before the early 1990s. "The system ran on its own and was only bent and moved by special interest forces," recalled one respondent. "The rest of the community, black and white, would damn the system at cocktail parties but do nothing about it."

One respondent called the board "the best show in town. It was televised once a month, and people tuned in just for the show." A third said, "The school board meetings had been raucous affairs full of people challenging and threatening each other and with very little agreement on anything. The school board meetings were just very, very rowdy affairs. You didn't want to see them on cable, they were X-rated."

However, by late 1992, community dissatisfaction started to coalesce in response to perceived board malfeasance. The board developed a reputation for incompetence: "The school system had consistently turned up on the bottom of all indicators and the school board was widely thought to have been inept and to have mismanaged the resources of the system." Another respondent remembered the system as corrupt and unable to convey a sense of forward progress. The board was "entrapped by the corruption of the system in general, which just stultifies any real reform. [The system] was really ossified, and unmoving."

Disgust with the board's antics and unproductivity spurred action across the spectrum of community groups. One respondent described Atlanta as "a town that doesn't like too much obvious aggression and yelling and carrying on." Board meetings "were regarded as comical. In particular, a couple of the board members, not all of them, were very offensive in the way they participated and communicated and the public was just outraged that they would be the folks leading the public school system." Board members were targeted by community leaders because the board's collective reputation had become a threat to the city's reputation:

The old board was turned out by a combination of groups. You had pretty widespread agreement, on the part of every faction in the voting district, that change needed to take place. A lot of the thrust for change came out of the business community, even though it could not have been successful without the widespread support of the people in the neighborhoods. [There was] a larger gathering of groups and individuals, something called the Atlanta Committee for Public Education. We could not have done this in Atlanta unless there had been agreement on the part of the black and white leadership.

The Atlanta Committee for Public Education mobilized the broadest possible support for cleaning up the board and refurbishing its reputation. It brought

a large number of groups together. The Chamber of Commerce and other business groups, neighborhood people, and other groups tend to protect their school turf, so to speak. So you have this tug of war going on for a long time around school issues. . . . I think that's why the Atlanta Committee was formed, because it's an interracial group so no one group has to stand out, so all groups work under the umbrella of the Atlanta Committee.

In fact, the effort to purge the board was described as a "window of opportunity" by one respondent, who said that racial tension normally constricted discussions of school policy. Until the board had sparked community-wide frustration, the racial divide actually protected board members by permitting them to serve as the voice of their respective communities:

It was a window of opportunity because, in a town like Atlanta, sometimes racial lines are drawn. The school system had become overwhelmingly black, it was operated by blacks who control the school system, and white people in the community were afraid to tee off on the system for fear they would roil the waters. The attitude of the black community was . . . "You guys took all your kids out, so shut up." . . . For many in the black community the school system represented a piece of the pie, so to speak, a piece of the power. . . . Whites were reluctant and apprehensive about a total onslaught on the system because they really weren't a part of the system aside from their money. They'd pulled most of their kids out.

However, when frustration with the board erupted, the board members were no longer protected by their bond with their constituents. Instead, the black and white communities cooperated to oust the sitting board: "The whole racial question could kind of be put aside and people could focus on the fact that everybody was being shortchanged."

In the fall of 1993, the community mobilized in an attempt to remake the board. Challengers defeated six of the nine incumbent board members and "overwhelmed" the remaining members. As in St. Louis, the citywide committee in Atlanta did not operate as a formal political entity, but it quietly orchestrated support for the reform slate:

> The new group just overwhelmed the rest of them. They didn't run as a slate, but you knew who the reform members were. They were highly identified by the groups that supported them as new members and reform members. Everyone, the newspapers and everything, knew these members represented a new group, a new order here. The Atlanta Committee did more behind the scenes, I don't think [the Committee] publicly endorsed anybody. But [Committee members] were all members of other groups that endorsed people. A lot of [people] were carrying joint memberships in a group called Good Government Atlanta, wearing two hats, and that group endorsed candidates. The Chamber of Commerce kind of had an education committee that had a group they supported, and they made it known who they were supporting.

The new board took power under the spotlight. Respondents noted that community interest in the schools "is growing and tremendous" and that "all eyes are on the school board." Faced with these pressures, the new board set out to rehabilitate its own reputation and to find a proactive superintendent who could cloak the district in the robes of progress. First, board members made it a point to restore decorum. The new board had "team players" eager "to do the best for the kids." One respondent said that the "greatest success" of the new board was "orderly school board meetings."

Second, board members made it a point to bring in a "new leadership team." They retired the old superintendent and the old executive team, allowing the new superintendent they had recruited to fill the spots. This superintendent was described as "very progressive, hands-on, articulate, . . . proactive and visionary." The board reportedly wanted to replace other senior administrators in order to encourage "new blood" and "new ideas." The Atlanta board was purged because its members became controversial and embarrassing. The result was a cataclysmic housecleaning engineered by the entire spectrum of community organizations. Clearly, the political cost of losing a community's confidence is high.

A Consensus for Reform

Needing to appear competent and cohesive, urban boards turn to the superintendent and expect the administration to produce a confidence-instilling agenda. This arrangement permits board members to focus their energy on satisfying constituent and ideological demands on less visible matters. Consequently, although school boards vary in their unity on most matters, they tend to be exceptionally unified on reform.

For instance, respondents reported that Duval County, Florida, had a deeply split board. It even voted 4–3 when deciding whether to bring in a facilitator to help the board "form more of a team environment." Respondents rated it a 5.0 on overall cohesion on a zero-to-ten scale, where zero indicated "no agreement" and a ten indicated "unanimity." Nonetheless, this fractured board was extremely cohesive in its support for each of the five reforms examined. Its average cohesion on reform measures was 8.3.

Like the Duval board, most boards in the sample were regarded as unified on reform issues. Board decisions on school reform proposals were always described as highly unified, with reported unity on the five reforms studied ranging from 8.0 to 8.8. By contrast, in only twelve of the fifty-seven districts was overall board cohesion deemed to be higher than an 8.0. Even though most school boards were considered fairly cohesive (mean board cohesion was 6.9), board decisions on reform were consistently reported to be about 20 percent more cohesive. In sum, school boards were extraordinarily unified when addressing school reform.[17]

Anecdotal evidence from districts including Amarillo, Texas; Fort Worth, Texas; Manchester, New Hampshire; and Milwaukee, Wisconsin supports this somewhat surprising data. The fact is that reports of board dissension on reform are exaggerated.

Contrary to the "public sector critique" presented in chapter 1, school

17. This holds true even in some surprising cases. For instance, the Oakland school board's 1996 decision to recognize "Black English" as a second language raised a national furor and was attacked by critics ranging from poet Maya Angelou to Richard Riley, U.S. secretary of education (*Los Angeles Times* 1996, 8A). However, the school board itself voted unanimously for the resolution to recognize "ebonics" (Sanchez 1996).

reform has not been done in by democratic conflict. The critique's implication that reforms will be hobbled by conflict endemic to the public sector does not fit the observed pattern of board consensus. The difficulties encountered by reform do not appear to be rooted in board conflict and ensuing paralysis. Board agreement on reform may be facile and shallow, but it is real.

Boards achieve consensus in a straightforward manner. The process of planning school reform is turned over to the superintendent, who eventually hammers out the details in informal discussions with the board and with union personnel until consensus is reached. "There's a lot of communication and phone calls on a personal level," one board member commented:

> [I]f there are major policy decisions to be made—we won't try to make it in a hurry at a weekly board meeting. We'll take a three or four hour bloc of time during a retreat and then have a study session. In the initial stage, concerns are raised, and then the administrative staff goes back and responds to those concerns. So, by the time it is brought to the board at a meeting, there's been a lot of . . . consensus and a comfort level.

Reforms that promise to create controversy on the board are buried. As mentioned previously, boards tend to work around reforms that could provoke conflict. One journalist respondent explained that curricular reform had not been proposed locally "because it is controversial and so it just has not come up. Some of these major curriculum battles took place in other school districts. The sex education battle really took place in a suburban district, that's where you get these real battles."

In districts with relatively untroubled schools, such as many suburban districts, school boards can draw upon a reservoir of goodwill rarely present in urban districts. Where school performance is deemed satisfactory, boards begin with more credibility. These boards can more safely engage in conflict over reform. In districts where school performance is deemed to be satisfactory, boards have less need to use reform to bolster their stature in the community.[18] In these districts board members either may demand less reform or be more willing to do battle over reform proposals.

18. Approximately 60 percent of urban superintendents in a 1994 study reported that school reform was a major issue, whereas only 20 percent of all superintendents felt that way (Kowalski 1995, 83). Reform is more important to policymakers in urban districts.

Apolitical Board Policy

The ability to dodge conflict is simplified for urban boards because "policy" is an elastic word in the world of school governance. School boards appear to conceive of policy in a formal, apolitical sense. Rather than emerging from contests over partisan measures, "policy" is what is written down in the manual. A board member clearly illustrated this perspective in the way she discussed policy: "The way we do our policy manual is that anybody can introduce a new policy, and we try to have at least an annual review of our policy manual to make sure that it's up to date on the legality of policy. We have the associate superintendent for personnel who oversees that." A board member describing her board's approach to policy portrayed a bureaucratic, administration-dominated enterprise: "We have had a routine review of policy by one of our central office administrators. We simply assigned him the job of going through our policy book and weeding out what wasn't effective anymore, and making changes in areas that were effective."

By treating "policy" as a formal husk rather than a vital concern, boards are able to desensitize it. Board members can address reforms to policy as technical or procedural—rather than partisan—concerns. This makes it easier for them to promote reforms while minimizing division. An apolitical view of policymaking characterizes many urban school systems, a point illustrated by the board member who related, "When I came on board, I was told that my department was policy, and I was handed ethics, sexual harassment, and smoking. They said, 'Here, fix these.'"

Handling policy in this manner enables administrators to introduce the substance of reforms through informal changes in practice or through budget manipulation. This takes the board members off the hook, permitting the board to collectively enact reform while requiring that individual members do nothing more than approve a line item or acquiesce in a modification of administrative practice. The administration is then free to pursue the substantive reform as it sees fit. Thus the board is the passive accomplice and the superintendent is the leader in the ceaseless drumbeat of stealth reform.

Boards tend to avoid controversy. Discussing policy on evaluation reform, one board member stated, "We probably just gave up on it for a while because it was so controversial. I think sometimes we tend to give up just so we don't get into an area where we can't get along with one another."

Boards avoid controversy by approaching change as an incremental affair and by using the budget to enact change without having to formally change policy. The previous respondent continued, "We brought [evaluation reform] back through the budget. . . . [W]hen things are proposed through the budget, like provisions for monitors or evaluators, then this can accomplish the evaluation change that the board wants to see, often without having to change the policy manual."

Contrary to the "micro-managing critique" discussed in chapter 1, reform activity is not usually the product of overreaching board members. The evidence suggests that school reform is initiated and shaped by administrators, and board members widely support these administrative initiatives. The desire to forge broad school board support may slow the pace at which administrators pursue reform. It also may prompt administrators to lower their sights and settle for lowest-common-denominator measures.

Unions: A Reactive Force

Teachers' unions are considered to be a powerful force in public schooling and have often been cited as a major impediment to urban reform.[19] In fact, respondents suggested that the unions played a reactive and surprisingly limited role in Third Wave reform at the local level. Unions helped to ensure that significant changes in district policy were rarely pursued, but they did not appear to slow the process of policy churn.

Like most government employee unions, teachers' unions "are mainly concerned with 'bread and butter' matters—pay and promotion policies, job security, pension systems, and grievance procedures."[20] During the 1980s, teachers unions "generally limited most of their demands to fairly traditional trade union issues of compensation, working conditions, and job security. Although these issues occasionally involved matters of educational policy . . . by and large the teachers' unions left purely educational issues . . . to the administration."[21]

19. See Chubb and Moe (1990); Hoxby (1996); Kritek and Clear (1993); Lieberman (1993, 1997); and Peterson (1993).
20. Banfield and Wilson (1963, 213).
21. Rury (1993, 4).

The evidence suggests that unions use contract language and the teachers' role as the classroom gatekeeper to determine the parameters of reform. In Chicago's dramatic school reform effort in 1988, the Chicago Teachers Union (CTU) opposed the legislation, but "it played a passive role once it secured safeguards to its contract."[22] Many teachers opposed merit pay and peer review in the early 1980s because these reforms threatened basic contractual principles; teachers were less concerned with the more pedagogical and curricular reforms that emerged after the mid-1980s.[23]

Because Third Wave reforms only rarely affected teachers' working hours, salaries, or job conditions, the unions' response to them may not have been typical of their responses to other reform efforts. Examinations of reforms that more directly affect teaching conditions may show a more prominent union role.

A Modest Effect on Reform Activity

The presence of a strong teachers' union appeared to mildly retard the rate of Third Wave reforms. The thirty districts with strong unions (where unions enrolled 90 percent or more of teachers) had slightly fewer proposed reforms than the twenty-six other districts and reported less attention to and less controversy over reform.[24] These strong union districts experienced 9 percent less reform (averaging 3.2 rather than 3.5 reforms on the zero-to-five composite scale), and 9 percent less attention to reform on the five-reform composite. Most interestingly, strong union districts also reported a modest 13 percent decrease in controversy.

These results do not differentiate between the nation's two dominant teachers' unions—the more reform-minded American Federation of Teachers (AFT) and the larger and more traditional National Education Association (NEA). The eighteen districts in which the AFT enrolled a majority of local teachers reported slightly more reform activity than the thirty in which the NEA enrolled a majority of teachers. Districts with an AFT majority also reported slightly less attention to the reform agenda and substantially less controversy over reform.[25]

---

22. Magat (1995, 163).
23. Bierlein (1993, 24).
24. The percentage of local teachers in a union was estimated by the union respondent.
25. The evidence that AFT locals were more supportive of reform than NEA locals is mixed. For instance, the union respondents from the NEA-majority districts and the AFT-majority dis-

Surprisingly, the unions were reported to be highly supportive of reform proposals.[26] For each kind of reform, the union was clearly seen as backing most proposals. Unions were regarded as supportive of evaluation reforms in 60 percent of districts, of time and day measures in 65 percent, of site-based management measures in 84 percent, of professional development measures in 88 percent, and of curriculum measures in 91 percent. Unions were less supportive of measures like school time and student evaluation that tampered with the routines of teachers' lives. Even on those measures, however, the union supported reform in more than 60 percent of districts.

A Limited Role in School Board Elections

Critics suspicious of union power might grant that unions are less hostile to reform than traditionally supposed, but only because unions dominate schools boards and therefore control the content of reform. This supposition would be incorrect. Four out of five school boards had a membership in which at least 80 percent of members had no previous experience teaching or working in a school system.

However, the suggestion that union control is exercised only through the physical presence of union personnel may oversimplify urban politics.[27] Unions are often thought to wield considerable influence in board elections. That does not appear to have been the case in the sample districts. No more than a handful of respondents mentioned the political strength of the teachers' union when asked to rate union influence on the school board. However, a number of respondents depicted union influence as overrated. One board member commented, "They'd like to think they have a lot of power, but I don't think they do." Another board member brushed aside claims of union power: "The union likes to think they have influence, but a concerted effort by any group can help you or hurt you." A union president said her union played a minimal role in board politics: "We usually don't get actively involved in [school board] campaigns. We usually interview and sometimes endorse, but recently we haven't even endorsed. We just present the information to the members and let them make their own decisions."

---

tricts reported similarly cordial relations with the district administration. Presumably, if the NEA locals are more obstructionist, their relationship with the administration ought to suffer.

26. For each issue where respondents indicated that a reform was proposed, they were asked whether the union had supported, not taken a position on, or opposed the reform. The district was scored according to the mean response of those respondents who indicated a proposal was made.

27. Jones (1983).

When unions get actively involved in board elections, their influence is described as surprisingly weak. One union president said, "The union is sometimes heavily involved. . . . [Our political action committee] has given up to a thousand or a couple of thousand [dollars] to some candidates. Very rarely do the candidates we back win. . . . When we do have partnerships, we have not been able to make those partnerships last past an election." Another union president said that visible union support actually hurt board candidates: "A lot of times union support can be the kiss of death."

Union influence in district politics is limited. Unions make financial contributions and are able to provide "foot soldiers, sign pounders, and coffee klatches," but they do not control school board elections. A board member pointed out that union strength is reduced because many urban district employees live in adjacent suburbs "and therefore don't vote." Despite their substantial organization and the low turnout for board elections, unions do not appear to control urban boards.

Influence through Contract Language

Unions primarily exert their influence through the district teachers' contract. One school board member noted that there had been no district-wide change in the school day "because of the union. But we did rework union contract language to permit schools to change the way they do business if sixty percent of the personnel at each site agree." In another district a union respondent indicated that site-based management had advanced when "restructuring [was] negotiated into the 1989 contract by the union with the former superintendent." A board member thus explained the crucial role played by the union contract in reform:

> One of the most crucial areas has been our negotiations with our unions, particularly the teachers' union. . . . [A]s we restructure, we've negotiated with teachers to change the contract to allow us to do the kinds of educational things we want to do. These are things such as changing time periods for classes, having different schedules at different schools, and all kinds of things that seem minor, but, if you're going to have block scheduling, it has to fit into the contract.

Unions supported Third Wave reforms largely because they had a significant voice in shaping reform. Administrators tend to write reforms in ways that fit into standing contract language, simultaneously ensuring that dramatic changes in district practice will not be considered.[28] In some districts the nature of the contract causes the union role to become more proactive. One union president described having a major role in the selection of the superintendent and district administrators, "We have been doing collaborative bargaining for the last 8 or 9 years, and it has changed . . . the whole way in which the union and the district interact, on a very positive note. I helped select the new super and every major administrator who was hired." The unions do little to slow the rush of reform, because their focus is on other, more immediate, concerns. However, union influence does help to ensure that significant changes that might fundamentally shift behavior or incentives in the teaching and learning core are not seriously considered.

Contrary to the implications of the "union critique" discussed in chapter 1, unions played a largely peripheral role in shaping the course of Third Wave school reform. If anything, a strong union presence may somewhat reduce the rate of reform. However, the union critique appears to be accurate when it suggests that unions reduce the effectiveness of reform. The mechanism of union influence is not a simple rejection of reform through political means, but the use of contract language to mold and restrict those reforms that are proposed. Reforms that do not cut very far into the organizational core become relatively more attractive to policymakers because they are less likely to stir union opposition.

State Governments: An Indirect Influence

Policy discussions of school reform during the past fifteen years have accorded state government a dominant role.[29] Other educational policy research has often implied a central state role through its focus on state action.[30] The policy community's tendency to focus on the states has been bolstered by interest in state-level questions of education finance. The

---

28. Peterson (1993, 285) noted that the Milwaukee Teachers' Education Association used their contract to control the reform process by "winning a collective bargaining agreement with the school board that made it possible for the association to challenge virtually any board or administrative decision it chose by alleging a violation of the agreement."

29. Doyle and Hartle (1985); Doyle, Cooper, and Trachtman (1991); Finn (1991, 1992); and Fiske (1984).

30. Firestone, Fuhrman, and Kirst (1991); Hearn and Griswold (1994); Johnson and Glasman (1983); and Odden and Clune (1995).

structure of the U.S. political system dictates that these issues are generally resolved at the state level, and a great deal of policy research has followed.[31]

At least for the sample districts during the 1992–95 period, however, the states played a more limited and less straightforward role in urban school reform than conventional accounts might imply. This limited role is consistent with the notion that Third Wave reforms called for more district-level activity than the state-centered First Wave of the mid-1980s. State activity also may have been restricted by tight finances: real educational spending by the states on instruction remained nearly flat during the early 1990s.[32] Finally, the moderate state role is consistent with the suggestion of some scholars that local districts can drastically alter state policies.[33] "The idea that state policy is uniformly implemented throughout a state is ludicrous," notes one scholar. "In practice, districts rarely adhere to the letter of state policy. Their allegiance to state dictates may be minimal to nonexistent."[34]

Reporting from a district-level perspective, respondents did not describe states as major influences on the Third Wave reform agenda. Respondents tended to emphasize funding when discussing the state role. Furthermore, when the state was discussed in terms of reform activity, more than a quarter of the reforms cited involved changing the role of the local school district (through mechanisms such as charter schools or accountability). The states were infrequently cited as the source of the changes in school practice encompassed by Third Wave reforms.

Reform: Only One Piece of the Agenda

From the district perspective, the state did not play a major role in driving Third Wave school reform. This may not be too surprising. State government has a multitude of responsibilities, and the nature of school practice is only one educational concern among many. As the results of state-level reform in the 1980s suggest, ambitious state educational initiatives can be more illusory than real.[35]

In order to assess the significance of state reform efforts from the perspective of the local districts, respondents were asked, "How has state action af-

31. See, for example, McCarthy (1994); Slavin (1994); Sparkman and Hartmeister (1995); Vergari (1995); Verstegen (1994); and Verstegen and McGuire (1991).
32. U.S. Department of Education (1996, table 165).
33. Cohen (1996a); Hertert (1996); Kirp and Driver (1995); and Willis and Peterson (1992).
34. Driscoll (1996, 421–22).
35. Cuban (1984a); and Fullan (1991).

fected local education policy during the last three years?" In an interview focused on school reform, respondents were asked to discuss the state's
biggest influence on local education policy during the 1992–95 period. In response, the interviewees primarily discussed money, particularly state aid
and funding formulas. More than half of the respondents mentioned influences not even peripherally related to increasing reform activity. Five to 10
percent of respondents cited the state as an impediment to reform because of
its policy flip-flopping or burdensome regulations, and 35 percent cited insufficient funding as inhibiting district reform. Fewer than 50 percent of respondents cited the state's promotion of educational change. In sum, when
asked explicitly about the state's role in "policy," barely a third of the responses addressed reforms or state mandates deemed to be part of the Third
Wave reforms.

The state's formal role may result in the state being credited for activity
that it pushed only indirectly. As a result, inadequate attention has been
paid to local district activity or to how districts influence the direction of
state policy. One-quarter to one-half of districts reported state-mandated
reform in each of the five policy areas.[36] Districts cited evaluation reform
as the reform most frequently mandated by state government (in 53 percent
of districts), while time-based changes were the least likely to be state
mandated (in 26 percent of districts). These data suggest that states were
responsible for somewhat less than half of the reform activity reported in
the sample districts. Upon a closer look, it turned out that even these mandates were not as mandatory as might be expected.

When asked, "How much pressure to act did the state put on the school
district?" respondents reported that the state had not pushed districts very
hard on the five reforms studied. Respondents rated state pressure on a
zero-to-ten scale, where zero meant the state exerted "no pressure" and a
ten that it "dictated policy." In districts where reform was proposed, state
pressure was rated as negligible, generally ranging from 2.1 for school time
and the school day to a 4.1 on site-based management. Only in the case of
evaluation reform did state pressure rate as high as a 5.3.

More revealing is the disagreement among districts within a state as to
whether a state had required action. Even respondents within a given district disagreed about whether the state had required reform. For instance, in
three California districts 20 percent or fewer of respondents said that the

---

36. The state was considered to have required reform in a policy area if the majority of answering respondents in a district reported that the state had required action.

state had required teacher development reform. On the other hand, in two other districts, more than 60 percent of the respondents said that it had. Similarly, in Texas there were two districts where 20 percent of respondents, or fewer, said the state had required curriculum reform. In two other districts, more than 60 percent said it had. If the respondents in a district cannot agree on whether the state required reform, and if different districts have strongly conflicting views as to whether the state required activity, it calls into question the impact of state mandates on reform.

Respondents who did cite the state as a source of Third Wave reforms often indicated the effect of mandates to stir district activity. For instance, a Seattle respondent thought a 1994 education bill had spurred reform by "stimulat[ing] the district's own curriculum reform and a lot of building-based management."

Brakes Not Engines

Far from being engines of school reform, the states sometimes hampered Third Wave reform efforts by creating funding uncertainty and undermining administrative leadership. Previous scholars have noted that state mandates have a history of "misdirection, lack of fiscal support, and shifting players, all of which end up clogging local reform efforts."[37] One New Jersey respondent explained that the state's efforts at monitoring had paralyzed reform activity. The state was

> completely and unquestionably out of control. The monitoring they were doing was so pervasive that it was destroying education in the state. You couldn't worry about anything except the state, monitoring was kind of all anybody had time to worry about.... You had to march in lock-step, with sign in sheets for faculty meetings so they could make sure everyone was there.

Some respondents suggested that the state slowed the rate of local reform. One Indianapolis respondent said the district had not acted on a measure because the school board is "waiting to see what" the state will do. A California administrator explained how a heralded state initiative slowed the pace of local activity:

37. Carter and Cunningham (1997, 66).

In the last six months, with pressure from the anti-public school far-right people, the new state superintendent has kind of gone sideways on [curriculum frameworks] . . . and now we're in a . . . hover position. It has taken the wind out of our sails. We've been out in the community saying, "This is what we want to do and what the state wants us to do," and now we're . . . out there with egg on our face in the community.

An administrator in a different district voiced similar frustration:

We had a very strong innovative approach, for instance, on a language arts framework that came down from the state. . . . But now, with the new election of the state superintendent for instruction and the pressure of more conservative groups, [the state] is saying, "Maybe we missed the boat and need to go back to basics." . . . We feel like we've been hung out to dry. The state was a backup for the things we wanted to do anyway, and now they've pulled the rug out. Now business can't go forward, we've got a new adoption list and now we've got to find out what their decisions are before we move forward with purchasing new math texts. It's extremely frustrating.

A Pittsburgh respondent said that local reform was caught up in policy confusion at the state level: "The new governor came on board and last month basically suspended the curriculum policy. So, after three years of massive fighting and one year of systemic planning, it was suspended."

A business community respondent said that the district's energies in recent years had been focused on warding off the state. The business community "is really waiting for the state to take over the district. We're waiting for that to happen, because there's almost no cooperation with the current administration and school board." Legislative policy reversals and the uncertainty of state funding may make significant and long-term reforms less attractive to local school system policymakers.

Conclusion

Third Wave school reform was driven by school boards and superintendents, with administrators bringing to the board proposals that had already been crafted to enjoy broad support. To make it easier to promote an active reform agenda with united board backing, boards tend to avoid writing explicit reform policies. As a result, reforms are often enacted informally, through changes in practice or modifications in the district budget. The dynamics of urban school districts encourage policymakers to welcome reforms but not to follow through on implementing them. As unstructured bodies composed of inexperienced but politically sensitive members, urban boards lack the skills or inclination to engage in the tedious business of supervising follow-through. The role of unions and state governments in Third Wave school reform has been exaggerated, though unions do play a role in discouraging policymakers from focusing on significant and difficult long-term changes. The next chapter depicts the extent of the reform activity generated by this system.

PART TWO

The Evidence

4

The Dizzying Pace of
Urban School Reform

THE COMMON INDICTMENT of urban schooling is that
nothing ever changes—a notion that is only half right.
While some observers believe schools are resistant to change, others claim
"that schools are being bombarded by change."[1] In fact, the evidence presented in this chapter shows that during the 1992–95 period there was a
great deal of reform activity in urban districts. The union, public sector,
and monopoly critiques discussed in chapter 1 do not square with these
findings; each implies that reform should be an infrequent occurrence. The
high rate of activity in the 1992–95 period, coupled with the lack of evident
progress noted by previous scholars, suggests that policymakers aggressively pursue reform but pay insufficient attention to making it work. This
high rate of activity is consistent with the implications of a symbolic explanation of reform, which suggests that urban policymakers have incentives
to be proactive reformers.

Far from being central to running an urban school district, reform is
largely peripheral to the daily grind of school management. This lack of
centrality helps to make reform an alluring forum for political leadership.
On more mundane and particularistic issues of district governance—like
attendance boundaries, school closings, or the distribution of capital outlays—local conflicts are more entrenched and explosive. The critical attention of the community is fixed on these financial and managerial concerns,
and community leaders have clear expectations and cues with which to
accurately assess district behavior. On reform issues, however, superintendents have much more room to shape and direct activity, particularly because their educational expertise carries more clout on these less contro-

1. Fullan (1991, 3).

versial issues.[2] Policymakers have a natural inclination to shift attention from pluralistic decisions rife with potential bad news to the friendlier confines of "progress" and "innovation." Defying the truism that agendas have limited space for policy initiatives, multiple school reform policies tend to move up or down a school district's agenda together.[3] This bundled movement is abetted by the public's tendency to approve almost any proposal that promises to remedy social problems and by the school administration's ability to dictate the pace of reform.[4]

Despite the high public profile of urban school reform in recent years, little is known about how much attention has been paid to local reforms, how controversial local efforts have been, or even how much district-level reform has taken place. This lack of information has made it difficult to assess urban school reform, contributing to the tendency to discuss reform in terms of anecdote and intention.

Reform Has a Low Profile on the Agenda

Because reforms are newsworthy and heavily promoted, the popular press sometimes conveys the false impression that reform dominates the day-to-day agenda of school systems. However, reform has limited significance in school district management, burdened as it is by federal mandates, state fiscal and performance pressures, and local demands. In fact, the community as a whole tends to take little interest in schooling. One respondent in Utica, New York, observed, "School board meetings are not well attended. Only when there's a major controversy, such as a school closing or a teacher contract, is there a conflict that gets people to come out."

Respondents were asked, "What have been the two leading issues in local schooling during the past three years, and why have they been important?"[5] Educational reform issues (shaded in figure 4-1) composed a distinct minority of responses.

2. This is quite similar to a president's ability to wield greater influence in foreign affairs than in domestic policy, given the different sets of institutional constraints and political expectations (Peterson 1994).

3. Kingdon (1984).

4. On the first point see Farah and Vale (1985); and Hess (1995).

5. Responses were coded by the author. The responses were initially coded into eighteen categories, which were then consolidated for presentation. The first two responses offered by each respondent were coded.

Figure 4-1. Leading Issues in Local Schooling

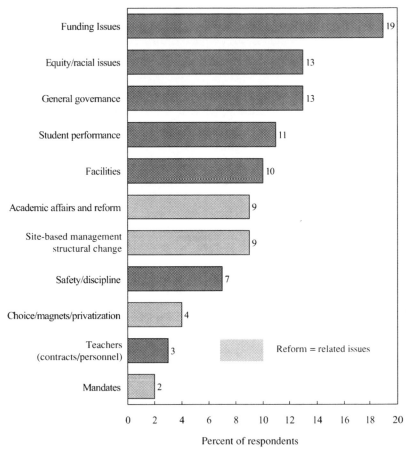

Source: Author's data.

More than three-quarters of responses had nothing to do with school reform. The most frequently cited issue was funding, a response consistent
with previous research.[6] Questions of equity (including desegregation),
general governance, and student performance were the next most frequently cited issues. References to any variant of the Third Wave reforms

6. National polls of superintendents in 1971, 1982, and 1992 found that they considered
school financing to be the most significant issue on the agenda. Similarly, school boards perceived
inadequate financing to be the greatest problem facing schools (Norton and others 1996, 16–20,
26).

made up less than 20 percent of total responses. Urban pressures shape the local agenda. One journalist explained that the leading local issues had been "a shooting in one of the buildings, which spurred a study and a lot of concern and new measures," and the need for new facilities, because "the school district recently had an eighty-one million dollar bond issue voted down."

Financial pressures frequently squeeze other concerns off of the agenda. One administrator said that funding had dominated the local school agenda "because we've been in an incredible financial crisis and had to cut back on programs." Another administrator said that "the two big issues were financing and . . . new laws, both federal and local, which cost us more money." A third respondent explained how human error had thrown the district into a fiscal crisis that demanded extensive attention from administrators:

> We had a financial crisis last fall. . . . There were some big mistakes made in the budgeting and accounting process. . . . For some reason, just human error, the budget the board passed was not posted properly. . . . What was distributed was a proposed budget from which a lot of money had been cut. The principals began spending off of the wrong budget, and they thought they had a lot more money than they had. . . . It cost some board members reelection. . . . For the last year that has been the biggest issue, the financial crisis.

In this environment reform provides a welcome respite to district policymakers. In fact, superintendents and school boards find it politically productive to push reform to a more prominent place on the school agenda in order to displace questions of funding, school closings, racial equity, and managerial malfeasance.

Reform Is Rarely Termed a Great Success

Respondents were asked a second open-ended question: "What has been the greatest success in [the district]'s school system during the past three years, and how was it achieved?"[7] The responses offer another view of how reform is perceived in local school affairs. It is not regarded as a particularly large source of district success.

7. Each respondent had one response coded. For those respondents who offered more than one success, the first one they mentioned was coded, unless they specified that they considered a subsequently mentioned success to be "the greatest success."

Figure 4-2. Successes in Local Schooling

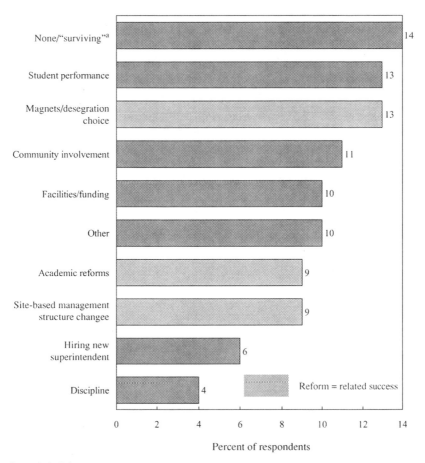

Source: Author's data.
a. The district's greatest success was "surviving."

School-based and classroom reforms make up about 18 percent of the cited successes; 14 percent of responses indicated that the district had no significant successes or that the district's greatest success was "surviving" (see figure 4-2).

Fewer than one in five respondents cited reforms dealing with classroom practice or school management, even though those reforms are explicitly promoted as the means to improving school performance. District

attention is disproportionately devoted to questions of funding, student retention, and other survival-related concerns. When contemplating district
achievements, respondents unintentionally illustrated how peripheral
school reform is. One Euclid, Ohio, respondent described the district's
greatest success as being the passage of a "bond issue which went to improve the existing physical plants. The schools themselves did a nice job of
getting around to all the groups in the city and explaining the need to maintain physical facilities." The respondent added, unprompted, "There's also
a lot of success with athletic programs." A board member in another district said, "With as many problems as there are, I have to stop and think for
a minute. Like all urban systems we have to deal primarily with problems."

Even small movements in test scores were cited as the greatest success,
while supposedly dramatic reform initiatives went unmentioned. "Test
scores and attendance are up a little, which is pretty modest as success
goes," said one respondent from Baltimore, a district acclaimed for several
innovations. Students' performance was cited by only 13 percent of respondents, usually in terms of attendance, retention, or test scores. Reform
was rarely described as having made a substantial impact on the school district's performance or on the school system as a whole.

Numerous Reforms Are Proposed

The marginal position of reform on the local education agenda might
suggest that little school reform took place during 1992 to 1995. In fact, an
immense amount of reform activity took place. It was measured by combining the responses of all observers in each sample district into a local index.[8] Because reform in any of the five areas requires significant outlays of
time and energy, it seemed unlikely that any district would try more than
one or maybe two of these reforms during this period.

The mean district had proposed reform in 3.35 of the five reform areas.[9]
Over two-thirds of districts proposed reforms in more than three of the five
policy areas, and the rest of the districts reported attempted reforms in at
least two areas. These figures only included initiatives that the respondents
reported in the context of the five reform areas studied. It seems likely that
districts were also pursuing other kinds of reforms. The sheer amount of

8. See chapter 1 for an explanation of how the index was created.
9. Respondents sometimes cited reforms that they later explained had been initiated before
1992. Because respondents were only asked to describe "the most significant" initiative proposed,
other initiatives may been launched. The figures for district activity should be treated as suggestive
rather than precise measurements.

school reform was apparent in the breadth of reform activity. Every type of reform except school time measures was reported by a majority of respondents in at least 65 percent of districts, and curriculum and site-based management reform were proposed in more than 85 percent of districts.

Because of the design of the study, even this depiction of widespread activity understates the number of initiatives being launched. During the interview, each respondent was asked whether a measure had been proposed in each of the five areas of reform. The respondent answered "yes" or "no," and then described the "most significant" proposal. Therefore, different respondents in each city could be reporting different initiatives as the "most significant" within each type of reform, but the various proposals were combined when determining the summary statistics on activity. Table 4-1 offers an example of how many different kinds of "most significant" proposals were reported in the Fullerton Elementary School District and Milwaukee Public Schools.

The Milwaukee respondents named three different "most significant" evaluation reforms and five different curriculum proposals. Could this disagreement simply be a product of the size of the Milwaukee system? Variation equal to Milwaukee's also showed up in smaller districts, such as the Fullerton, California, Elementary School District with 10,470 students. The number of distinct initiatives in Milwaukee and Fullerton is somewhat higher than the norm, but it demonstrates that districts are actually proposing more activity than the summary figures suggest.

In short, the extremely high levels of activity described thus far actually understate the number of significant initiatives that were proposed. Figure 4-3 displays the total number of reforms initiated in each district.[10] Only Third Wave initiatives cited by at least one respondent as "significant" and launched between 1992 and 1995 were counted. In the mean district 11.4 different reforms were proposed—a pace of one significant reform every three months! Seventy-five percent of districts proposed at least ten significant initiatives. More than one in three districts had proposed thirteen or more initiatives, a pace of better than one every three months.

Reform may be proceeding in two different ways. Districts may be enacting multiple reforms in a burst of coordinated activity, or they may be

10. The number was calculated by coding a respondent's description of a reform initiative as representing one of several categories of activity within that reform. (The initial presumption had been that respondents in a district would all describe the same type of initiative as the "most significant" measure for each type of reform. That rarely proved to be the case.) The total number of different initiatives cited by respondents in each district was then summed up.

Table 4-1. "Most Significant" Proposals Reported in Fullerton Elementary School District and in Milwaukee Public Schools

Site	Curriculum proposals	Evaluation proposals
Fullerton Elementary School District in California	Restructure framework Change system's mechanics Increase hands-on learning/student orientation Increase critical thinking in curriculum	Use portfolios Use more tests and evaluation Revise tests Increase school-site role
Milwaukee Public Schools	Increase graduation requirements Increase multiculturalism Increase critical thinking in curriculum Overhaul books Modify values (sex) education	Use portfolios Use graduation tests Modify promotion policies

Source: Author's data.

continually initiating sequential initiatives. Ambiguities in the data make it impossible to answer this question definitively, but the summary results suggest that activity is continuous. Respondents in thirty-five of the fifty-seven sample districts reported that a "significant" reform was proposed in each year of the 1992–95 period. Respondents in nine other districts reported that a "significant" measure was proposed in every year of the 1991–94 period. In sum, more than 75 percent of the sample districts reported "significant" proposals in at least four consecutive years during 1991 to 1995. This behavior was evident in the active and less active districts. Too much should not be made of these findings, because respondents were often imprecise about dates. However, the data appear to rule out the notion that activity is primarily launched in coordinated bursts of reform.

Almost Everything Is Enacted

Policymakers pursue reform in a manner that seeks to reduce conflict and satisfy both the local community and educational professionals. Measures are vetted and written within the parameters of the union contract, minimizing the likelihood that the union will actively oppose reform proposals. Additionally, the superintendent and the board have an incentive to steer away from reforms likely to ignite an adverse local reaction. As a

Figure 4-3. Number of Reforms Initiated in Each District

Number of initiatives (N = 57)

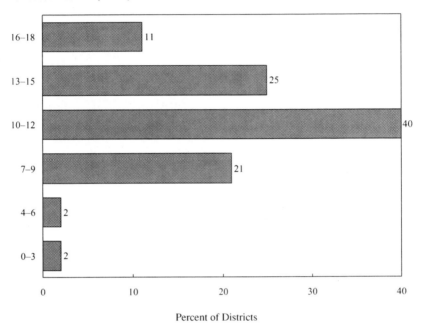

Percent of Districts

Source: Author's data.

consequence, most reform proposals are enacted. About 90 percent of proposals were reported by a majority of respondents to have been enacted. In fact, 72 percent of time and school day measures, 89 percent of evaluation measures, 90 percent of professional development measures, 91 percent of curriculum measures, and 93 percent of site-based management measures were enacted.[11]

School systems operate very differently from state or national governments, where dozens of measures are proposed for each bill that passes. In

11. These extremely high passage rates contrast with the adversarial model evident in more professional legislatures, where many measures are proposed and never addressed, much less passed. The high rates could partially be a function of question wording or the design of the questionnaire, though the anecdotal evidence strongly contradicts this possibility. Further, the assumption that respondents will necessarily focus on enacted measures when contemplating the "most significant" proposal is flawed on two counts. First, the respondents were generally "inside" players who keep abreast of school affairs; they probably would have heard of major proposals, enacted or not. Second, rejected measures might very well attract more notoriety than enacted ones; respondents could easily have been biased toward citing *rejected* proposals.

most urban districts the superintendent enjoys broad leeway.[12] The board is averse to confrontation over reform. One journalist explained that the local board had not proposed a certain reform "because it is controversial and so it just has not come up."

This kind of unanimity emerges from an informal process of discussion, which takes place without partisan politics, out of the public eye, and under the guidance of the school administration. A union president explained his district's policymaking process as "a mish-mash where we all work on each other and out of that comes policy." By law that school board had to do all of its business in open meetings. The president emphasized that

> board members talk to each other. They discuss things in ones and twos, because more than two cannot meet in the same room to discuss anything dealing with board policy. Do they talk on the telephone? Sure. We're a little incestuous town here. Everybody knows everybody else. . . . [T]he board has to make all decisions in the open as far as policy goes.

Another union president offered a more conspiratorial view of board cooperation, "This board violates the laws, so confidentially, privately, I can say that everything is done in private. We don't get the agenda until the board meeting ends, which is illegal in New Jersey. Our board's the type that you don't know what the decision will be until you're actually there that night." A board member indicated that even that state's open meeting law did not impede this informal bargaining:

> There is even an injunction that states that school board members cannot make decisions by telephone or by meeting together, but I don't think that prohibits us from doing so. My legal question is, "When does a decision become a decision?" I don't think [the law] prohibits us from asking for information from other board members or giving information. . . . I don't think the injunction has had any effect whatsoever on our policy-making ability.

A great deal of reform is hammered out informally by board members and administrators, and reform proposals rarely emerge until the system's leadership is ready to enact them with consensus support from the board.

12. Zeigler, Kehoe, and Reisman (1985).

Constant Reform Is Expected

When respondents indicated that no proposal had been made in any of the five policy areas, they were asked if a particular reason came to mind. The explanations for why districts did not act were then tallied by summing up individual responses across all five reform areas. The responses demonstrate zero evidence that districts slow the pace of reform after a burst of activity.

Naturally, it was expected that respondents would explain inaction by saying that reform was unnecessary. However, few respondents suggested that the district did not act because no action was necessary, because the district was occupied with other matters, or because the relevant aspects of district practice were satisfactory. Given the frenetic rate of activity, respondents also were expected to explain current inactivity by pointing to an initiative launched before 1992. Reforms like site-based management and evaluation had already been tried in the First and Second Wave of school reforms in the 1980s.

In fact, respondents considered constant change to be the norm. Only a handful of respondents indicated that no action was taken on a reform because action was not needed. Just 11 percent of respondents said an untried reform was not needed or not being considered.[13] Only 3 percent of respondents indicated that a given reform was not considered because it had already been done. Reforms are not necessarily enacted because they will solve particular problems. Rather, reforms are proposed, enacted, and then reintroduced in a continuous process that is largely divorced from efforts to improve teaching and learning. Reform does not represent a district's dramatic break with the status quo. Despite the common belief that reform is the key to shattering the status quo, the truth is that a state of perpetual reform is the status quo.

Reform Agendas Are Elastic

Studies of political agendas have shown that the number of issues that attract national attention at one time are limited. The size of the agenda is

13. This reflects the finding by Wagner (1994, 251) that school community members believe reform to be necessary, without ever discussing the reasons why it was needed: "One of the most startling and unexpected findings of my research in these three schools was that while most adults shared a commitment to educational change, they had never discussed why we need fundamental educational reform." People assume the need for reform and operate on that assumption.

Table 4-2. Positive Correlation among Reform Proposals

Proposal	Day and time	Curriculum	Evaluation	Professional development
Curriculum	.04			
Evaluation	.22	.03		
Professional development	.18	.01	−.06	
Site-based management	.30	.12	.05	.23

Source: Author's data. $N = 57$.

limited by the capacities of the executive and legislative branches and by the tendency for changing circumstances to shove new issues into the spotlight.[14] The rise of one issue generally means the fall of another. After all, a school board can work through only so many measures, and a school district has only so much time, money, and staff.

On the other hand, the political pressure on policymakers in particularly vulnerable situations to appear proactive may counteract the limitations imposed by finite resources. A political explanation of reform suggests that superintendents who choose to propose one reform are actually more likely to propose others. This implies that policymakers are pursuing reform for reform's sake, and not because particular initiatives have been scrutinized and carefully selected as appropriate to the district's needs.

The positive correlations in table 4-2 show that the presence of one reform proposal made other proposals slightly more likely. Negative correlations would have suggested that reforms crowd one another off of the agenda.

Nine of the ten correlations in table 4-2 were positive, and four were 0.18 or higher. Districts that proposed one kind of reform were somewhat more likely to propose others. There is no evidence that proposing one kind of reform inhibited a district's willingness to also pursue other kinds of reform.

Another issue concerns space on the district's broader education agenda. Because the various school reforms are methods of tackling problems within one policy area, an increase in public attention to one initiative may or may not have the traditional negative effect on attention paid to other reform initiatives. For instance, while the rise of education on an urban district's agenda may reduce the attention paid to crime, an increase in

14. Light (1983); and Kingdon (1984).

Table 4-3. The Elasticity of the Reform Proposals

Proposal	Day and time	Curriculum	Evaluation	Professional development
Curriculum	.31			
Evaluation	.32	.20		
Professional development	.09	.25	.24	
Site-based management	.25	.02	.15	.30

Source: Author's data. $N = 57$.

attention paid to curricular reform may not necessarily reduce attention to evaluation reform—because the attention paid to all education reform may increase. Table 4-3 emphasizes the elasticity of the district agenda, showing that there is a moderately positive correlation between the attention paid to each of the five kinds of reform.[15] The correlations are all positive, and are 0.20 or greater in seven of the ten cases.

Both reform activity and public attention to reform are bundled. Increased public attention to one reform signaled more attention to all reforms. One of the truisms of government and political campaigning is that the public attends to a limited number of issues at a time. This is not the case with school reform. When reform is pushed onto the agenda, the attention that is paid to all reforms increases. Because policymakers are able to tackle everything at once, and because they have political incentives to do so, the risk that they will initiate more activity than they can manage is increased.

As the above correlations imply, there is a strong relationship between activity and public attention to reform. The number of proposals made in a district was very strongly associated with the mean amount of attention paid to the Third Wave reforms in that district ($R = .48$).[16] This strong correlation indicates that attention and activity tend to track each other. Given the leading role in reform that respondents accorded to policymakers, this relationship suggests that attention tends to follow activity, rather than activity being a response to community-generated attention. Presumably,

15. Respondents were asked, within each of the five issue streams, how much attention the reform had received in the local community. Respondents rated attention on a zero-to-ten scale. A zero meant that the issue had received "no attention" and a ten that it had received "a great deal of attention."

16. Naturally, public attention to the reforms and controversy over them were strongly related ($R = .63$).

media coverage and community discussion of proposals increase attention paid to reform. Politically, this is significant because it means that reform initiatives are more likely to attract notice, without which they would be symbolically irrelevant.

Conclusion

During the 1992–95 sample period, urban school districts pursued a great deal of reform—a finding that may shock those calling for more change in urban districts. This evidence, however, comports with a 1994 Council of Great City Schools study in which "virtually all member school districts" reported involvement with district-wide reforms that year.[17] The typical urban district pursued reform in at least three of the five areas and proposed more than eleven "significant" initiatives. Because almost all proposed measures were enacted, administrative personnel and teaching faculty were forced to cope with a river of reform efforts. All of this reform was largely an inside game, promoted and driven by superintendents and board members. Reform had a relatively low profile on the school districts' broader agenda, which was dominated by the day-to-day crush of financial concerns, crises, and management issues. Reforms were not considered as discrete approaches to improving school performance. Instead, they tended to be addressed and proposed en masse.

17. Kowalski (1995, 126).

5

A Political Explanation
of Policy Selection

A MID THE FLOOD of reform activity, some proposals
appear to prosper while others do not. Why are some
measures proposed and enacted more widely than others? Why do education policymakers "decide to push for or promote [some] particular
changes" rather than others?[1] The technocratic presumption is that reforms
are utilized primarily for their ability to improve teaching and learning and
are considered and adopted on that basis. The "union" and the "monopoly"
critiques discussed in chapter 1 each suggest that reform will be shaped by
forces that are unrelated to the political appeal of the proposals.

In fact, professional and institutional incentives discourage
policymakers from proposing those reforms most likely to alter teaching
and learning significantly, while encouraging them to pursue more symbolic measures. This predicament occurs because policymakers are worried about how reform will play in the short term in the local district and in
the professional community, and consequently they emphasize showy and
less controversial measures. The reforms most likely to produce substantive improvement, however, are the time-consuming, unglamorous, and
difficult-to-implement school-level efforts.[2]

Because research on district-level education reform has not compared
the fate of multiple reforms, it has not been possible to examine whether
some reforms are more popular with policymakers. The very question of
popularity is somewhat offensive, since professional educators are presumed to be focused on helping children learn. This chapter examines how
the nature of specific reforms affects the diffusion of these measures. In the

---

1. Fullan (1991, 17).
2. Fullan (1993); McLaughlin (1991b); and Odden (1991b).

broader political science literature on diffusion and agenda setting, researchers have generally paid little attention to how the nature of an innovation itself affects policymaking.

Research into policy diffusion and agenda-setting has examined why certain policies spread and why certain issues gain public prominence. However, traditional theories are of less help in the current study, because most systematic research has focused on which realms of policy are in the media spotlight or how much total activity takes place.[3] Fewer studies have examined why certain policy proposals are selected within a given policy realm, and practical considerations have prevented those studies from exploring the fate of same-realm policy initiatives across a large number of governmental units. Agenda-setting research has focused more on why policy realms move up and down in the public eye than on why proposals move up and down within a policy realm. In fact, the substance of policy proposals has generally been treated as a less significant part of the larger question of how and why policy realms jockey for agenda position.

Certain kinds of proposals are more likely to help superintendents maintain their professional reputation and community prestige. Because there is no rigorous measurement of school system output, because the effects of policy change are lagged, and because turnover of school administrators is extremely high, superintendents can rarely be held accountable for the effectiveness of their proposals. Consequently, when superintendents push proposals, questions of oversight and effective implementation become secondary to those of visibility, dramatic effect, and cost. As a result, the easiest and most politically attractive solutions get replicated and thrust into the public consciousness as widely hailed and endorsed remedies.

Little systematic research has explored the question of why one particular approach is selected rather than another within a given policy arena. For instance, John Kingdon notes that policy proposals are one of the three streams shaping the position of the policy realm on the national agenda, and that it is important a proposal be available when a window of opportunity opens for policy action.[4] However, the determinants of the policies likely to be available when the policy window opens are not addressed. Lacking empirical data, Michael Fullan is forced to vaguely conclude that "innovations can be adopted for symbolic political or personal reasons: to

3. Baumgartner (1989); Baumgartner and Jones (1993); Jones (1994).
4. Kingdon (1984).

appease community pressure, to appear innovative, to gain more resources."[5] This chapter empirically explores the reasons why some education reforms may be preferred to others.

The Determinants of Policy Diffusion

There is a tendency in educational history for certain types of reform to
cyclically rise and fall in popularity.[6] Scholars have proposed theories explaining the kinds of reform that will enjoy the broadest appeal, but they
have not collected comparative data to empirically test these theories. For
instance, measures that add on to existing arrangements in the schools are
more likely to last than are measures that attempt to change established patterns of behavior. Systematic data on the rates at which administrators pursue "add-on" proposals have not been collected, however.

Analysis of policy diffusion has traditionally been rooted in the differences between distributive, redistributive, and regulatory politics. Research that has explained why redistributive policies fare better in some
states than in others has focused on why policies with particular ends are
selected.[7] That is a different question than explaining why different means
are elected to accomplish a given goal. The reforms studied here do not
have distributive implications because they are all different means of pursuing the common end of educational improvement, rather than policies
with divergent substantive goals. Only a handful of studies have looked at
differences in adoption of proposals that represented varying means to a
common end, and these have generally not compared the fate of specific
proposals.[8] The impact of initiative characteristics on policy activity has
rarely been examined.

---

5. Fullan (1991, 28).
6. See Cuban (1984, 1995) and Tyack and Cuban (1995).
7. Sharkansky and Hofferbert (1969).
8. Canon and Blum (1981) studied the diffusion of twenty-three innovative tort doctrines
across the state court systems, but they did not attempt to differentiate how they fared. Although
Menzel and Feller (1977) studied innovation in air pollution control agencies and in state highway
agencies in their ten-state sample, they attempted no comparisons. Thompson (1981) separated
workmen's compensation policy into two dimensions (a nineteen-item compliance index and relative average benefit levels for each state), but he did not attempt to compare the fate of the items
studied. McCrone and Cnudde (1969) examined four kinds of welfare policies, but they limited
themselves to determinants of spending levels and did not compare the fates of policies. Khator
(1993) looked at a number of dimensions of recycling policy, but determined only whether states
had adopted more or less recycling.

Early research on policy diffusion explored how policy innovations spread across state governments.[9] Subsequent scholars have inquired whether certain governments tend to innovate earlier than others, whether this pattern tends to be static, and what traits distinguish early innovators and late innovators.[10] Research studying the rate at which innovations spread has rarely examined whether the policy itself affects diffusion. Instead, the focus has been on how institutions and context explain where, when, and why something is enacted. Further, the diffusion literature has generally focused on formal adoption and spending levels and has paid less attention to policy dimensions not revealed in fiscal data.

A Political Explanation of Reform Selection

Other things being equal, superintendents will attempt those reforms that produce the quickest and most positive feedback. Positive feedback is a function of two factors: how visible the proposal is and how controversial the proposal is likely to be.[11] Because superintendents intend for reform to rally community support and enhance their professional reputations, measures that attract notice and engender little conflict are most attractive. Politically vulnerable policymakers need reform to generate the greatest possible sense of progress with the least amount of disruption or adverse publicity. Assuming that policymakers prefer measures that attract more attention with less controversy, the relative attractiveness of reforms can be plotted on a two-by-two matrix (see table 5-1).

This systemic bias favors policies with more public relations value, even though the most visible and least controversial measures may not be the most effective route to improved teaching and learning. Proposals that are packaged for public acceptance may have little to do with the tedious process of improving school performance.

---

9. Gray (1973a, 1973b) and Walker (1969, 1973).

10. Berman and Martin (1992); Berry and Berry (1990, 1992); Glick (1981); Opheim (1991); Ringquist (1993, 1994); Roeder (1979); Savage (1978); Skalaban (1992); and Skocpol and others (1993).

11. In many cases professional support for a reform helps to make it less controversial and, to a lesser extent, more visible. Crain, Katz, and Rosenthal (1969) conclude that the water fluoridation movement suffered because it moved before professional medical opinion had coalesced in support of fluoridation. In this case, however, all five types of reform enjoyed relatively strong support within the professional education community.

Table 5-1. Political Attractiveness of Reform

	Relative controversy	
Visibility	Low	High
High	Attractive	Mixed
Low	Mixed	Unattractive

Visibility and Controversy

Respondents rated reform visibility by scoring the attention paid to each of the five reforms in the local district. Attention was rated on a zero-to-ten scale, where zero meant the reform had received "no attention" and ten "a great deal." Site-based management (SBM) received the most public attention of the five policy proposals, with a composite rating across the fifty-seven sample districts of 7.0. School day and time proposals attracted the least attention, with a fifty-seven-district composite rating of 4.3. The difference between attention to SBM and to school time was statistically significant at $p < .01$. Attention paid to the other three types of reform fell between those two extremes.

Politically attractive reforms are made more useful if the proposed measure is noticed by the community. An SBM proposal increased the attention paid to site-based management significantly. SBM proposals and attention correlated at 0.58, which was the biggest impact of any reform proposal on the attention paid to that reform. A proposed day and time initiative increased attention paid to day and time matters by just 0.30, the weakest connection of activity and attention among the five kinds of reform. The connection between the stimulus (proposing a measure) and the response (attention to the measure) was greater for SBM than for more decentralized and mundane scheduling measures.

Policymakers seeking to reassure the community and enhance their professional reputations receive greater benefits from more visible measures. However, the strong correlation between attention and controversy (see chapter 4) means that measures that attract notice are also likely to generate controversy. Other things being equal, a superintendent will prefer measures where the gap between attention and controversy is large.[12] Contro-

---

12. As Meranto (1970, 11) noted more than a quarter-century ago, "The fact that a school conflict becomes public is most unfortunate from the educators' perspective. . . . Conflict . . . may weaken the public's confidence in the schools, thus endangering financial support."

versy was measured on a zero-to-ten scale, where zero meant the reform had caused "no controversy" and a ten that it had caused "a great deal." Relative controversiality was measured by subtracting the composite score for controversy from the composite for attention paid to the reform. In the mean district the attention paid to SBM exceeded the controversy over SBM by 2.1 points. The attention paid to the school day exceeded its controversiality by just 1.0 points, substantially less than the margin on SBM. Controversiality for curriculum and professional development fell between that for SBM and school time. Evaluation was slightly more controversial than school time (with a gap of 0.7 between attention and controversy). SBM measures stirred up less conflict, relative to the attention attracted, than did any other type of reform.

The Political Appeal of Reforms

The results on visibility and relative controversy are presented in the two-by-two matrix in table 5-2. Measures that attract more notice and are relatively less controversial are the most attractive to policymakers. SBM and evaluation received the most attention of the five kinds of reform, while professional development and scheduling received the least. In table 5-2, SBM and evaluation are the more politically appealing, high-visibility reforms, while professional development and scheduling are the less appealing, low-visibility measures. Professional development and SBM were less controversial at any given level of attention and more politically appealing, while evaluation and scheduling were much more controversial and less appealing to policymakers.

Measures with a greater political pay-off (visibility) and less risk of negative fallout (controversy) are more politically attractive. SBM is clearly the most politically attractive reform for policymakers, while the least palatable reform is scheduling, which attracts little notice while provoking a relatively high degree of controversy.[13] The rest of the chapter examines SBM and scheduling as examples of politically attractive and unattractive reforms. Scheduling is used here as a short-hand reference for the complex of proposals relating to school time and the school day.

13. More than 95 percent of the nation's fifty largest school districts had adopted some form of SBM by 1993. See Wohlstetter, Mohrman, and Robertson (1997, 202).

Table 5-2. Visibility and Controversiality of Four Reform Proposals

	Controversiality	
Visibility	Less	More
High	Site-based management (SBM)	Evaluation
Low	Professional development	Day and time

Ambition and Breadth

SBM is visible and attractive partly because it is perceived by observers as a bigger and bolder gambit than is scheduling reform. Respondents' descriptions of the two types of reform help explain why this is so.[14] Districtwide reforms are a more powerful symbolic statement than are measures piloted in a few schools. SBM measures were described as districtwide by a majority of local respondents in 63 percent of the forty-nine districts where a proposal was reported, while scheduling initiatives were districtwide in just 11 percent of the eighteen active districts.

SBM measures were also regarded by local respondents as more ambitious than scheduling measures. This is politically ideal, because school policymakers want to get the credit for being risk-takers and innovators. Respondents were asked to rate the relative ambition of each proposal on a zero-to-ten scale, where zero meant "not ambitious" and a ten "very ambitious." SBM proposals rated a composite 8.0 in the forty-nine active districts, 27 percent higher than the 6.3 rating for scheduling proposals in the eighteen active districts. SBM proposals were rated an 8 or higher in 59 percent of the active districts, nearly three times the 22 percent of districts that rated scheduling proposals as that ambitious.

SBM is also attractive because it is less controversial, due in part because such measures tend to be less ambitious and are perceived as less costly than scheduling reforms. Site-based management is perceived as a less ambitious reform than scheduling reforms, and its cost is seen as less

---

14. The following data on SBM and school time proposals include only those districts where a majority of respondents answered affirmatively the question "Has a reform been proposed in this area?" Excluding those districts where a majority of respondents did not report a proposal kept outlier responses (for example, from the one respondent who said a proposal had been made in a district where no one else reported a proposal) from skewing the overall results. The ratings used in the following analysis are district means generated by averaging the answers from multiple respondents.

Table 5-3. Measure of Actual Ambition of Two Reform Proposals[a]
Percent unless otherwise noted

Measure of actual ambition	Scheduling	Site-based management
Over midpoint of scale	44	8
In bottom third of scale	17	35
Number of districts reporting each reform	18	49

Source: Author's data.

a. "Actual ambition" was coded by the author based on respondents' descriptions of the "most significant reform" proposal that they cited for each policy area. All descriptions were coded by the author during the winter of 1995–96, before the data analysis conducted in this chapter. Each response for actual ambition was coded on a zero-to-three scale where a three indicated the measure was "very ambitious," a two that it was "moderately ambitious," a one that it was "somewhat ambitious," and a zero that it was "not ambitious." District ratings are an average of local respondents who described a proposal.

onerous. The proposal descriptions offered by respondents, however, suggest that scheduling reforms are really more ambitious (see table 5-3). By proposing an SBM measure, policymakers were able to appear to be aggressive innovators, while they may have actually reduced the number of expected problems.

Consistent with the implication that scheduling reforms require more work than SBM reforms, local respondents also reported cost to be a more significant factor for scheduling reforms. Lower costs make a policy more politically attractive to policymakers. On a zero-to-ten scale, where zero meant cost was "not a factor" and ten meant cost was a "major concern," scheduling proposals were rated as above average (higher than a five) 50 percent of the time in the eighteen active districts. By comparison, cost was as large a concern for SBM proposals less than 25 percent of the time in the forty-nine active districts. Compared with scheduling measures, SBM proposals delivered more visible and impressive reform at a lower perceived cost and with less apparent trouble.

The Policy Areas: Comparing SBM and Scheduling Reforms

The five types of reform examined were selected because of their prominence among the Third Wave restructuring reforms that dominated education circles in the early 1990s. Unlike the reforms of the 1980s that had emphasized a state-directed approach, the Third Wave reforms presented an excellent opportunity for an aggressive and visible role at the district level. District-level reforms are the most useful to superintendents as political symbols because state-level mandates often shift credit to the governor or state superintendent. District-level reform offers a chance for local actors to take visible, dramatic action.

The ensuing analysis focuses on two of those reforms, school time and SBM reforms, as examples of politically unattractive and attractive reform. While SBM reforms were more politically palatable, there is no evidence they were more effective at improving school performance than school day and time measures. In fact, some educators argue that the more problematic time and scheduling reforms may have more significant education conse-quences. The following discussion is not an attempt to weigh the relative merits of SBM and school scheduling reform, nor is it an effort to assess the pedagogical or practical impact of these reforms. Rather, it is intended to suggest that the evidentiary record during the 1992–95 period offered little reason for district policymakers to believe that SBM was significantly more likely than scheduling and time reforms to improve school perfor-mance or student outcomes.

The School Day and Calendar Reforms: Low Visibility, High Conflict

School day and calendar measures are politically unattractive. These measures are often not very visible, they can be conflictual, they tend not to have a dramatic districtwide impact, and they are considered costly by re-spondents. Changing the school day, week, or year forces logistical changes on teachers and community members, creating inconveniences and disrupting established routines. This causes problems for district policymakers. As noted earlier, the most politically successful reforms are generally those that add on to existing arrangements rather than impose di-rect costs by attempting to change routines and behavior.[15] The *Encyclope-dia of Educational Research* notes that "many school improvement efforts involving organizational reforms founder because of scheduling difficul-ties."[16]

Some educational researchers have argued that unless schools change the schedule of the school day, they "cannot improve the quality of teach-ing and learning."[17] Support for reforming school time is rooted in "an in-creasing disenchantment with impersonal, time-based, calendar-based learning arrangements." John Clarke and Russell Agne believe that modi-

15. Kirst and Meister (1985); Powell, Farrar, and Cohen (1985); Tyack and Cuban (1995); and Wilson (1989, 218–32).
16. MacIver (1992, 1125).
17. Clarke and Agne (1997, 343).

fying the current school calendar and school day is necessary because "the 180-day school year, marching from August to July . . . reinforces the drudgery of an eight-period day. . . . The conventional calendar freezes in place the idea that learning occurs through regular exposure to a content area rather than through engagement in a focused learning activity."[18]

Logistical questions are particularly important because they determine how effectively teachers will utilize new pedagogies and curricula, and how much time teachers will have to train and become accustomed to proposed reforms.[19] Edward Miller has argued that "the schedule—the organization of time in school—is basic to a whole universe of pedagogical and workplace issues at the heart of school reform." For example, "school decision making, curriculum planning, instructional and administrative operations . . . are defined by and organized around the calendar. . . . The calendar and its adjuncts, the clock and the schedule, exert a pervasive influence on both the organization of schools and the thinking of those who work and study in them."[20]

Scheduling reforms may be significant precisely because they force changes in the "grammar" of schooling. This promises to upset the comfortable routine in which parents, teachers, and community members operate. Respondents offered numerous illustrations of the adverse reactions provoked by proposals to reform scheduling. In Palo Alto, California, a year-round calendar encountered heated parental opposition. One respondent recalled, "The first school to attempt [to switch] was the elementary school at Stanford, and the parents went bananas. We didn't expect that. It took the principal and all of us by surprise." An administrator, in a district with "for the most part, minimal participation by parents" recalled how the district's decision to move to a year-round calendar "created a firestorm, with all sorts of community members getting involved to try to stop the thing. They thought we ought to stay with the traditional calendar. The biggest issue has been: What's going to happen to kids during intersessions?" One board member noted, "Parents don't like the fact that teacher workdays mean students don't go to school. It's a tough call for many working parents to provide baby-sitting for their kids." A business community re-

18. Clarke and Agne (1997, 346). See also Murphy (1991, 63).
19. MacIver (1992, 1129). Changes in the school day can be intended to give teachers more time for professional development. A respondent in Euclid, Ohio, noted that the district had added "a team preparation period at the middle school level by trimming each class," so that teacher teams would have more time to coordinate and prepare.
20. Spady (1988, 4–5). See also Miller (1992, 6).

spondent said that local reforms in school time were not proposed because "every time there's a discussion about something as simple as changing the start of the school year, even for snow days, everybody in the town goes off. When the issue of time comes up, the concern is: How will it affect the logistics of picking kids up and dropping them off for working parents?"

Another disincentive for policymakers to alter the school day is potential conflict with teachers about provisions in their union contract. One minority community respondent reported that the superintendent favored reforming the school day but "was told by the school board to oppose it" because of "the opposition from the teachers. Basically, right now, there is a certain amount of comfort with what the teachers have. I don't think the teachers like change." One board member said that change in the school day "has been controversial when we talk about it as a union issue."

Site-Based Management: High Visibility, Low Conflict

Site-based management proposals seek to shift decisionmaking from the central administration to individual school sites. In terms of political appeal, SBM is everything that school scheduling is not. It is highly visible, appears to be ambitious, can be superimposed on existing arrangements, is less likely to inconvenience teachers or the community, and is not considered costly. By definition, SBM proposals tend to be districtwide, making them more visible. Even if a superintendent's predecessor has promulgated SBM, superintendents frequently initiate new activity in order to claim ownership of the measure. One administrator related that the prior superintendent had "set up governing councils at the schools." Rather than continuing with that approach, however, the new superintendent worked out "a new version of the site management policy that's not implemented yet."

SBM is politically ideal because it creates the impression of dramatic change, while permitting policymakers to pursue this reform with only minimal disruption of school routines. SBM measures present a minimal threat to teachers, because there are "reasons to doubt whether changes in structure connect directly with what teachers do in the classroom." As a consequence, little research suggests that "changes in school organization lead directly to changes in teaching practice."[21] A 1990 review of dozens of studies examining SBM initiatives found "little evidence that school-based management alters relationships, renews school organizations, or develops

21. Elmore, Peterson, and McCarthy (1996, 8, 213).

the qualities of academically effective schools." Neither was there evidence that SBM improves "the attitudes of administrators and teachers or the instructional component of schools" or "student achievement."[22]

Betty Malen, Rodney Ogawa, and Jennifer Kranz did find that "school-based management initiatives . . . have been enacted, rescinded, and reenacted for decades. The documentary data suggest that these initiatives tend to surface during periods of intense stress" and "may operate primarily as a symbolic response."[23] In fact, an emphasis on "structural change" often distracts attention "from the more fundamental problems of changing teaching practice."[24]

The visible promise to radically alter local governing arrangements could make SBM highly controversial. However, SBM measures tend to be piecemeal, only partially implemented, and more symbolic than concrete, all of which helps to avoid potential conflict. The central administrators theoretically threatened by SBM did not provoke significant conflict. Central administrators may be crucial to the effective implementation of policies, but they have a minimal role in the political calculus of education policy. SBM was the least controversial of the five kinds of reform, perhaps because the administrators realized that SBM reforms contained little substance. Research has found implementation of SBM initiatives to be ineffectual because of "the modest financial support for planning sessions, staff development activities or new program costs and the inability of teachers to exert significant influence on significant issues." Additionally, site managers rarely use SBM opportunities to tackle substantive issues. Instead, the subjects that councils consider are frequently characterized as "routine, blasé, trivial, peripheral."[25]

Why then did site-based management receive so much attention? And why was it considered so ambitious by the respondents? Malen and her colleagues concluded that SBM serves a symbolic purpose, because troubled systems facing "multiple, complex and competing demands" seek ambiguous reforms that will "quell conflict and restore confidence . . . and reestablish legitimacy" without provoking opposition. Under these conditions, "structural adjustments can be symbolically potent. . . . They can signal that the system is trying to improve, [and] . . . can foster stability and

22. Malen, Ogawa, and Kranz (1990, 289, 321, 323). See also Murphy and Beck (1995) and Wohlstetter (1995).

23. Malen, Ogawa, and Kranz (1990, 296, 327).

24. Elmore, Peterson, and McCarthy (1996, 237).

25. Malen, Ogawa, and Kranz (1990, 305, 312).

re-establish legitimacy without imposing new financial burdens on the system."[26] Richard Elmore, Penelope Peterson, and Sarah McCarthy have noted that "reformers focus on changing structures because these changes have a visible impact on the schools. . . . From the perspective of outsiders—administrators, parents, policy makers—schools involved in structural change appear to be 'doing something.'. . . For these reasons, structural change is seductive and energizing."[27]

Respondents indicated that a wide range of plans and arrangements came under the rubric of SBM. The plans shared union support and a lack of clarity as to decisionmaking authority at the site. A Palo Alto, California, respondent reported a "significant" SBM reform, but could only describe it vaguely, saying, "What we keep talking about is site-based management decision-making, but there is not a clear policy on what that means. . . . We're trying to get something in place, but what is site-based decision-making is not yet clear."

Testing a Political Theory of Policy Selection

A theory of political policy selection suggests that actors will favor symbolically potent reforms and produce greater activity on these reforms than on substantive reforms. Symbolic reforms, however, are likely to prove less effective.

Local Actors

SBM measures are more attractive than school time measures largely because they are relatively uncontroversial. SBM measures also appear to promise quicker improvement. SBM measures are less controversial because they cause less disruption in the lives of education stakeholders, particularly the teachers, than do scheduling measures. One administrator summed up the union response to demanding changes quite simply: "The union is overworked and no one likes change."

Unions are more tolerant of SBM than of scheduling measures for two reasons. First, unions have a significant role in shaping governance proposals through their contract. One union respondent illustrated how contract-reliant SBM reform can be: "We just finished negotiating with the [school] committee to review the [SBM] models and to move into getting [shared

---

26. Malen, Ogawa, and Kranz (1990, 325–26).
27. Elmore, Peterson, and McCarthy (1996, 237–38).

governance] to the sites. Hopefully, the year after this coming year we'll be moving to implementation." An administrator in another district said the administration had "given away" control of SBM reform to the union in the contract:

> [SBM] is even part of the teacher contract. See, we give away every-thing. The contract dictates the percentage [of teachers] that have to support site-based control for a school to be site-based managed. [The contract] sets up a structure for SBM. [SBM] is pretty structured and controlled . . . because the union was afraid that principals would be in charge.

Education policymakers are less concerned with instituting a focused SBM policy than with minimizing conflict and attracting broad community support. Politically, SBM is attractive because—surprisingly—it appears to enjoy union support and to be broadly acceptable. Union leaders are rel-atively comfortable with SBM, perhaps because they have learned that SBM proposals are largely symbolic and produce much less day-to-day disruption in the classroom than do alternative reforms. Although anec-dotal evidence may suggest that unions are opposed to SBM proposals, un-ions in the sample supported SBM reform proposals much more strongly than they did changes in the school day or calendar.

In the forty-nine districts where a majority of respondents reported that a reform was proposed, the union opposed the SBM proposal in just 6 per-cent of the districts. Unions were more than six times as likely to oppose scheduling reforms, opposing them in 39 percent of the eighteen active dis-tricts. Mean union support for SBM was 7.6 (on a zero-to-ten scale, where ten indicated strong support and a zero strong opposition). This score was nearly 50 percent higher than the 5.2 support for scheduling reforms. Even scheduling measures were backed by the union most of the time, because proposals were constrained by contract language. However, as one admin-istrator explained, "Changing the school day is very controversial in school with the staff." A superintendent ran much less risk of provoking union op-position by addressing school governance issues than by changing the school day.

Community groups consistently preferred SBM proposals to scheduling measures. Respondents reporting a proposal were asked to evaluate the po-sition of several local groups on a zero-to-ten scale, where ten indicated strong support for and a zero strong opposition to each measure. Parent teacher associations (PTAs), whose members interact with the schools regularly and have to worry about release schedules and childcare arrangements, had the strongest preference for SBM relative to time proposals. PTAs were about 25 percent more supportive of SBM proposals than of scheduling measures. Business organizations, local newspapers, and race organizations all were more supportive of SBM measures than of school day and time measures by margins. Greater community support for SBM than for scheduling reflects the political attributes of the two types of reform and explains the greater incentives for policymakers to favor SBM.

Reflecting the preferences of the teachers' union and community groups, superintendents in the sample strongly preferred SBM measures to scheduling measures. Respondents rated superintendents' support for each reform on a zero-to-ten scale, where zero indicated strong opposition to the proposal and a ten indicated strong support. In 61 percent of districts, superintendents' support for SBM reform was rated an 8 or higher, which was more than twice the 28 percent rate at which superintendents strongly backed scheduling reform.

Superintendents' support for SBM rated a mean of 8.6, compared with 8.1 for scheduling proposals, the lowest level of support for any of the five reform types. The scheduling figure is still high because superintendents supported all reform proposals. However, given their uniformly high level of support for reforms, the 0.5 gap is not insignificant. Furthermore, superintendents pushed SBM reforms more energetically than those involving the school day. Respondents were asked "how much influence the superintendent has exerted" on behalf of each reform, where a zero meant "no influence" on the measure and a ten "a great deal of influence." Superintendents' support was rated a 6.5 for scheduling proposals, but 8.1 for SBM proposals, meaning that superintendents pushed SBM measures about 25 percent more vigorously than scheduling measures.

Proposal and Enactment

Consistent with its broader support, SBM was proposed more frequently and enacted at a higher rate than was scheduling reform. A majority of respondents reported that SBM was proposed in 86 percent of the fifty-seven sample districts, while scheduling measures were proposed in just 32 percent of districts. This huge disparity in proposal rates is not the product of state legislation mandating SBM activity. In districts that did not report state-required activity on SBM and scheduling, the disparity actually increases slightly. SBM measures were proposed in 75 percent of the forty-seven districts where the state did not require SBM activity; scheduling reform was proposed in just 17 percent of the thirty-two districts where mandated change was not reported.[28]

SBM measures, once proposed, were enacted at a very high rate. In fact, SBM proposals were reportedly enacted in 100 percent of the forty-nine districts where a proposal was made. Scheduling proposals were still quite successful, like all school reforms, but the 61 percent success rate in the eighteen active districts did not approach the unanimous success of SBM measures.

A majority of respondents in 86 percent of the fifty-seven districts reported that SBM measures were proposed and enacted, while school day and calendar measures were reported to enjoy similar success in just 19 percent of the districts. The relative unpopularity of school time and day measures is not a new finding. A study of reform initiatives in the 1980s found that a few were not very popular, "the most striking being the suggestion to increase the school year to 200 or even 220 days" and a second being "lengthen[ing] the school day."[29] The costs of tackling school day and time issues are intimidating, and the rewards are few, particularly at the local level.

Outcomes

Superintendents and community groups consistently support site-based management more strongly than scheduling reform, with the result that SBM measures are proposed and enacted at rates dramatically higher than school time measures. This state of affairs can be interpreted to support either a reformist or a political explanation of school reform. The traditional reformist understanding of school reform implies that SBM attracts more support and is more prevalent because it is believed to be more effective at improving school performance. In contrast, the political theory of policy selection hypothesizes that SBM is favored because it is a more attractive symbolic political statement. If SBM was not perceived as any more successful than scheduling reform, even as it was being supported and utilized much more widely, the case for a political interpretation of policy selection becomes relatively persuasive.

28. Activity in a district was coded as state mandated if a majority of respondents reporting a reform proposal answered "yes" when asked if the state had required the reform.
29. Firestone, Fuhrman, and Kirst (1991, 236).

Evaluations of how respondents gauged the central administration support, the degree of implementation, and the reform efficacy of each measure offer evidence on the perceived efficacy of the reforms studied. Assessing the impact of even a single school reform in a single district is a difficult business, and assessing the impact of amorphous reforms across fifty-seven large districts is nearly impossible.[30] Measuring reform implementation or success on a zero-to-ten scale is obviously a very rough measure. On the other hand, most efforts to measure large-scale policy consequences are approximations of a hard-to-observe process. Assuming that the impressions of community observers who have been paying close attention to local education for an extended period—the average respondent had been following local schooling for nearly twenty years—have some meaning, comparing their evaluations of the two reforms ought to produce unbiased and meaningful information. While obviously blunt, this approach permits comparative study of activity in over fifty districts, providing a necessary complement to the existent work on school reform.

CENTRAL OFFICE SUPPORT.   When it comes to school reform, there is a divergence of interests between the superintendent, as head of the school bureaucracy, and the members of that bureaucracy. The superintendent, pressed to demonstrate visible evidence of energetic leadership within a constrained time period, has incentives to be a policy entrepreneur. Lower level bureaucrats have incentives to preserve order, predictability, and the security of their positions.[31] The natural reticence of bureaucrats when confronted with reform is greatly accelerated in the case of SBM, which threatens to throw the central administration into turmoil and to imperil the jobs of administrators. Bureaucratic resistance can consign a reform to likely failure, because "the seriousness and purposefulness with which the district administration undertakes its tasks are likely to be transmitted to school staffs and on down."[32] Therefore, opposition from the central administrators makes it less likely that a measure will produce positive results.

District administrative support for each reform was assessed by asking those respondents who had reported that a proposal was enacted, "How committed is the central administration to this policy?" Respondents an-

30. Simon and May (1995).
31. Wilson (1989).
32. Purkey and Smith (1985, 385).

swered on a zero-to-ten scale, where a zero indicated the administration was "not committed" and a ten that it was "very committed" to the proposal.[33]

Central office personnel supported scheduling reform much more strongly than SBM reform. Scheduling measures received complete central office support (a composite ten out of ten) in 35 percent of the seventeen districts reporting activity, while SBM received complete support in just 2 percent of the forty-nine active districts. Mean central office support for school day and time measures was reported to be 8.4 across the seventeen districts, about 18 percent higher than the 7.1 reported for SBM measures. Successfully implementing policies with low levels of central office support is difficult, and SBM was not popular among administrators because of "concerns about turf and turf control."

IMPLEMENTATION.   Implementation is crucial. Research has found that "the more completely projects were implemented, the more likely they were to be sustained" and the more likely they were to improve school performance.[34] Measures that are not implemented are not going to prove effective. The extent to which reforms were implemented was measured by asking respondents who reported that a proposal had been enacted, "How thoroughly has this reform been implemented at the school level?" Respondents answered on a zero-to-ten scale, where zero indicated the policy was "not at all implemented" and a ten meant it was "completely in place."

Although SBM was proposed three times as often, scheduling reforms were reported to be implemented much more thoroughly. Respondents reported that scheduling reforms were completely implemented (a ten out of ten) in 35 percent of the seventeen active districts, while SBM reforms were completely implemented in just 4 percent of the forty-nine active districts. School day and calendar reforms were rated a 7.4 for implementation, while SBM reforms were rated a 6.6. One Atlanta respondent's criticism of site-based management illustrates the difficulty that districts have in making SBM effective: "They've been in the process allegedly of doing

33. This question was designed to gather information on the behavior of central office personnel. Separate questions measured superintendents' support for each policy. However, the superintendent is the head of the central administration, so the response on the "central administration" probably includes an evaluation of the superintendent. The fact that the central administration supported scheduling reform much more strongly than SBM reform—even though superintendents supported SBM reform more strongly—suggests strong resistance by central administrators to SBM.

34. Purkey and Smith (1985, 384).

this for a long time. You hear bits and pieces and snippets of it, but I don't know if there is any school that's fully engaged in it. But they've been talking about it forever."

PERCEIVED SUCCESS.   The evaluations of reform success reflect the judgments of those involved in urban education policy. Did district policymakers believe that SBM was more effective than scheduling reform? The answer is no.

Consistent with the weak levels of support from administrators and poor implementation, SBM initiatives were regarded as less successful than were school day initiatives. In fact, the same respondents who reported higher levels of community support for SBM and dramatically higher levels of SBM activity also reported SBM initiatives as having been substantially less successful than were school day measures. SBM measures were enacted at a feverish rate, even though they were not considered particularly successful.

The reported success of policies was compared using composite ratings from the question, "Thus far, how successfully has the policy achieved its stated goals?" Respondents answered on a zero-to-ten scale, where zero meant the policy had been "not at all successful" and a ten meant it had been "very successful."[35]

SBM measures were not considered to be particularly effective, despite their high level of community support. Describing the district's experience with SBM, one board member said,

> [P]eople have been riding on this for a long time, and I've never seen a district do it well. . . . You've got to deal with the principals' authority issue, you've got to train parents. . . . [E]ven if you take away the board member resistance and administrative resistance . . . you still have a difficult proposition . . . We were not going to walk down the Chicago path. . . . We saw the Miami story, and there was no increase in student performance. [We saw] the limited results and pretty serious headaches that evolved in some of the big experiments that took place early on.

SBM proposals were deemed to be substantially less successful than school day and calendar reforms. Overall, scheduling reforms were rated

35. Respondents were evaluating reforms only in terms of the reform's stated goals—rather than on some kind of universal scale. However, comparing the "success" of reforms in any more abstract fashion requires information unavailable from the current study.

as 19 percent more successful than SBM reforms. School time reforms were rated a 6.9 on the zero-to-ten scale, while SBM reforms were rated a composite 5.7. Scheduling reforms were viewed as being at least 70 percent successful in half of the sixteen districts where they were enacted, while SBM proposals were considered to be that successful in just 14 percent of the forty-nine active districts.

SBM initiatives' minimal effects were described by a Long Beach, California, respondent: "Sixty to seventy percent of schools have done [SBM]. But my value judgment is that it's not effective site-based management. They may have a team, it may be in order, but do I think it's working? Absolutely not. They're still discussing parking spaces. I would put three or four schools out of eighty-five in the successful category."

Superintendents support SBM reforms more energetically than scheduling reforms, and propose and enact SBM measures at a much higher rate, despite the mixed results from research and higher rate of success attributed to scheduling proposals. Policymakers were not simply opting, in overwhelming numbers, for one of two reforms thought to be equally promising. Policymakers chose, by a wide margin, a reform reported to be somewhat less successful.

This evidence suggests that the "monopoly critique" discussed in chapter 1 is incorrect. School reform is not failing because school systems are unconcerned with public preferences. Rather than policymakers being inattentive to community concerns, they are selecting some reforms precisely because they are appealing to the public. Of course, attention to pleasing the local and professional communities on the symbolically potent issue of reform does not mean that policymakers are sensitive to these pressures on less visible elements of system management.

Conclusion

Urban superintendents and school boards have strong incentives to prefer visible, dramatic, and relatively painless school reforms. Pressed by short-term time constraints to win public prestige and build their professional reputations, superintendents opt for reforms that will generate the most positive political feedback. Consistent with a political theory of school reform, the more visible and less controversial SBM measures are supported much more widely and are employed much more frequently than are less politically salable school day and time reforms. As educational scholar Theodore Kowalski has observed, "Urban school leaders frequently point to recent efforts to implement popular ideas such as in-district choice or site-based management as evidence that their organizations are not standing still."[36]

Policymakers' preference for SBM measures does not appear to be attributable to SBM's track record. Neither the literature available in the early and mid-1990s, nor the evaluations by respondents suggests that SBM measures were deemed more likely to improve school performance or more successful at improving school performance than were day and time measures. Policymakers benefit politically from measures, like SBM, that are not likely to be implemented immediately or to have an immediate effect. Formal measures with clear implications, such as competency testing, can provoke controversy and leave little wiggle-room to defuse conflict. More informal measures, or formally announced measures that can be eased into place and modified to avoid conflict, are more politically useful. This behavior may actually hinder school system performance. The danger is that "focusing on structural changes draws attention away from the more fundamental problems" and "is likely to increase disillusionment and cynicism about school reform."[37]

Education policymakers in urban districts want to improve teaching and learning. The evidence presented in this chapter does not impugn their motives. However, when selecting from a menu of policy options, they will choose reforms that maximize political impact and minimize potential adverse reaction—not necessarily the reforms most likely to improve school performance.

36. Kowalski (1995, 126)
37. Elmore, Peterson, and McCarthy (1996, 242).

6

Community Context and
Urban School Reform

IN RECENT DECADES practitioners and academics have
reached a consensus that community context affects
school reform.[1] How and why context matters have not been studied, however. The knowledge we do have is largely the product of case studies and
has not been comparatively tested using a large number of districts. This
chapter examines why context matters and what it is about context that
matters by studying the effects of several demographic and fiscal factors on
the school reform agenda.

Reform is promoted as a tool to remedy identifiable problems in schooling. As a result, if it is about enhancing student performance, reform should
emerge from a deliberative process in which needs are defined and addressed as policy problems. There is little evidence of that behavior. Instead, the responsiveness of the reform agenda to public pressures strongly
suggests that policymakers are more focused on reassuring anxious communities and protecting themselves than on initiating long-term fixes. This
responsiveness to political imperatives does not mean that policymakers
are unconcerned with local problems, but simply that reform is subsumed
in the district's broader political process.

There are currently two general understandings of how context affects
district governance. The "one best system" analysis suggests that all urban
school districts have similar institutional arrangements that insulate them
from the broader community. This bureaucracy-oriented analysis implies
urban districts will address reform in similar ways. The second understand-

---

1. For instance, see the Consortium for Policy Research in Education (1996); Doll (1996);
Fuhrman, Clune, and Elmore (1991); Fullan (1991); Hanson (1996); Johnson (1996); Marsh and
Crocker (1991); Marsh and Odden (1991); McLaughlin (1991a); and Wallace (1996).

ing of context is as a constraint rather than as a motivating force: context will influence policy implementation, but it will primarily play a reactive role. I propose a third view—a political understanding of school reform. It differs from the other two views by conceptualizing local context as a proactive force that causes reform activity to vary across districts in response to local pressures.

The "One Best System" Analysis

The insights in David Tyack's book *The One Best System: A History of American Urban Education*, published in 1974, inspired this type of analysis, which emphasizes the interdistrict similarities in governance structures among urban school systems.[2] According to this view, urban systems are so hamstrung by bureaucracy that they are highly insulated from the external community. Local conditions are rendered unimportant. John Chubb and Terry Moe assume this homogeneity when they treat all urban public schools as similar for purposes of analysis in their widely discussed book *Politics, Markets, and America's Schools*.[3] The isolation and rigidity of public school systems are implied in other work on school governance structures as well. These scholars suggest that the link between school policy, school boards, and the public is very tenuous.[4] The "one best system" analysis implies that there will be minimal systematic variation in school reform across urban districts, because these districts are governed by homogenous bureaucracies insulated from local pressures.

The "Context as Constraint" Analysis

A second school of thought presumes that context has important implications, particularly in terms of policy implementation, but it addresses context primarily as a passive factor that policymakers must accommodate.[5] Little attention is paid to how local context shapes policymakers' behavior through its influence on incentives. Implicitly assuming that local policymakers are single-minded seekers of educational performance, research on contextual effects has rarely explored what determines the re-

---

2. Tyack (1974).
3. Chubb and Moe (1990).
4. Finn (1991) and Zeigler and Jennings (1974).
5. See, for instance, Fuhrman, Clune, and Elmore (1991); Odden (1991a, 1991b); Pressman and Wildavsky (1984); and Sabatier and Mazamanian (1981).

forms that are proposed or considered in a district. Research has rarely addressed these inputs, instead emphasizing how contextual constraints affect the decisions that are made and thereby shape the results of the policy process. Contextual analysis has emphasized the need for policymakers to take account of local constraints, but it has not examined how context shapes the behavior of the policymakers themselves.[6] This chapter attempts to build upon the current understanding of context by exploring its proactive role. To what extent does context alter the political pressures that inspire policymakers to pursue reform?

Local Context and Reform

Urban school bureaucracies, although designed with the intention of taking politics out of schooling, have remained political.[7] District policymakers are subject to political pressures from their local and professional communities. Community conditions shape the local political constraints, thereby modifying the incentives for policymakers to pursue school reform.

If school reform is largely a political response to political pressures, the rate of reform activity can be expected to vary systematically as environmental pressures vary across districts. Initiatives will be more likely in the most troubled districts, because these are the districts where communities require the most reassurance—regardless of whether these districts have the resources or capacity to make reform work. On the other hand, if school reform is simply a technocrat's tool, school reforms should be targeted to particular educational problems and largely insulated from the local political environment.[8] Because previous researchers have not comparatively and explicitly examined the causal dimensions of context, they have not been able to measure how local political factors shape the reform agenda. The "monopoly critique," and other analyses that emphasize the insulation of urban school systems, inaccurately depict the nature and consequences of policymakers' responsiveness.

This analysis utilizes the composite ratings for each sample district, which were generated by determining the mean score of all local re-

6. Fullan (1991, 1993).
7. See Tyack (1974) on this design.
8. It could be argued that demographics will correlate with a need for a specific reform, but few respondents indicated a reform had been targeted that deliberately.

sponses. Ordinary least squares regression was used to perform the analysis. A linear model was appropriate because the creation of composite district values made the measures of school reform into continuous distributions.

Explanatory Variables: Measures of Context

School reform is heavily influenced by three kinds of contextual forces: demand pressures, supply pressures, and community polarization. These forces are operationalized in an analytic model using seven explanatory variables. Five measures of demand pressures in the district are used: the adult education level, the poverty rate, the total school district enrollment, the percentage of district students enrolled in public school, and the rate of local retail growth from 1987–92. Supply-side pressure is measured using the district's per pupil spending rate. Community polarization is measured using the black population percentage in the district.[9]

Demand-Side Pressures

School policymakers will promote more reform activity in districts that are closely scrutinized, troubled, or where producing demonstrable improvement is difficult.

EDUCATIONAL ATTAINMENT OF THE ADULT COMMUNITY.   The more education adults have, the more demanding they are of educational quality.[10] Consequently, it is hypothesized that communities with more educated adults are more demanding of school performance. One administrator summed up this pressure succinctly, "It's hard to make [spending] reductions in a community where one-third of the people have doctorates— expectations here are high." The educated are more willing to lean on school administrators and get involved in decisionmaking. The adult population in the Palo Alto Unified District topped the sample with a 96 percent high school completion rate. A respondent from this district thus described the pressure that a highly educated community brings to bear on the school system:

9. When the individual is the unit of observation, these seven explanatory variables suffer from problems of prior causality. However, in this analysis the behavior of community members is of less interest than how school policymakers respond to community characteristics.

10. Elam (1978) and Elam, Rose, and Gallup (1994).

We have a full board room at every board meeting, and the board meets twice a month or more. The papers are full of letters to editor. Whenever we advertise for parents to join committees, we have people standing in line to get on those committees. . . . The PTA is involved in everything. Our site councils are like mini-school boards and people apply from all over. It's very impressive. It's overwhelming for some of our staff who aren't used to everyone looking over your shoulder. . . . I spend half my life arguing with [the community].

Another respondent noted, "The better educated and more worldly tend to look into schools more closely. . . . People at the higher end of the socio-economic spectrum, if their children are placed at poorer schools, they remove their children from the schools and send them to private schools." In response to the increased demand for school quality, school officials work harder to demonstrate their commitment.

Community educational attainment was measured using the 1990 census figure reporting the percentage of district adults age twenty and over who had completed high school.

POVERTY RATE.   The poverty rate is frequently used as a rough barometer of community wealth. It may be more useful, however, to view poverty in American cities as the most easily measured "manifestation of a much more general deterioration in American society and culture."[11] Residents of poor inner city neighborhoods "confront a broad spectrum of irritations, inconveniences, affronts, and anxieties."[12] The poverty rate is a proxy for the associated ills of crime, gangs, drugs, broken families, teenage pregnancy, and unemployment that are part of "a spreading underclass culture."[13] All of these problems, explained one respondent, mean that urban districts are forced to perform "educational triage." Indeed, researchers have noted that "when schools are plagued by problems—poor academic performance, drugs, violence, absenteeism, high drop-out rates—public officials come under intense pressure to take corrective action in the form of new policies."[14]

11. Peterson (1991, 8).
12. Crenson 1983, 114).
13. Peterson (1991, 8).
14. Chubb and Moe (1990, 63).

In this study per pupil spending and the rate of local economic growth are controlled for separately. Therefore, the poverty variable largely reflects the extent of the "underclass culture" rather than the simple lack of wealth in high-poverty districts. Poverty was measured using the percentage of district residents with 1989 incomes below the poverty level, as reported in the 1990 census.

Respondents from high-poverty districts often traced school system problems to "underclass culture" problems. One administrator said one of the system's leading issues was "discipline, because, with increased gang activity and the more challenging students we're serving, it's more difficult to focus on classrooms and education." A board member in another district observed that "gang violence" was a central concern: "In fact, we were one of the first school districts to start our own state certified police department." Districts contending with gangs and operating police departments find it difficult to focus on students' performance. Schools in communities with high rates of poverty also have more troubled students and adverse environmental conditions, both of which make it difficult to demonstrate performance. One administrator, when asked about the leading local educational issues, cited "a dramatic increase in family poverty. It's increased the demands on urban school districts, and resources are being reduced." Another respondent said, "Sometimes students [are tested] on the presumption they're all starting from the same place. I don't think that's the case with any group of people, particularly in urban districts."

DISTRICT ENROLLMENT.   The leadership in large districts finds it more difficult to connect with the community and to display concrete progress on educational reforms. Superintendents' decisions in large systems have to work their way through an extended administrative hierarchy to many more schools and classrooms, while parents and the community have a more difficult time assessing the district's overall performance. In smaller communities, with fewer schools and less distance between the leadership and the public, the community possesses more firsthand information on the schools. This makes media and public relations cues less important in forming views of school system performance.[15]

In smaller communities residents can more easily learn about school affairs through interaction with friends, colleagues, and neighbors. Parents and community participants in larger districts are forced to rely more on

15. Carmines and Stimson (1989).

formal institutions like daily newspapers, television stations, the PTA, and school communications.[16] In a district with only a handful of schools—like Euclid, Ohio, with eight schools or Malden, Massachusetts, with twelve—parents and the general community are more likely to have a first-hand impression of the district's performance, and it is more likely to be positive.[17] As one administrator noted, "When you talk to a person about their individual school, they think it's great, an eight to a ten. When they look at the system as a whole, because it's so large . . . it's a five or a six. People view the system and their school very differently. We're the largest business in the county by a long shot, and people look at us that way." Because the community in a large district feels a weaker connection to the schools, policymakers work harder at taking actions that will translate clearly through the formal media.[18]

District size was measured using the district's total public school enrollment, as reported in the 1990 census.

PUBLIC ENROLLMENT PERCENTAGE.   Communities that enroll a greater percentage of their children in the public schools have a greater incentive to pay attention to school affairs.[19] Because more parents have a stake in the schools in these districts, the salience of educational issues is raised. School policymakers face heightened scrutiny and more pressure to demonstrate competence, so they turn to reform in an attempt to strengthen their vulnerable position. Conversely, in districts with a low public enroll-

16. Each journalist respondent was asked about the role of the local media in school affairs. In the sixteen districts with more than 50,000 students, newspapers and local television were both considered to be much more influential than in the twenty-two districts with fewer than 20,000 students. Local television was rated 89 percent more influential and newspapers 24 percent more influential in the large districts. Additionally, media attention to school affairs was reported to be 15 percent higher in the larger districts.

17. A parent visiting one school in Euclid has observed more than 10 percent of the system's schools. A parent making the same effort in Detroit (259 schools) or Philadelphia (256 schools) would have seen less than one-half of 1 percent of the district's schools. On the greater likelihood of a positive impression, see Elam, Rose, and Gallup (1994).

18. Respondents in large districts could have a tendency to report more reform simply because more of everything is taking place. However, respondents may not be as acquainted with the full range of activity in a large system. This would bias the reported number of proposals downward, so the nature of any possible effect is unclear.

19. Public enrollment percentage indicates the percentage of school-age children who are not in private schools. The vast majority of private school students attend relatively inexpensive parochial schools. See Bryk, Lee, and Holland (1993). Therefore, public enrollment percentage is primarily a function of idiosyncratic local factors, particularly the size of the local Catholic population and not of local wealth.

ment percentage, widespread utilization of private schools reduces community interest and scrutiny. As one business leader explained:

> The business community . . . pays lip service to the need for improved public education, but does very little more than pay lip service. One reason is that . . . there is a very high level of private school attendance. And for that reason, maybe among others, the level of energy and commitment among people of means and substance is less than it otherwise would be, because they have their kids in private school.

A similar point was made by a board member in a Sun Belt district:

> This district used to be, 20 years ago, 70 to 75 percent Anglo, mostly middle class. . . . And essentially . . . white students left the district over 18 years. We have a pretty rich array of private schools. . . . A lot of parent groups and good citizens groups and business types who were heavily committed to this district years ago, a lot of their interest and commitment and investment has left, and that hurt the district.

The public school enrollment percentage was determined by dividing the number of students in the district's public schools by the total number of students enrolled in all schools in the district, according to the 1990 census.

LOCAL RETAIL GROWTH.   The metropolitan area's economic health influences the problems that confront the local school district. Districts with a growing local economy find non-educational problems less pressing, so local organizations and community members pay more attention to school affairs. Educational problems, aside from those involving infrastructure, are less immediate and less visible than are most urban problems. Consequently, the school system's prominence on the public agenda is partly a function of other community needs. A healthy rate of local growth reduces the number of concerns competing for the attention of community organizations, thus allowing them to pay more attention to education. Retail growth does not single out the school system so much as lessen the salience of other concerns, increasing relative demand for school performance. Interest in schooling grows, but without the insistent expectations for dramatic improvement produced by the other demand variables.

Growth in the local city's retail trade was measured for the 1987 to 1992 period, the five-year period immediately preceding the years (1992–95) for which the dependent variables were collected.[20] The data were collected from the 1995 *City and County Data Book.*

Supply-Side Pressures

School administrators are more likely to pursue school reform when confronted with "supply-side" pressures, which increase the resources at a school district's disposal. Increased resources, other things being equal, permit administrators to attempt more reform. At any given level of demand-driven pressure, administrators have an incentive to use additional resources to demonstrate their commitment to school improvement and bolster their community prestige and professional reputation. The measure of district resources used here is district instructional spending per pupil. Districts that spend more dollars per student have, other things being equal, more money that they can afford to invest in reform proposals. A respondent discussed how important funding was to a restructuring effort led by the superintendent: "a significant factor . . . was the superintendent's ability to rally the Pittsburgh Foundation, private and corporate clienteles in the city, and to engage them in supplying private funds to support a number of the initiatives. . . . [W]e couldn't have done it without the external funding."

Policymakers in cash-strapped districts often find it relatively more difficult to pursue reform. One board member admitted not knowing the superintendent's position on evaluation reform:

> I know it sounds crazy, but we have some major financial problems and major facilities problems, and that's where our attention goes. It's a shame, but there's little focus on education now because of those problems. . . . Because anything and everything we look at costs money, there's not a lot of attention to these reforms. It seems we do very little because we don't have any money.

Per pupil spending was measured in terms of current instructional spending per pupil in 1989, as reported by school districts in the 1990 census.

---

20. Retail growth data were not available by school district, so the growth rate was calculated based on growth in the dominant local city.

Community Polarization

Reform proposals are more likely to engender conflict in communities with substantial racial divisions. If reforms measures are intended to reassure the public and defuse criticism, they should be less likely in these communities where they may actually increase tension.[21]

Racial homogeneity or heterogeneity affects reform activity because social homogeneity is related to political uncertainty. In homogeneous communities, where conflicts of interest are fewer and factions less sharply defined than in heterogeneous communities, "the threats and costs of political uncertainty are low."[22] The opposite is true in heterogeneous school districts.

Equity concerns can make innovation extremely controversial if a significant and visible element of the community feels wronged. In polarized districts administrators have an incentive to avoid potentially disruptive reforms. Questions in most areas of urban public policy, including education, feature fierce disputes about racial equity. The polarization between black and white is particularly stark, because a long history of exclusion and segregation has engendered a strong group-based demand for educational equity among blacks.[23] The skin color of students is obvious, and racial composition is easily counted, making inequities highly visible. The result is that educational initiatives can easily provoke conflict in communities with large black populations.[24]

Respondents suggested that the black community is extremely concerned about inequities any reform activity might produce. One administrator said that the minority leadership opposed site-based management reform "because we have certain site-based management members,

21. Readers may be surprised that the predicted effects of black population and poverty are different, because they are often portrayed as having similar effects upon policy. The symbolic argument here hypothesizes that school policymakers in impoverished communities feel increased pressure to demonstrate a clear sense of motion, while an increased black population causes policymakers to exercise greater caution.

22. Chubb and Moe (1990, 62).

23. Katznelson and Weir (1985). In Cleveland in 1995 the issue of changing the elected school board, which was predominantly black, to an appointed board was promoted by the nonpartisan Citizens' League. Outraged, the president of the Cleveland NAACP declared, "The Citizens' League's searing evaluations of the candidates and its haughty recommendation to abolish the board or replace it with 'anointed' members is not only an insult to American democracy, but reeks of elitism and a combination plantation [and] 'Bell Curve' mentality." See Stephens (1995a, 1B).

24. Rich (1996).

particularly minorities, who want every student on the same page at the same hour. They say, 'What's good for one school is good for all,' and they support strict top-down management to make sure of it." Administrators in racially split districts will be particularly leery of reforms like site-based management or evaluation that can segment the community.

The possibility that reform efforts will backfire makes administrators more cautious and discourages reform activity. Because it is never perfectly clear in advance which proposals will be viewed as inequitable, administrators in heavily black districts are likely to walk gingerly and feel the community out carefully before proposing many kinds of reform. In the most difficult situations, racial and desegregation concerns can pervade district management, lending a racial calculus to every decision. Said one union respondent, "The desegregation agreement has clouded every issue that we've tried to talk about." A respondent in Tyler, Texas, illustrated how equity concerns plagued a bond issue for facilities and technology that promised to benefit the entire district:

> We have overcrowded schools and crumbling facilities. But the bond issue has been put on hold because . . . the U.S. Department of Justice decided they didn't like the racial makeup on our campuses and wouldn't give us clearance to go ahead and have a bond election. . . . The black north Tyler community has been very influential. Basically, they're the ones that sicced the U.S. Department of Justice on us and that killed the 38 million dollar bond issue. . . . No facilities, no technology, no re-roofs, no classroom additions, no new libraries.

The black percentage of the school district population was measured using the 1990 census.

Correlations among the Explanatory Variables

Table 6-1 shows that some of the explanatory variables are moderately correlated, but none of the correlations is stronger than 0.69. Only three correlations are 0.49 or higher, and none of the three is surprising. Education and poverty have a strong negative correlation (–0.59), while poverty and black population percentage have a strong positive correlation (0.69). The third strong correlation is the negative one (–0.57) between the percentage of students enrolled in public school and expenditures per pupil. Because district budgets are only partially based on enrollment, changes in

Table 6-1. Correlations among the Explanatory Variables

Variable	Adult education level	Poverty rate	Total school district enrollment	District students enrolled in public schools (percent)	Retail growth rate, 1987–92	Black population in district (percent)
Poverty rate	-.59	1.00				
Black population percentage in the district	-.40	.69				1.00
Retail growth rate, 1987–92	.23	-.20			1.00	-.20
Total school district enrollment	-.35	.38	1.00		.04	.49
Percentage of district students enrolled in public schools	-.41	.40	.06	1.00	.19	.16
Per pupil spending	.12	-.11	-.18	-.57	-.18	-.02

Source: Author's data. $N = 51$.

student population are not matched by changes in funding. Districts that lose students are left, in the short term, with more dollars per pupil, and districts that gain students have fewer dollars per pupil.

The Dependent Variables

Three key variables were used to analyze the reform agenda in this chapter. A fourth variable measuring perceived local performance is also examined to gauge how the perceived need for reform varied with district context. The value for each dependent variable in each district represented the mean response produced by averaging the evaluations of all respondents in a given district.

The first variable measured (on a zero-to-ten scale) how the respondent thought the community would rate the performance of the schools. Respondents were intentionally asked to evaluate community sentiment rather than their own feelings. This question measured perceived performance, not actual performance.

The second variable measured how many different kinds of reforms (zero to five) were proposed during 1992 to 1995. Respondents were asked about these five reforms: modifications in the school day and school calendar, curricular reform, evaluation reform, teacher development reform, and site-based management. For each kind of reform, respondents were asked whether a reform proposal was made. Therefore, each respondent provided five "yes-no" responses. To produce a district composite, the percentage of answering respondents in each district who reported a proposal being made was used as the measure of reform activity.[25] This approach effectively created a continuum for each of the five types of reform. The five scores were then aggregated into a districtwide composite.[26]

Two other variables assessed the attitudinal agenda of school reform. One measured how much attention respondents said each of the five kinds of reform attracted. (Attention was measured on a zero-to-ten thermometer for each reform proposal and then summed, so the combined reported attention in each district ranged from zero to fifty.) The second variable mea-

25. Respondents who answered "don't know" when asked whether a proposal was made were excluded.

26. A district where every respondent said that every reform proposal had been made would score a 5 on the composite reform activity measure; a district where every respondent reported that no proposal had been made in each area would score a composite 0.

sured how much controversy attended reform in each district. It was measured in the same way as attention.[27]

The Effects of Context

All analyses in this chapter use the same seven-variable model. For discussion purposes the results of the full model are presented together for each of the explanatory variables. (See appendix D for the full results for each regression.)

To simplify interpretation and ensure compatibility across districts of different sizes, the effects of all seven explanatory variables are discussed in terms of percentage point changes in the variable. Rather than talking about the effect of an absolute change in a variable (for example, a $100 per pupil spending increase or 7,000 more students enrolled), effects are discussed in terms of a 10 percentage point change in each variable.[28] It is important to recognize that the impact of a 10 percentage point change is not constant across different variables. For instance, poverty rates in the sample districts ranged from 3 percent to 32 percent, while the percentages created from the raw figures for per pupil spending and student enrollment produced ranges from 0 percent to 100 percent (see table 6-2). Consequently, a 10 percentage point change in poverty rate is much more significant than a 10 percentage point change in total enrollment.[29] Ranges for the explanatory variables are presented in table 6-2.

The dependent variables were measured using constructed scales. Since these scales do not measure concrete quantities, they have no concrete meaning. Different scales were used, which makes compatibility among the variables difficult. To simplify the analysis and to make it easier to

27. The proposing of reforms and the attention and controversy generated by reform proposals are linked, but distinct, events. Unlike the broader political agenda, where public attention or focusing events often bring reform proposals to the forefront, agenda formation in school reform is dominated by proposals initiated by system policymakers. On political agenda setting see Baumgartner and Jones (1993) and Kingdon (1984). Respondents described almost all reform proposals as initiated by policymakers, while almost no activity was attributed to external pressure. The community is primarily reacting to initiatives put forward by policymakers.

28. A 10 percentage point change, rather than a 10 percent change, is used because a percentage point is a constant number. For instance, a 10 percent increase from 30 percent is 3 percent, and a 10 percent increase from 70 percent is 7 percent; a 10 percentage point change has a constant size.

29. To simplify comparison across the seven variables, the effects of student enrollment and per pupil spending are discussed in terms of a 20 percentage point increase.

Table 6-2. Descriptive Statistics for the Explanatory Variables
Percent unless otherwise specified

Variable	Mean	Standard deviation	Number of observations	Sample minimum	Sample maximum	Range in percentage points
Percent of adults over age 19 in the district who had completed high school	74	9	57	45	96	51
Poverty rate	16	7	57	3	32	29
Public school enrollment	82	6	57	69	93	24
Number of students enrolled	45,661	46,248	56	5,360	189,450	100
Retail growth, 1987–92	13	15	52	–14	62	86
Per pupil spending	$4,833	$1,314	56	$2,780	$8,570	100
Black population percentage	22	21	57	1	85	84

Source: Author's data.

compare effects across variables, all effects are presented as a percentage change in the dependent variable.

State efforts at reform are not an explanatory variable in this chapter. Omitted variable bias would result from this omission only if state reform activity correlated with the district-level variables used to explain reform.[30] Since neither the data nor previous research suggest that state reform efforts correlate with the characteristics of urban districts in the state, there is no omitted variable bias—even though state reform activity affects district reform.

Educated Communities: Playing to a Full House

More educated communities have higher expectations of their schools, but also have a more positive view of them (see table 6-3). The level of high school completion among the local adult population in the sample ranged from a high of 96 percent of adults age nineteen and over in Palo Alto, California, to a low of 45 percent in Santa Ana, California.

Increased satisfaction normally reduces the demand for change because a satisfactory status quo makes any change more likely to be for the worse. Nonetheless, a 10 percentage point increase in district education increased the number of areas in which reforms were proposed by 5.2 percent ($p < 0.05$). More educated districts exhibited more satisfaction with their school systems, but they still produce heightened levels of reform activity.

Educated communities produced this higher rate of reform because school administrators were scrutinized more carefully. More educated districts paid more attention to proposals for reform. A ten percentage point increase in community education boosted the amount of attention paid to the five reform areas by 2.8 percent ($p < 0.05$). A respondent in California's Berkeley Unified District, where the 92 percent rate of adult high school completion was second highest in the sample, said, "There's too much participation, if anything. We have an activist population. There's enormous interest at the board level, in terms of serving on district-wide committees, school committees, raising money for schools. . . . You can't make a move without raising public concern." A different Berkeley Unified respondent said, "The community is always watching and com-

---

30. King, Keohane, and Verba (1994, 169) note: "We can safely omit control variables, even if they have a strong influence on the dependent variable, as long as they do not vary with the included explanatory variable."

Table 6-3. Effect of Dependent Variables on School Reform

Dependent variable	Units	Effect of a 10 percentage point increase in high school completion among adults over 19	Standard error	Percentage change caused by a 10 percentage point increase in high school completion among adults over 19
Adult education level				
Perceived school district performance	0 to 10	0.52[a]	(0.20)	+5.2
Total number of proposals	0 to 5	0.26[a]	(0.12)	+5.2
Total amount of issue attention	0 to 50	1.42[a]	(0.63)	+2.8
Total amount of issue controversy	0 to 50	0.99	(0.88)	+2.0
Poverty rate				
Perceived school district performance	0 to 10	−0.82[a]	(0.32)	−8.2%
Total number of proposals	0 to 5	0.38[a]	(0.18)	+7.6%
Total amount of issue attention	0 to 50	−0.88	(0.99)	−1.8%
Total amount of issue controversy	0 to 50	1.94	(1.40)	+3.9%
District size				
Perceived school district performance	0 to 10	−0.03	(0.04)	−0.6%
Total number of proposals	0 to 5	0.12[b]	(0.02)	+4.4%
Total amount of issue attention	0 to 50	0.45[b]	(0.12)	+1.7%
Total amount of issue controversy	0 to 50	0.43[a]	(0.17)	+1.6%
Public enrollment percentage				
Perceived school district performance	0 to 10	0.84[a]	(0.32)	+8.4%
Total number of proposals	0 to 5	0.32[c]	(0.18)	+6.4%
Total amount of issue attention	0 to 50	2.88[b]	(0.98)	+5.8%
Total amount of issue controversy	0 to 50	3.16[a]	(1.38)	+6.3%

Table 6-3. continued

Dependent variable	Units	Effect of a 10 percentage point increase in high school completion among adults over 19	Standard error	Percentage change caused by a 10 percentage point increase in high school completion among adults over 19
Retail growth				
Perceived school district performance	0 to 10	0.60	(1.03)	+ 6.0%
Total number of proposals	0 to 5	0.73	(0.59)	+14.6%
Total amount of issue attention	0 to 50	1.16[b]	(0.32)	+ 2.3%
Total amount of issue controversy	0 to 50	1.30[b]	(0.45)	+ 2.6%
Per pupil spending				
Perceived school district performance	0 to 10	0.04	(0.13)	+0.2%
Total number of proposals	0 to 5	0.14[c]	(0.08)	+1.6%
Total amount of issue attention	0 to 50	0.21	(0.41)	+0.2%
Total amount of issue controversy	0 to 50	0.47	(0.57)	+0.5%
Black population percentage				
Perceived school district performance	0 to 10	0.27	(0.99)	+2.7%
Total number of proposals	0 to 5	−0.14[a]	(0.06)	−2.8%
Total amount of issue attention	0 to 50	0.49	(0.31)	+1.0%
Total amount of issue controversy	0 to 50	−0.64	(0.43)	−1.3%

Source: Author's data. $N = 51$.
a. Less than 5 percent.
b. Less than 1 percent.
c. Less than 10 percent.

menting, so it's very difficult to accomplish any change in Berkeley without a lot of process. That's how we do business. If we don't, they sue us."

Conversely, less educated communities exert less pressure. A respondent said of his community's lack of involvement in school affairs: "The interest has been sporadic and in pockets. Malden [Massachusetts] has historically been a white collar community, and there's been a shift in makeup to blue-collar and immigrants. Now a lot of people defer to the so-called experts and don't question what's going on."

Poor Communities: Problems of Underclass Culture

Districts with high poverty rates seek to produce satisfactory educational output in an environment that makes effective education very difficult. Policymakers in these districts are under particular pressure to do something constructive because of widespread dissatisfaction with the schools. Table 6-3 shows that a 10 percentage point increase in the poverty rate reduced the perceived performance of a district's schools by a very strong -8.2 percent ($p < 0.05$).[31] The lowest poverty rate in the sample was for Warren, Michigan, which had a 3 percent poverty rate in 1989. The highest rate, 32 percent, was reported for San Antonio.

Seen as performing poorly, impoverished districts pursue much more reform activity. An administrator in a district with a poverty rate of over 20 percent explained the pressures on his district, and how administrators respond:

> State initiated proficiency testing ... has ... thrown you into the limelight with little box scores in the newspaper which compare you to other districts. . . . You do what you have to do to make it look better, whether you want to or not. In an urban district, where you have some problems out of your control, it would be tough to do well [in the box scores] even if we did a perfect job. We have kids who don't even show up to take the test, and those kinds of problems make it real tough to compare [urban kids] to their suburban counterparts. So you do what you have to do to get those scores up, and it's driven a lot things.

31. Of the seventeen districts that had poverty rates over 20 percent, the mean reported performance score for the school district was a 4.9. Among the thirteen districts with poverty rates under 10 percent, the mean was a 6.9.

Policymakers do two things to assuage public concern in high-poverty districts. They try to provide proof of performance, "to get those scores up," as the respondent said. But, as the respondent indicated, getting scores up "would be tough to do . . . even if we did a perfect job." So policymakers "do what they have to do to make it look better" by promoting reform. Administrators in impoverished areas engaged in significantly more reform than did those in other districts. A 10 percentage point increase in the poverty rate produced a 7.6 percent increase in the number of reform types that were proposed (p < .05). Administrators use promising reforms to compensate for the trouble they have producing tangible improvement in an obstacle-strewn environment.

Large Districts: Trying to Tackle the Octopus

Districts that enroll many students are less manageable than smaller districts. The sheer numbers of students and schools make it more difficult for leaders to control the system or to demonstrate to community members that they are improving teaching and learning. The largest district in the study was Philadelphia with 189,450 students, and the smallest was Euclid, Ohio, with 5,360. A 10 percentage point increase in students was equal to about 18,409 students.

Compared with small districts, large districts pursue more reform and generate more attention and controversy. A 20 percentage point increase in the number of students enrolled in a district produced an 8.8 percent increase in proposed reforms (p < 0.01), a 3.4 percent (p < 0.01) increase in attention to the reform agenda, and a 3.2 percent (p < 0.05) increase in controversy over reform.[32]

32. Because the largest district in the sample had 189,451 students, and the smallest district had 5,357, a 20 percentage point increase is equal to just under 37,000 students. A 20 percentage point change is used here and for the spending variable because the real effect of enrollment and per pupil spending is understated by a 10 percentage point change. Converting the effects of enrollment and spending from raw numbers into percentages for the purposes of presentation means that there are districts ranging from the zero to the 100th percentile. The other five explanatory variables were measured as percentages and therefore span only a fraction of that distance. For instance, poverty stretches only from 3 percent to 32 percent. This means that the percentage difference between the district with the lowest (3 percent) and the highest (32 percent) poverty rate is 29 percent, or only about one-third as much as the measured difference between the districts with the smallest (0 percent) and the largest (100 percent) enrollments. In order to compare the effect of similarly significant increases, it is useful to present those variables converted from raw numbers in terms of a 20 percentage point increase.

One respondent in Duval County, Florida, with more than 106,000 students, described local frustration with attempting significant change in such a large system:

> There is a general sense of frustration about really getting anything done in education that makes a difference. Over the years, people have become so frustrated and debilitated in trying to make a difference in the public school system that people say, "Why should we try? It's a big octopus and I'm not interested in wrestling with that animal."

Unable to "really get anything done," or to trust the community's ability to accurately assess their performance, school policymakers turn to extensive reform efforts.

Public School Enrollment: Attracting Local Scrutiny

In districts where a large percentage of students is enrolled in the public schools, the salience of educational issues is high. The district with the smallest percentage of children in public schools was Philadelphia, which enrolled just 68 percent of all district students. The district with the greatest percentage of students in public schools was Santa Ana, California, which enrolled 93 percent of local students.

Public school enrollment rates are, at best, a vague approximation of school quality. Public enrollment is primarily a function of the opportunities to utilize affordable private schooling, which is largely determined by local culture. One respondent in Albany, New York, explained that local private school enrollment is not a function of public school performance but of tradition. However, he said, "I don't think that's untypical. Albany has a long tradition of private and parochial education. . . . That's a tradition that's a couple hundred years old in this area. Albany is home of one of the oldest girls' schools in the country. The Catholic church is very strong here."

Perceived school performance increased by a strong 8.4 percent for each 10 percentage point increase in the public enrollment percentage (see table 6-3). While this suggests that public enrollment tracks perceived school quality to some degree, it also reflects the finding that parents are consistently more positive toward schools that their children attend.[33] One admin-

33. Sorting out these effects, which will help address the important question of how responsive education consumers are to perceived school quality, requires further research. Education re-

istrator summarized this point: "It's very difficult to motivate support in the general citizenry, but we get very good support from our parents." A respondent in the Pasadena Unified District blamed weak public school support on high enrollment in private schools, rather than blaming low enrollment on the weak support: "I would say the interest [in our schools] is low, relative to other communities in the area. It's because in the city of Pasadena . . . a very high percentage of kids go to private school. So citizens do not support the public schools very well."

An increased rate of public enrollment produced more reform proposals, attention, and controversy. This is similar to the effects of well educated, impoverished, or large school communities. The effects of public enrollment percentage were very strong. A 10 percentage point increase in the public school enrollment percentage increased the number of reform areas proposed by 6.4 percent ($p < 0.10$). Attention and controversy rose as the number of proposals increased, which was different from the pattern for poverty or district size, where district activity went largely unnoticed. In districts with high rates of public enrollment, as in more educated districts, the lack of economic or size-related distractions meant that the attention paid to reform tracked the rate of reform activity much more closely. A 10 percentage point increase in public enrollment elevated the attitudinal agenda, raising attention to reform by 5.8 percent ($p < 0.01$) and controversy by 6.3 percent ($p < 0.05$). A respondent in Albany, New York, which had the third highest rate of private enrollment, said, "Many of the most interested and committed parents were devoting their energies much more to private or parochial schools than to the public schools."

Retail Growth: A Higher Profile

The attention paid to education reform fluctuates with the severity of competing political concerns, such as crime, and crumbling infrastructure, municipal services, and particularly economic conditions. Cities varied a great deal in rates of growth, with the retail trade growth rate during 1987 to 1992 ranging from a decline of −14 percent in Malden, Massachusetts, to an increase of 62 percent in Pinellas County, Florida.

Districts with vibrant local economies pay more attention to education reform, and experience more controversy over it, but they do not appear to

searchers are still unsure about the extent to which a lack of information (Bridge 1978) and limited market power (Wells 1993) mute the market response to school quality.

propose more reform activity (see table 6-3). It is easier for districts with healthy economies to pay attention to education, since the competing problems are less severe. A 10 percentage point increase in retail growth produced a 2.3 percent increase ($p < 0.01$) in attention to reform and a 2.6 percent ($p < 0.01$) increase in controversy. The attitudinal agenda is largely a product of how much competition exists for space on the local agenda. Faster growing districts pay more attention to school reform, while more reform is actually proposed in the troubled districts.

Per Pupil Spending: Giving Policymakers More Slack

The most accurate measure of the resources available to a school system is the amount of money it spends per pupil. Systems with more resources per student are able to engage in more activity, even though the demands for action are unchanged. Additional revenue, from any source, becomes a spur to reform efforts, since policymakers face many incentives to embark upon reform efforts and almost no incentives to curtail them. The lowest rate of spending reported in the sample was $2,780 per pupil by Salt Lake City, Utah, and the highest figure was the $8,570 spent on each pupil by Cambridge, Massachusetts.[34] A 10 percentage point change in per pupil spending was equal to about $579.

Because spending enhances the resources at the disposal of the system leadership, it increases their ability to attempt reforms—and does so without increasing either attention or controversy (see table 6-3). Normally, attention and controversy correlate strongly with the rate at which measures are proposed. However, consistent with the hypothesis that funding is a "supply-side" measure that increases reform activity without attracting community notice, attention and controversy remained flat while reform activity increased.[35] A 20 percentage point higher rate of per pupil spending (about $1,160) produced a 3.2 percent increase in the number of areas in which reforms were proposed ($p < 0.10$). Districts with more money pro-

34. Like the figures for student enrollment, the figures for spending were raw numbers rather than percentages. To compare the effects of spending with the effects of other variables, the distance between Salt Lake City and Cambridge had to be converted into a percentile. A 10 percentage point change in spending understates the actual spending, relative to a similar change in other variables. Although the distance from Salt Lake City to Cambridge is 100 percentage points, the range for most other variables is between 25 and 70 percentage points. To compensate, results for spending are presented using a 20 percentage point change.

35. This is analogous to the way that enhancing the supply of an economic good will make a greater amount of that good available, and at lower price than it was originally available.

duced more reform without significantly increasing the amount of attention or controversy generated by school reform.[36] Extra resources permit administrators in high-spending districts to initiate additional reforms, and they naturally do so.

Black Population: The Equity Trap

A larger percentage of black residents increases the risk that any proposed reform will ignite community conflict. A history of segregation, unequal opportunity, and poor achievement means that black constituents demand evidence of educational improvement, while remaining highly sensitive to issues of equity. Their concern for equity, however, dominates.[37] Sample districts varied widely in the percentage of their population that was black—from Warren, Michigan, with 1 percent black, to Gary, Indiana, with 85 percent.

Districts with a larger percentage of black residents proposed less reform, implying that administrators grow "gun shy" as the black population increases. As table 6-3 shows, a 10 percentage point increase in black population reduced the number of areas in which reforms were proposed by −2.8 percent ($p < 0.05$). This is a modest change, but it is especially interesting because so many Third Wave reforms paid particular attention to meeting the needs and improving the education of minority students (through measures such as multicultural education and portfolio assessment).

As expected, districts with large black populations do not propose as many reforms as do other districts because of the increased risk that any reform will provoke conflict. A teachers' union respondent complained that the district changed the test it used "and, every time you do that, the scores

36. In fact, simple levels of attention and controversy are lower in those districts that spend more per pupil. Higher spending districts propose more reform, but there is no evidence that the broader public notices. The mean levels of attention and of controversy were roughly 8 percent lower in the twenty-nine districts that spent more than $4,500 per pupil than in the twenty-seven that spent less than $4,500.

37. The black community may doubt the willingness of school policymakers, even sympathetic ones, to address inequities. One respondent described the local NAACP's mistrust of the school board because of its past actions: "Most of the acts by the school board that convinced the NAACP that the board was not acting in good faith took place in 1990 to 1993 or 1994, before the new [school board] majority was in place. I think the people in the majority now really understand the position of the NAACP and are willing to work with the NAACP. But at this time, the NAACP is so frustrated that I don't think they're sure that they want to work with the board anymore."

drop. And they dropped by more in the African American than in the white community. . . . [W]e're now gun-shy when a measure might have racial overtones." Seven years after the reform effort, the district was still "gun-shy." A respondent from a race organization said that desegregation concerns had nearly paralyzed education reform in his 47 percent black district:

> Desegregation is the lion's share of . . . school policy, because we wind up reacting to the judge's order and to busing. It's a real distraction. At this particular point, the issues of student achievement and a new superintendent, and building new schools are tied up in the court. . . . When we sit down and talk about what we mean by quality education, the issue always gets drawn to desegregation. It's a major issue that complicates the effort to talk about educational issues . . . and that has affected the district's ability to pursue other kinds of educational policy.

An Urban League respondent explained how the racial calculus can make school reform into a political minefield:

> Sometimes racial lines are drawn. The school system had become overwhelmingly black and it was operated by blacks who control the school system, and the white people in the community were afraid to tee off on the system for fear they would roil the waters. The attitude of the black community was that, "You guys took all your kids out of the schools, so shut up." . . . For many in the black community, the school system represented a piece of the pie, so to speak, a piece of the power.

Black population percentage had only small effects on the local attitudinal agenda. Administrators in districts with large black populations are working to calm the roiling waters of racial suspicion by moving slowly and carefully vetting proposed reforms, but they are nonetheless negotiating a very difficult and sensitive situation. Table 6-3 shows the outcome of this balancing act. A 10 percentage point increase in black population increased attention to education reform by a slight amount, 1.0 percent ($p < 0.15$), while reducing controversy by -1.3 percent ($p < 0.15$). Although neither large nor certain, these effects are suggestive. Rather than the reduced rate of local activity producing a decrease in attention to reform, as

Table 6-4. Contextual Effects and Reform Activity

District	Total number of proposals[a]	Total attention[b]	Total controversy[b]
Mean district	3.35	29.3	22.6
District with a 10 percentage point increase in total enrollment, the percentage of students in public schools, and the percentage of adults in the district with high school diplomas	4.15	34.5	26.6
Projected increase	23	18	18

Source: Author's data.
a. 0 to 5 units.
b. 0 to 50 units.

is the norm, a large black population actually produced a slight bump in attention. Districts with a large black population pay more attention to reform, even as fewer reforms are proposed. They also find reform less controversial, despite the fact that attention to reform is increasing and that controversy and attention are very strongly correlated ($R = 0.63$).

It appears that policymakers in districts with large black populations are behaving differently from those in less potentially divisive districts. They propose fewer measures, while appearing to be more careful about assessing the community's feelings before proposing a measure (hence the greater attention). These districts also are more likely to put forward relatively uncontroversial measures.[38]

Conclusion

Contextual effects have a significant impact on the rate of reform. Table 6-4 demonstrates these effects by comparing the prominence of the reform agenda in the mean district and in a slightly larger and more educated community where more students use the public schools. Increasing total enrollment, the percentage of students in public schools, and the percentage of adults with high school diplomas each by 10 percentage points produced a dramatic 23 percent increase in reform activity in the hypothetical district.

38. This evidence suggests that policymakers will be more circumspect about pushing reform, not necessarily that they engage in formal negotiations with minority populations. For instance, Cuban (1976, 106) observed that big-city school chiefs did not pursue "active negotiations with civil rights leaders" during the desegregation conflicts of the 1960s.

The most surprising thing about the causal effect of context is how much it matters. Given the tenuous links between voters and school districts and the nonpartisan design of school systems, school reform is often discussed as though it is relatively insulated from local pressures.[39] Especially with so much reform activity attributed to the states, traditional views of school reform suggest that little systematic variation among a set of urban districts is to be expected.

Context matters because school policymakers are reliant upon community resources and support. The indirect ties linking the community and the school system are significant. Economic, educational, and racial factors have large and significant effects on many elements of the school system and consequently affect the incentives that encourage policymakers to manipulate school reform as a political tool. The working environment of policymakers is shaped in large part by the community's interest in school affairs. Increased interest is a boon because it produces more public support, but that support comes at the cost of heightened expectations. Factors that increase scrutiny in a district, and those that make it more difficult for the schools to demonstrate performance, produce more reform proposals and more attention to reform.

39. See Zeigler and Jennings (1974); Meier and Stewart (1991); and Tyack (1974) for discussions of apathy and the nonpartisan design of urban school systems.

7

The Effectiveness of
Urban School Reform

A S WAS NOTED in chapter 1, education scholars agree that most educational reforms have failed to improve school performance. Of the "dizzying array of educational reforms" introduced since the 1960s, "few are still with us, at least in their original form."[1] Frustrated advocates of reform have responded by promoting increasingly large and expensive reform efforts. Yet, after decades of effort, the problem of "'scaling up'—of translating the successful practices of a few exemplary models into the widespread adoption of those practices—has never been solved."[2] School systems have consistently demonstrated an inability to make systemic reform work:

> A significant body of circumstantial evidence points to a deep, systemic incapacity of U.S. schools, and the practitioners who work in them, to develop, incorporate, and extend new ideas about teaching and learning in anything but a small fraction of schools and classrooms. . . . Innovations that require large changes in the core of educational practice seldom penetrate more than a fraction of schools, and seldom last for very long when they do.[3]

Despite the dismal record of school reform, a whirlwind of reform activity characterized the sample districts in the 1992–95 period. In fact, the frenetic pace of activity is an important reason why reforms do not deliver the promised results on a large scale. The evidence presented in this chapter

---

1. Brouillette (1996, xi).
2. Miller (1996, 1).
3. Elmore (1996, 1–2).

strongly suggests that policy churn in school districts has significantly impeded the implementation and success of reforms.

Why do observers continue to tolerate and encourage reforms despite little evidence that they work? A large part of the reason may be the difficulty in actually determining the effectiveness of reforms, and the belief of policymakers that reforms are more successful than they actually are. The counterproductive rate of policy churn and turnover of superintendents is perpetuated by a lack of objective performance criteria and by an exaggerated sense of progress among administrators and other insiders.

When one reform fails, reformers pursue another. They assume that something eventually will work. The result is increasingly ambitious attempts at organizational change promoted with insufficient regard to organizational culture or to implementation. David Tyack and William Tobin have observed this myopia: "Reformers believe that their innovations will change schools, but it is important to recognize that schools change reforms."[4]

The key to improving teaching and learning through new initiatives is thorough implementation and the cultivation of expertise.[5] These are difficult tasks in the best of circumstances, and urban school districts do not present the best of circumstances.[6] The short-term emphasis of urban district management, aggravated by rapid leadership turnover and overburdened reform agendas, make the thorny problems of implementation and fostering long-term organizational development nearly insoluble.

Massive difficulties block efforts to put policy into practice.[7] Scholars of school reform have explained the checkered history of reform by pointing to conflicts between higher governments and school systems, the lack of local commitment to reforms initiated outside the district, the lack of attention to the need for "mutual adaptation" among actors, and a lack of input from educators.[8] Inattention to implementation and a failure to provide the resources necessary to make new programs productive have prevented reforms from delivering the promised returns.

Implementing change is an onerous and time-consuming task, one for which district leadership is ill equipped.[9] Superintendents entering a

4. Tyack and Tobin (1994, 458).

5. Carter and Cunningham (1997); Elmore, Peterson, and McCarthy (1996); Fullan (1991); Murphy (1991); Odden (1991a).

6. OECD (1996, 149).

7. For instance, see work by Nakamura (1991), Pressman and Wildavsky (1984), and Sabatier and Mazmanian (1981).

8. Odden (1991a) and Tyack and Cuban (1995).

9. Hersey and Blanchard (1977).

district are expected to rapidly demonstrate that problems are being effectively tackled, even though "the odds are stacked against new superintendents from the start. Teachers are suspicious of formal authority, wary of being abandoned and . . . prefer investing in what they know rather than submitting to the dubious judgment of the latest administrative expert."[10] The lack of information on costs and benefits aggravates the tendency to focus on the promise of improvement, rather than on the outcomes of reform.

The Study of Policy Implementation and Effectiveness

Implementation is judged "by observing the difference between intended and actual consequences."[11] Determining the intended consequences and the actual effects of a particular education reform is immensely difficult. Therefore, most studies look intensively at only a handful of schools or school districts.

In this study a very different approach was used in order to assess the validity of the relatively obvious, but generally unheeded, proposition that districts that do more will not do it as well. Much more complex models of implementation are useful and appropriate, but the testing of more refined hypotheses must await the collection of more finely grained data on district-level reform. Respondents' evaluations of implementation and reform success were used to compare reform performance across districts. This approach is obviously imperfect. Clear and precise measures of implementation or program success are hard to come by, particularly for multiple locales. Respondents were asked to use imperfect information to summarize a complex phenomena in a simple manner. Nonetheless, because it reveals the nature of multiple reform efforts in a large number of districts with some uniformity, this approach is a valid complement to the more precise studies that have been done on small numbers of districts.[12]

Several elements made this methodology particularly useful. First, respondents were selected for their relationship to local education, and the mean respondent reported following local education for nearly twenty years. The respondents had a wealth of knowledge about their local school systems. Second, respondents were not asked for their opinions, but to

10. Johnson (1996, 149).
11. Pressman and Wildavsky (1984, xv).
12. For more complex models of implementation, see Sabatier and Mazmanian (1981).

evaluate a particular, observable phenomenon: the implementation and success of specified reforms. Third, any biases ought to have been equally distributed across school districts, since the same types of respondents were used across the sample districts. Finally, because the evaluations are not being used to assess the absolute performance of any reform—but only the relative performance of the five reforms—it is not a problem if respondents systematically rate reform too high or too low. Though flawed, the respondent evaluations are useful and relevant.

Resources, Time, and Commitment

More than anything else, effective school reform requires that the school system focus on making the desired changes work. This requires resources, time, and commitment. Particularly important are the support of the school community, especially the principal, and the availability of necessary resources.[13] Few of these resources are available in districts that churn out reforms one after the other year after year.

Reviewing the literature on effective schools, Stewart Purkey and Marshall Smith noted that schools require "additional time, money, and information if their staffs are to break old habits."[14] So long as faculty believe that changes are only a short-term intrusion on the pattern of school life, there is little incentive to take reforms seriously and to invest summers in designing new curricula or Saturday mornings in workshops on new instructional tools. On the other hand, if districts make resources and expertise available to those faculty involved in an initiative, and successfully convince faculty and administrators that the measure will be in place for the long haul, then reforms are much more likely to impact teaching and learning. The key to determining the effectiveness of any given reform—no matter how refined—is the training and the commitment of classroom personnel.[15]

Resources

Making reform work requires an infusion of resources for training and support. Reformers have paid, "little, if any, attention . . . to the financial . . . requirements for putting recommendations into practice."[16] Insufficient

13. Johnson and Pajares (1996).
14. Purkey and Smith (1985, 384).
15. Mirel (1994) and Pauly (1991).
16. Ginsberg and Wimpelberg (1987, 358).

attention to the dollar costs and opportunity costs of reform have shortchanged the implementation of reform. As Joseph Murphy has scathingly noted, "If information on the costs of initiatives is limited and somewhat misleading, data to compare the cost-benefits of different reform measures are conspicuous by their absence."[17] Lacking data on the real costs of reform, reformers can dramatically underestimate the price tags of their proposals. Adequate resources are simply not available when it comes time to carry new initiatives into thousands of individual classrooms. For instance, the cost of delivering the Texas Teacher Test was ten times higher than anticipated. The program cost $35.6 million—rather than the $3.0 million price tag included in the official state reports.[18] Successive attempts at reform have each imposed the start-up costs of program design without producing the long-term benefits of successful reform.

By underestimating the financial resources necessary to make change work, districts wind up providing staff training and support that is "woefully inadequate" or totally absent.[19] Previous research has found that staff development is critical to successfully implement restructuring, yet the mundane matters of resource allocation and training are consistently shortchanged.[20]

Time

Effective reform requires districts to make a long-term commitment to a specific program of change, and to provide teachers an opportunity to use that time. Discussing the effective implementation of SBM in one school, participants said the most valuable resource was "time for face-to-face talk."[21] An extended time horizon is necessary to provide opportunities for organizational learning and coordination, and because faculty and staff are much more likely to make a real commitment to reform if they believe that their efforts will have lasting impact. For instance, those districts that have successfully empowered professionals and decentralized operations have usually taken at least five years to do so.[22]

17. Murphy (1991, 80).
18. Shepard and Kreitzer (1987).
19. Murphy (1991, 91).
20. David (1989); Elmore, Peterson, and McCarthy (1996); and Murphy (1991).
21. Johnson and Pajares (1996, 616).
22. David (1989) and Murphy (1991). Clarke and Agne (1997, 342) report, "Ask any teacher what makes change so hard to consider. The answer is invariable: 'We don't have the time.' The embedded systems—grading systems, report cards, graduation requirements, departmental organi-

Because of conflicting social goals and poor accountability measures, attempts to change public sector organizations generally require an especially long period of time. Uncertainty about how to improve teaching and learning aggravates these problems in urban school systems. The pressure on superintendents to produce quick and noticeable results disregards the fact that long-term efforts are required to effectively change complex public organizations. As Tony Wagner has observed:

> Even with greater consensus, collaboration, and outside help, change is neither quick nor easy. . . . [T]he scarcest resource in the change process is time, even more than money. Time for teachers to meet to discuss students' needs, observe each other's classes, assess their work, design new curricula, visit other schools, and attend workshops. . . . Time—perhaps five years—to rethink the purposes of education, reinvent teaching and learning, and create new school cultures.[23]

Commitment

Time is necessary for successful reform, but time alone is insufficient without consistent and clear leadership. Long-term commitment, focused energies, and stable leadership play a vital role in school restructuring. Although the length of time a reform has been in place matters, stable leadership and attention to follow-through are at least as important:

> While consistency and cumulative learning require time . . . schools can, and frequently do, wander aimlessly from one innovation to another over long periods of time, gaining little in the way of cumulative understanding and little common learning among teachers. . . . It is more important to know what schools do over time to reinforce new forms of practice than it is to know . . . how long they have been engaged in change.[24]

Margaret Johnson and Frank Pajares, discussing the effective implementation of site-based management in one school, note the importance of

---

zations, and teacher contracts, for example—that frustrate change are trivial in contrast to the limits of time."

23. Wagner (1994, 269).

24. Elmore, Peterson, and McCarthy (1996, 218).

sustained and energetic leadership from the principal. In particular, the principal consistently attempted to expand training opportunities in the second and third years of the project, rather than move on to new concerns.[25]

Previous Research on Reform and Performance

It is possible that resources, time, and commitment could be present in a coordinated, multifaceted effort at school improvement. Districts that launch mutually reinforcing measures may enjoy exceptional performance. This study has little to say about that argument, because there is little evidence that urban districts are operating in that manner. Education research tends to focus on those schools that are islands of exceptional effectiveness in a sea of chaos. This study is different because it focuses on the environment in which schools operate.

Previous research on how the amount of reform affects school performance has studied outcomes at the school level—a very different task than studying initiatives at the district level. The incentives for individual schools to engage in symbolic behavior are far weaker. Some schools always succeed in any context, and these schools are characterized by qualities of leadership, culture, and teacher commitment that reforms seek to replicate in other schools.[26] These high-performing schools are likely to be characterized by some reform activity, but are they successful because of the reforms? Achieving focus, by whatever means, is a key to effective school performance, and it is not clear that reform efforts cause schools to achieve focus. In fact, a moderate level of reform and restructuring may be a consequence of effective school leadership.

Schools and urban districts operate in very different institutional contexts, but a few findings from school-level research are relevant here. Recent studies of school-level reform have suggested that some reform may be healthy but that too much reform may negatively affect school outcomes.[27] Neither study focused on urban schools, which labor under conditions that greatly handicap the performance of reform.

Valerie Lee and Julia Smith analyzed data on student performance and school behavior from 820 secondary schools. They argued that schools em-

25. Johnson and Pajares (1996).
26. Bryk, Lee, and Holland (1993) and Elmore (1996).
27. Kyle (1993) and Lee and Smith (1994).

ploying a coherent and focused reform strategy enjoyed the best results. Schools that attempted more than three reforms enjoyed inferior results to schools that attempted three. It appears that embracing "too many reforms—perhaps to give the appearance of climbing on the 'reform bandwagon'—is counterproductive." Schools that attempted two or fewer reforms also fared poorly, suggesting that the passivity characteristic of some inert schools has negative effects. Lee and Smith conclude: "It seems clear that schools with a commitment to restructuring as we have defined it should decide on a modest number of reform strategies, should work hard to see that these reforms are engaged profoundly in the school, should continue their commitment to those particular reforms over a sustained period, and should not attempt too many reforms simultaneously."[28]

Regina Kyle studied the experience with reform of a school district in Kentucky. Kyle found that schools in the early stages of reform, particularly those schools that tried a wide range of reforms, had worse student outcomes than schools that engaged in no reform and much worse outcomes than those with sustained commitment to a few reforms. Anthony Bryk and his colleagues found similar results in examining Chicago elementary schools after the Chicago school restructuring. They noted that "'showcase' schools with many new programs, multiple 'add-ons' with little coordination, and little attention to strengthening the organizational core" compared unfavorably to schools with more focus and discipline.[29]

While moderate reform activity may be very helpful, the sample districts in this study did not pursue reform in a moderate or focused fashion. Their high rates of activity were reported to substantively reduce the implementation and value of reform initiatives.

The Effects of Hyperactive Reform Agendas

It is easier to devote resources, time, and commitment to specific reform proposals in districts where only a few changes are pursued and the leadership is stable. Therefore, these districts are expected to implement reforms more thoroughly and enjoy more success with any given reform. Too much activity prevents leaders from selecting appropriate reforms and focusing upon implementing and refining those measures.

28. Lee and Smith (1994, 32, 33).
29. Bryk and others (1993).

Less Reform Yields More Success

The mean district reported 3.35 reform proposals on the zero-to-five composite scale, but the median was slightly higher than that. To examine the effect of high levels of reform activity, I compared the fate of reforms in districts that attempted 3.5 or fewer reform proposals with the fate of reforms in districts attempting more than 3.5 proposals.

Respondents who reported that a proposal had been enacted were asked, "How thoroughly has this reform been implemented at the school level?" Respondents answered on a zero-to-ten scale, where zero indicated the policy was "not at all implemented" and a ten meant it was "completely in place." The reported success of policies was compared, using composite ratings from the question, "Thus far, how successfully has the policy achieved its stated goals?" Respondents answered on a zero—ten scale, where zero indicated "not at all successful" and a ten "very successful." District composites for each type of reform were used in this analysis.

Districts that attempted less reform were reported to have implemented the measures they did attempt more thoroughly. For the fifty-eight reforms reported by a majority of local respondents to have been locally initiated and proposed after the beginning of 1992, districts attempting less reform were rated 25 percent more successful at implementing the reforms they proposed. The advantage enjoyed by low-activity districts was equally pronounced for the reported success of reforms. Low-activity districts were reported to have been more successful with every one of the five types of reform. Overall, reforms were reported to be 25 percent more successful in low-activity districts.

One traditional explanation for the failure of urban school reform has been the insuperable obstacles presented by urban environments. While these problems are central to the dynamic driving the school reform treadmill, they do not explain the relatively inferior performance of high-activity districts. The environmental critique implies that the performance of reform should be primarily a function of urban difficulties, and the evidence does show that wealthier districts fare better with reform. However, low-activity districts outperform high-activity districts, even among urban districts in similar economic situations.

The thirty-seven locally initiated reforms proposed after 1992 in districts with a median household income below the sample mean ($27,806 in 1989) were implemented 36 percent more thoroughly in low-activity than in high-activity districts. The measures were also 24 percent more successful in low-activity low-income districts (n = 35). Similarly, reforms were implemented 3 percent more thoroughly and were 27 percent more successful in low-activity high-income districts (n = 21). Reduced reform activity appears to improve implementation much more strongly in low-income districts than in wealthy ones. Since poorer districts have more extreme problems and fewer resources with which to solve them, it is reasonable that poor districts reap greater benefits from focused efforts. If anything, the political problems of school reform appear to aggravate inequities between the haves and the have-nots.

Perhaps those districts that launch *everything* at once are pursuing a comprehensive strategy and will outperform districts pursuing piecemeal reform. The effects of policy churn can be more clearly illustrated by comparing the outcomes of reform in extremely low-activity districts with high-activity and extremely high-activity districts. There were thirty-two reforms reported by a majority of local respondents to have been locally initiated and proposed after the beginning of 1992 in districts that proposed either 2.5 or fewer reforms or more than 3.5 reforms (see table 7-1). The results in this table should be interpreted cautiously because of the limited sample size.

Reforms in extremely low-activity districts (2.5 or fewer proposals) were 61 percent more successful than reforms in standard high-activity districts (more than 3.5 but fewer than 4.0 proposals). Districts that did much less did it much, much better. Interestingly, the few reforms attempted in extremely high-activity districts (4.0 or more proposals) fared 33 percent better than those in standard high-activity districts. This provides some evidence for the proposition that districts benefit by pursuing comprehensive reforms that tackle everything in an integrated fashion. However, measures in the extreme low-activity districts still fared 21 percent better than those in extremely high-activity districts. The evidence strongly suggests that more active districts implement reform less thoroughly and that their reforms fare relatively poorly.

Leadership Stability Makes Reform More Effective

Districts where superintendents frequently leave office have difficulty sustaining commitment to specific reforms. Leadership turnover disrupts administrative support and increases emphasis on initiating—rather than executing—reform. The need to design and launch new initiatives reduces the resources available to diagnose problems and implement remedies.

Table 7-1. Impact of Activity Level on Reform Performance[a]

Total number of reforms enacted in the district	Average success	Number of observations
4.0 or more	6.5	5
More than 3.5 but fewer than 4.0	4.9	20
2.5 or fewer	7.9	7

Source: Author's data.

a. The reported success of policies was compared by using composite ratings. Respondents who reported that a reform had been enacted were asked, "Thus far, how successfully has the policy achieved its stated goals?" Respondents answered on a zero-to-ten scale, where zero meant the policy had been "not at all successful" and ten meant it had been "very successful." District composites for each type of reform were used.

New superintendents want to try new approaches, but "innovations take time to stabilize themselves."[30] As one respondent said, "The new superintendent that came in 1990 wanted every reform we've talked about to be implemented immediately." The problems caused by churning leadership prompted a concerned former superintendent to write in 1976, "If the record of the past seven years continues, most big-city superintendents will not remain in their positions long enough to accomplish anything."[31]

The longevity of superintendents' tenure had a strongly positive impact on implementation. Districts where the superintendent had been in place five years were compared with those where the superintendent had been in place three years or less. The forty-six relevant reforms were implemented 39 percent more thoroughly in the more stable districts. Results similarly showed that reforms initiated in districts with long-term superintendents were rated as 31 percent more successful than in districts where the superintendent had been in three years or less.

Stable leadership even improved the performance of reforms that had been enacted only within the past three years. If new superintendents bring energy and vigor, a high rate of turnover ought to produce more thorough implementation and more successful reform. There is no evidence of this. Veteran superintendents can devote attention to planning and implementing local initiatives. Short-term superintendents devote less time to implementing reforms and making them successful—whether the reforms are theirs or their predecessors.

The problem with rapid leadership turnover is aggravated by the tendency of unstable districts to replace superintendents with a successor who

30. Carter and Cunningham (1997, 73).
31. Scott (1976, 347).

will bring "fresh ideas," lending reform a stop-and-start quality that makes consistent focus nearly impossible. One respondent in Duluth, Minnesota, described the problem:

> Seven or eight years ago, a long-term superintendent retired. Since that time we've had a warm fuzzy superintendent, then an interim kind of "Let's stick to the basics and watch our finances" superintendent, followed by a corporation that changed its internal leadership three times in less than a year, an external person that had local ties coming from a district that was much like ours, [and] an internal person.

Do superintendents with short tenure have a poor track record simply because they are trying to initiate so many measures, and not because they are any less attentive than veterans to making reform work? Is there evidence that leadership instability and policy churn actually have independent negative effects on the fate of reform? The answer is yes. Even in districts that are highly active in reform, veteran superintendents produced superior implementation and outcomes.

Twenty-three locally initiated reforms were proposed after the beginning of 1992 in high-activity districts. The reforms enacted in districts where superintendents had been in office for four or more years were 40 percent more thoroughly implemented than were those in districts where the superintendent had been in three years or less. Reforms were also considered to be dramatically more successful when the superintendent was in place for four or more years. The reforms enacted in districts with veteran superintendents were rated as 48 percent more successful than those in districts with less stable leadership. Even in districts pursuing a heavy load of reform, stable leadership had a large and positive impact on the implementation and success of reform.

How Observers View Reform

Why have communities and board members continued to tolerate and to endorse rapid leadership turnover and frenetic reform activity, despite its counterproductive results? The answer is quite simple. The greater effectiveness of low-activity and low-turnover districts has not been recognized because it is difficult for observers to accurately assess the results of any educational program—which is one of the factors driving policy churn in the first place. Lacking hard evidence with which to evaluate reform, observers rely on cues that appear to carry an implicit pro-reform bias.

The Bias for Reform

When respondents were questioned about each of the five types of reform specifically, they tended to evaluate any proposal as ambitious and successful. These seemed to assume that any professionally endorsed change could only improve matters. While observers have some faith that their general dissatisfaction with urban schooling and the fate of school reform is justified, they evince no faith in their ability to evaluate the worth of any specific proposal or program. Tugged by hopes that change will make things better and that respected professional reformers know what they are doing, observers seize any reason to positively evaluate the fate of each and every reform initiative.[32]

Reforms are considered to be more successful than they actually are because observers lack hard evidence for making a sound critical assessment. Reforms also enjoy the advantage of being favorably regarded by influential educational policymakers. It is the administrators, board members, and union leaders who frequently have a hand in crafting reforms. Consequently, these actors can be expected to evaluate the results of their handiwork more positively than will outside observers with no personal stake in the school system.[33] Because it is these individuals who disproportionately influence local educational policy, the tendency toward proactivity is encouraged.

The result of observers' limited understanding of school reform is a heavy reliance on professional educators, reformers, and the media to frame the way in which reform is judged. Observers rate highly reforms of questionable effectiveness for three main reasons. First, they have a hard

32. Although it is nearly impossible for an observer to objectively assess just how successful a reform is, that inefficiency does not necessarily bias comparative results. Because the same types of respondents were used in each district, bias should not be a problem when comparing different districts. Particularly when responses are aggregated across a large body of respondents, as in this case, it is likely that the relative ratings are unbiased—since ratings of each reform are subjected to similar upward pressure. Consequently, while the actual rating of reform outcomes ought to be interpreted with caution, as should the ratings for any one district, the relative *ratings* are much more reliable.

33. Stake (1986).

time judging individual reforms apart from their overall view of the district leadership. Second, they judge both district performance and specific reforms on the basis of simple and visible cues, rather than according to any outcome criteria. Third, taking their lead from the professional educators and the reformers, observers select their cues primarily on the basis of perceived leadership input and their sense of community enthusiasm.

Proxy Measures of Success

Lacking empirical evidence that a given reform did or did not work, respondents used five kinds of proxies to evaluate reform, each of which reflected publicity and inputs more than results: strong and visible leadership, the dramatic nature and visibility of proposals, a sense that community support was increasing or that the district's atmosphere had improved, the number of schools in which the program was enacted, and the number of awards earned.

Respondents frequently mentioned visible leadership as self-evident proof that reforms were effective. Strong leadership was deemed a measure of reform success, rather than a means to an end. One journalist discussed reform success primarily in terms of the superintendent's stature and activity: "The superintendent has some national stature. . . . He's pushing a lot of reform. So far as math reform, he's putting a lot of emphasis on math and science. And he's decentralized the school system." A board member painted a rosy view of district reform efforts because of a "strong superintendent and administrative staff that bring innovative or current policy change recommendations to a school board that is supportive." A Pittsburgh respondent praised local restructuring efforts as the most significant success in "fifty years" yet pointed to no outcome effects of the reform initiative. The respondent presumed the large and ambitious reform effort was, by definition, good:

> Our greatest success, I believe has been the restructuring effort led by the superintendent. Three years ago the district went through an entire reorganization when the budget was balanced. Between 500 and 800 parents and community leaders got involved in the process. Now we're through the third wave and the decision is to continue and move on, so that's probably the most significant thing in the last fifty years in Pittsburgh, much less the last two or three.

Second, respondents judged reforms according to the drama and visibility of the proposal. For instance, one respondent discussed successful new tenure standards strictly in terms of program visibility:

We developed, with the teachers' association, tenure standards . . . based on the national professional standards. . . . We're traveling about state talking about it. . . . We spent a ton to mail out parent input documents and the parents love it, they can tell us how they feel and how the students feel. . . . It's a lot more work for the principals, but they say they like it.

One board respondent proudly described the existence of a new school for troubled students, terming the school "very successful" without once mentioning the performance of the school. Establishing the school was a self-evident mark of success: "This is the real success story. We . . . established [a special campus] dealing with students who have been expelled. We bring them back into the system now on a restricted basis, and they and their parents have to sign contracts on what they will do in order to get back into school."

One respondent cited a school restructuring initiative as the district's greatest success based on the ambitiousness of the proposal, even while acknowledging that he could not judge the proposal's impact: "I can't say it's a success yet, because they just started the new system, the move to site-based management, but it's clearly the biggest thing that's happened." Another respondent said, somewhat tautologically, that a reform initiative was successful because it was a dramatic initiative: "[We're] restructuring the entire school system to go to the middle school concept. . . . [T]he fact that we are making such a massive move in a school system that's the area and size of Rhode Island, that's very good."

Third, respondents considered reforms a success if they increased optimism in the community or spurred community support. One Long Beach respondent deemed a school uniform policy to be successful because "there was a definite change of the wind. . . . The uniform policy was basically hearing the community saying, 'We want you to do something.'" One board respondent indicated that the reform process itself was his district's greatest success: "Our 'Educational Summit' has been our most notable success" because it brought "the stakeholders in the community together, close to 3000 people, in a process of diagnosis and prescription for the problems facing us."

Fourth, respondents judged reform success based on how many schools the reform was in or how fast the reform was spreading. A typical response was offered by a board member who boasted of the district's record in curricular reform. "We're a school district that has intentionally expanded gifted and talented education," he said. "For instance, we have gone successfully from one international baccalaureate site to three."

Finally, respondents cited state or national awards, grants won, or other honors as evidence that the district's reforms were working. Even those grants that were intended to prompt reform were interpreted as successful examples of reform in their own right. Unable to assess outcomes or results, respondents assumed that an honor or award was irrefutable proof that a reform was working—even though honors and awards are generally awarded by committees that must evaluate programs from a distance, and must often rely primarily on publicity and stated intentions. One respondent related with pride that the system had the majority of its schools honored by the governor's new program: "The governor introduced a centennial schools program, and thirty of our thirty-six schools have been designated." A board member in another district said the district had been successful in professional development because "we have successfully written and received some grants for teachers in science and technology." A Memphis respondent emphasized the district's ability to win recognition and outside money: "Recently, the city was selected to become an American Schools Development Corporation System. It gets to test some new reform strategies. That's pretty big news to school people. . . . The district also won a fifteen million dollar grant from the [National Science Foundation]."

Observers of local school systems rely upon these kinds of proxies when assessing reform. Therefore, they have trouble judging the performance of any particular initiative. They simply presume that reform produces improvement. Presuming that reform produces improvement—even as they voice displeasure with system performance, with past reforms, and while citing little evidence that reforms are working, observers rate the implementation and success of reform in glowing terms. This helps to explain why a lackluster record has not discredited frenetic reform efforts.[34]

34. There is no evidence that relying upon proxies to measure the success of reforms impeded the ability of respondents to answer other queries in an unbiased manner. The foregoing discussion offers no reason to suspect bias in the responses regarding the behavior of local actors, the rate of reform activity, the visibility and nature of the reform agenda, or the policy process.

Assessment Difficulties

It is immensely difficult for respondents to accurately gauge the success of any given reform initiative, especially in the short term.[35] That is both the allure and the problem with school reform from the district leadership's perspective. It is difficult for anyone—and especially for outsiders—to determine whether reform is actually effective. The resulting presumption that any reform is good reform maximizes the rewards for dramatic and visible efforts and minimizes the rewards for painstaking accomplishments.

Inconsistencies in respondents' answers illustrate how difficult it is to judge specific reform measures. Respondents frequently had trouble naming the district's "greatest recent success," but evaluated specific reforms very positively when prompted on each type of reform. A business community respondent admitted, "I can't think of anything I would tout as a great success." Nonetheless, this respondent reported that a "significant" curriculum reform had been enacted, and he rated it a six out of ten when asked how successful it had been.

An administrator had a similar response when asked to name the district's greatest success in the past three years: "I'm trying to think how best to say this, but I guess there really hasn't been one. We've been so preoccupied with the state investigation and all these issues, that there haven't really been any noticeable successes." However, this respondent reported that "significant" school day and professional development reforms had been enacted and rated their success an eight and a seven out of ten, respectively. Then there was the Palo Alto, California, respondent who, when asked for the district's greatest success in the past three years, said, "I'm going to pass on that one, which is unbelievably revealing, isn't it? They've tried a lot of things, but I'm not sure, honestly speaking, they can say they were successful." However, when asked about specific types of reform, the respondent reported there had been a "significant" SBM reform that rated a seven out of ten for success.

While respondents like these reported that the district had achieved no successes but rated individual reforms as successful, other respondents cited something educationally peripheral (such as "surviving" or winning a sporting title) as the district's greatest success, but rated the success of spe-

35. See the discussion of this point in chapter 1. Also see discussions by Fullan (1991), Kirst and Jung (1991), and Sarason (1982).

cific "significant" reforms quite highly. These responses suggest that how respondents judge the success of "significant" reforms is not necessarily linked to how they evaluate the performance of the system as a whole.

An administrator, who termed a school time measure a ten and a professional development reform a six in terms of success, failed to mention these reforms when discussing the district's greatest success in the past three years. Instead, the administrator described the success as the district's ability to "go forward with major building projects and major organizational changes in the way we address education closures forced by declining enrollment and financial constraints." Similarly, an administrator in a different district rated a professional development reform an eight for success and an SBM measure a six, but described the district's greatest recent success by saying, "There's such a financial disaster that I don't know how to answer. The biggest success is just managing to stay alive in the financial crush."

A board member gave the distinct impression that nothing productive had transpired in the district in the previous three years. When asked to describe the district's greatest recent success, the board member said,

> I don't know that, in the past three years, we can look at one thing and call it a tremendous success. We have been able to live within our budgetary constraints. Nevertheless, programs go wanting. Employee groups feel they are not getting due compensation, and, even if we have additional security in our schools, the perception out there is that [the schools] are not as safe as they would like them to be. If we look at the dropout rate and academic achievement records, there appears to be no significant change, and so I don't believe we can call that any greater success.

However, this same respondent, when answering those questions that asked specifically about specific reforms, proceeded to rate as relatively successful "significant" reform initiatives in school time and student evaluation (rating the reforms a seven for success in both cases).

One union respondent discussed in bleak terms the district's record on site-based management reform:

> We had [SBM] in our district once and it failed, and now they're bringing it back. . . . They're going to put site-based management in 25 schools in the fall, and they claim it's going to work this time. The

first time, basic implementation failed. It was not implemented well or thought out well. It was just poor delivery, and they claim they're going to make up for that this time. . . . You have to train people, but they didn't want to train people.

Nonetheless, this respondent rated the SBM initiative a ten on implementation and a ten for success.

The fundamental difficulty in evaluating the success of school reform was best reflected by a Seattle respondent. The respondent termed a reform successful, while declaring in the same sentence that no change had been produced in output measures: "I think the [administrators] are committed to the reforms. The reforms have been successful, but I haven't seen any change towards improving current scores." Despite seeing no movement in the output measure he chose to cite, the respondent deemed the reforms successful. One wonders what it takes to convince someone that a reform is unsuccessful.

Discussing a new evaluation measure that students were required to take, a business community respondent clearly enunciated the nature of the dilemma: "If the goal is, 'Do they have to take it?' then yes, it's been successful. If the question is whether they're really learning due to it, then the answer is, 'No,' because about 75% of ninth graders get an F or a D." So long as this confusion about whether reform should be judged according to activity or outcomes is present, efforts to accurately assess the performance of school reform measures will be an immensely difficult task.

Different Perspectives of Insiders and Outsiders

School system insiders (administrators, school board members, and teacher union respondents in this study) do not promote policy churn maliciously. They pursue reform because their institutional position compels them to do so. However, these external pressures are reinforced and aggravated by the tendency of reformers to overestimate the effectiveness of their efforts. Insiders tend to be personally invested in and affiliated with reform, while the outsiders tend to be uninvolved or to have a much more tenuous connection to reform. As a result, school system insiders wind up viewing education reform differently than do outsiders.

Because there is no concrete way to measure school reform, it is not possible to determine whether system insiders are evaluating reform in "too positive" or outsiders in "too negative" a fashion. However, the fact

that insiders evaluated the ambition, implementation, and success of reform efforts far more positively than did system outsiders calls into doubt
their ability to evaluate reform efforts objectively.

The different perspectives from which insiders and outsiders consider
education reform is illustrated by these responses from two St. Louis residents. In discussing a major bill to reform education in Missouri, the in-
sider focused upon the act's educational promise: "Senate bill 380 . . . calls
for exact standards in 43 or 44 different areas of performance." The outsider viewed the bill as little more than another political dispute over funding: "The bill shifted money from the richer schools, but the city schools
have argued that they were supposed to get 17 million dollars which they
didn't get. [The city schools] say the rural schools came out a lot better."

INSIDERS CONSIDER REFORMS MORE AMBITIOUS AND EFFECTIVE.
Each time they reported that a reform was proposed, respondents were
asked to judge "how ambitious" the proposal was on a zero-to-ten scale. Insiders reported reforms to be 12 percent more ambitious than did outsiders,
rating reforms an average of 8.2 as opposed to a 7.3 for outsiders. Insiders
reported the ambition of the average reform proposal to be higher than did
outsiders for each of the five types of reform.

Insiders also viewed reforms as having been more thoroughly implemented than did outsiders. Each time they reported that a reform was enacted, respondents were asked to evaluate "how thoroughly the reform was
implemented," using a zero-to-ten scale. Insiders reported implementation
as being 13 percent more complete than did system outsiders. Insiders
evaluated implementation to be 7.0 on average, while outsiders rated it a
6.2. The only reform for which outsiders evaluated implementation more
highly was the symbolically potent SBM (see chapter 5), which promises
visible and dramatic change.

The rosy view of policymakers and system insiders is clearly shown in
table 7-2. Insiders viewed school reform as substantially more successful
than did outsiders. Respondents were asked to rate the success of each reform that they reported had been enacted, using a zero-to-ten scale to evaluate "how successful the measure had been." Overall, insiders rated reforms as 21 percent more successful, in terms of their stated goals, than did
outsiders. Outsiders rated no type of reform as more successful than a 5.5,
while insiders rated every type of reform at 5.9 or higher.

JOURNALISTS AND ADMINISTRATORS DISAGREE ON THE SUCCESS OF
REFORM.   Comparing the views of administrators and journalists on the

Table 7-2. A Comparison of District Insiders' and Outsiders' View of Reform Initiatives[a]

Type of respondent	Day and time	Curriculum	Evaluation	Professional development	Site-based management	Weighted average
District insiders	7.4	6.4	6.3	6.5	5.9	6.3
	(35)	(96)	(81)	(94)	(122)	(428)
District outsiders	5.2	4.9	4.7	5.5	5.4	5.2
	(26)	(62)	(48)	(45)	(83)	(264)

Source: Author's data.

a. Numbers of respondents are in parentheses. Respondents were asked to rate the success of each reform that they reported had been enacted, using a zero-to-ten scale to evaluate "how successful the measure had been." Insiders are administrators, school board members, and the presidents of teachers' unions. Outsiders are journalists, business community members, and minority organization members. Insiders regard reform as more successful by 21 percent.

success of reform offers the most explicit illustration of the insider-outsider gap. Of all respondents, administrators have the most interest in viewing reforms as successful, while journalists have the least stake in the outcomes of reform. Not surprisingly, administrators viewed reform efforts as 40 percent more successful than did journalists. Journalists rated the average reform as less than 50 percent successful (at 4.7 out of 10), while administrators rated each of the five types of reform as more than 60 percent successful (at 6.6).

All of the differences were not between insiders and outsiders. For instance, unions were markedly more critical of reform than were administrators. This was particularly true for reforms on which the union felt it had not been accorded a full and fair voice. Because administrators generally have a larger personal stake in reform than do union leaders, they naturally tend to be more optimistic. In one district the administrator evaluated an SBM measure as the district's greatest success in the past three years, while the union respondent denounced the measure as a sham. The administrator said,

We've had success in reform. We've moved to decentralize the district into smaller units. About 200,000 kids and 240 campuses were decentralized to get smaller units closer to the communities. . . . [E]ach school has a decision-making committee made up of parents, teachers, and administrators. This really has helped in looking at the needs of each campus.

The union president voiced a critical perspective of the same reform,

> There was a state law which required that every campus have an
> SBM committee, that every district would submit to Texas a plan. . . .
> The principals held onto power like I'd never seen. We had stuffed
> ballot boxes and had to send people out of the central office to over-
> see school elections. We had behavior that I would have been
> ashamed of in fifth graders. We had one election that had to be done
> four times and the central office finally said, "The heck with
> it." They've taken power away from teachers and now they've lost
> interest.

Ironically, the business community respondent disagreed with both of
these evaluations, saying he was unable to judge the success of the SBM
initiative because "it's too early to tell."

In large part evaluations of success and implementation are shaped by
the relation of the respondent to the reform. This bias may have caused
greater distortions in prior research than has been previously recognized,
because most studies of implementation and program evaluation tend to focus on the opinions, concerns, and judgments of experts and insiders.
These individuals are likely to view the success of reforms from an exceptionally positive perspective.

Conclusion

Implementation is crucial to the effectiveness of any organizational reform. However, attention to implementation is short-changed because of
the institutional and professional pressures that shape school district
policymaking. The high rate of reform activity in urban school districts significantly reduced the implementation and perceived success of individual
reforms in the districts studied. Additionally, rapid executive turnover had
an independent and negative impact on implementation and perceived success.

Why are suboptimal reform behaviors perpetuated? There are two crucial reasons. First, it is difficult for observers to accurately assess the effectiveness of reform, so they give almost any reform the benefit of the doubt.
That helps explain the extremely high overall rating given to reform by respondents in the survey. Respondents who could think of no significant
recent successes in the local district gave high ratings when asked to discuss specific reform initiatives. Since all reform tends to be regarded favorably, the incentives for policymakers to take action—any action—are

strengthened. Unable to assess actual school performance, most observers rely upon a series of imperfect proxies, the most accessible of which are isolated and anecdotal successes.[36] Second, system insiders, who exert disproportionate influence on local education policy, have a much more favorable view of reform than do outsiders.

36. Popkin (1991).

PART THREE

The Possibilities

8

The Spinning Wheels
of Reform:
Getting Unstuck

THIS STUDY BEGAN with a question that has long troubled the educational community: why have such energetic reform efforts yielded so little change in urban school districts? The answer is both radical and embarrassingly obvious. Reform—rather than being the remedy to what ails urban schools—has been a distraction and a hindrance. Reform is an expensive endeavor requiring time, money, and energy. By absorbing these resources, reform imposes significant monetary and opportunity costs on urban school systems.[1] Reform, at least as it has traditionally been conceived and enacted, is only tangentially about improving urban education.[2] School reform is primarily the consequence of district policymakers' attempting to operate in a hostile political environment. Unfortunately, the efforts of these policymakers have undermined school-level stability, focus, consistency, enthusiasm, trust, and commitment—the keys to effective schooling. This spinning of wheels has aggravated the sad plight of urban education.

Most reform is not a serious attempt to change teaching and learning in the classroom but is intended to bolster the stature of the district policymakers.[3] The evidence on five Third Wave reforms in fifty-seven ur-

---

1. Cuban (1984).

2. This argument will not come as a shock to those familiar with the work of Barth (1980,1991); Chubb and Moe (1990); Cuban (1976, 1984, 1988); Elmore (1991a, 1991b, 1997); Fullan (1991); Orlich (1989); Plank (1988); Rich (1996); Sarason (1982); and Tyack and Cuban (1995); among others. Nonetheless, this perspective is nearly invisible in the ongoing policy debates about urban education.

3. Pauly (1991, 2) writes: "Although it may seem hard to believe, education policy research has paid little attention to the influence of classrooms on education. Instead, the search for ideas about how to improve our schools has focused on quick fixes; researchers looked for the best curriculum, the best textbook, the best instructional method."

ban districts during 1992 to 1995 supports this political understanding of school reform. The amount of reform taking place, the nature of that reform, which reforms and where they are proposed, and the consequences of this activity are all consistent with a political interpretation. The great irony is that the sheer amount of activity—the fact that reform is the status quo—impedes the ability of any particular reform to have a lasting effect.

The Obstacles to Effective Reform

Highly touted reforms, found to be effective when attempted in small-scale studies, often produce disappointing results when attempted on a larger scale.[4] Reforms have not necessarily been misguided or ineffective. Rather, excessive and weakly supported reform activity has made it exceedingly difficult for reforms to take root and flourish—regardless of the design of any given initiative.

To say that school reform has been a disappointment does not mean that every effort has fallen short. Reforms will sometimes take hold when they happen to "match the inclinations, strengths, and preference of people in a particular classroom."[5] However, policymakers, academics, and consultants have no incentive to acknowledge that the law of averages means some policy initiatives somewhere are bound to work. "Worr[ied] about the public's reaction if we suddenly declare that on critical matters of pedagogy, we just 'aren't sure,'" administrators use perceived successes as opportunities to proclaim their expertise.[6]

Policy Churn

The constant proposing and enacting of new measures—the spinning of wheels—by urban districts ensures that only the rare measure receives sustained support. Meanwhile, administrators, faculty, and community members are distracted and frustrated by one new plan after another. In fact, policy churn may not just distract and frustrate policymakers but actually reduce school performance and student outcomes. Future research needs to explore this alarming possibility.[7]

4. Even though a new approach may work in one school, \'93the same program, used in another school, [may fail] to repeat the earlier success, and at the original site, the initial results typically fade away after a year or two.\'94 See Pauly (1991, 25).

5. Pauly (1991, 112).

6. Sagor (1996, 83).

7. Because of its broad scope, this study cannot account for a great deal of variation from one school district to another. A few districts do produce sustained improvement. There is a need for

Reforms directed from the top of the system rarely foster the class-room-level or school-level commitment essential to making change work.[8] Instead, efforts to reform schools from the top tend to be hobbled by vague conceptions of how teaching and learning will be improved by the initiative:

> Changes are often not explicitly connected to fundamental changes in the way knowledge is constructed, nor to the division of responsibility between teacher and student. . . . Schools, then, might be "changing" all the time . . . and never change in any fundamental way what teachers and students actually do when they are together in the classroom.[9]

Rapid leadership turnover and the constant search for new solutions have meant that "commitments to programs of ex-superintendents dry up and the programs are abandoned." As a result, "staff become disillusioned and resist further change."[10] The problem has not been that "nothing ever changes," but that too much change is being pursued too often.

In effect, policy churn punishes those teachers who are willing to throw themselves into reform efforts. These are the very teachers who are most committed to teaching and their professional responsibilities. Meanwhile, the teachers who are the intended targets of reform are able to ride out the successive waves of reform behind the closed doors of their classrooms. Teachers who take reform at face value, investing their time and energy in the new proposals, find their efforts wasted when reforms rapidly fall out of fashion. These teachers disrupt their classrooms and lesson plans by attempting to teach in unfamiliar ways rather than refining methods with which they are comfortable. Because each regime initiates new reforms, within a few years this entire process starts again. Veteran teachers quickly learn to close their classroom doors and simply wait for each reform push to recede.[11] This helps to ensure that each successive wave of reform is largely manned by new teachers lacking in institutional memory.

---

research that examines in more detail the environmental, institutional, and leadership qualities that characterize these districts. In addition, my method of data collection may understate or exaggerate the extent of policy activity in specific districts. This may make it difficult to identify with precision those districts that are pursuing systemic reform in a disciplined manner. Efforts to tally up reform initiatives may depict these districts as overextended or unfocused, when they in fact are not. This also is an issue that calls for additional scrutiny.

8. Johnson (1996).
9. Elmore (1996, 3).
10. Carter and Cunningham (1997, 7).
11. Johnson (1996).

The inability of urban districts to replicate isolated success on a widespread basis cannot be taken as a repudiation of the reform proposals themselves. On the other hand, the promises and programs produced by the professional reform community have only aggravated the perverse incentives driving short-term political leadership and policy churn. By continuously promising and marketing quicker and better ways to improve schools, reformers increase the pressure to pursue new initiatives while encouraging the public to hold unrealistic expectations.

Disregarding the realities of urban districts, critics of reform have focused on the symptoms rather than the causes of policy churn. Policymakers, they argue, should adopt reforms that are more coherent and holistic, emphasize implementation and training, stop tinkering at the margins, focus on the purpose of schooling, and clarify and define objectives before moving forward.[12] The critics are right on all these counts, but their advice ignores the reality of policymakers' situation. In fact, there is little practical incentive for superintendents to abide by this advice, and those who try are likely to wind up out of a job long before their efforts come to fruition.

Political Isolation

Inattention to the messy task of supporting change in the classroom is part of a larger phenomenon: school administrators' apparent distaste for politics and the business of managing conflict.[13] For years superintendents have sought professional status and nonpartisan governance structures in order to insulate themselves from the pressures that permeate municipal government. They believed that a nonpolitical stance would mean more benefits, respect, and professional authority for school administrators. In reality, the result has been a nonpartisan and bureaucratic school administration headed by a politically isolated superintendent. Superintendents often aggravate this exposed position by evincing a distaste for politics and by viewing politics as antithetical to "educational" issues. The irony is that

12. Firestone, Fuhrman, and Kirst (1991); Fullan (1991); Sizer (1996a); and Hess and McNergney (1998).

13. Carter and Cunningham (1997, 43\9644) note that educators \93tend to scorn anything that even smacks of being political.\94 Jack Kaufhold (1993, 42), a former superintendent, thus expressed his distaste for politics: \93If I\92d wanted to be a politician, I would have majored in political science and taken a law degree instead of a doctorate in education. . . . I don\92t want to be a politician. . . . I wanted to help kids and provide the best possible education for them.\94

superintendents try to bolster their credibility and avoid politics by wielding school reform in a flagrantly political fashion.[14]

Superintendents, whether they like it or not, are political figures. Politics and public education are inextricably intertwined, and pretending that matters are otherwise does not help. Superintendents who foreswear a political role sacrifice useful tools and weaken their institutional position. It is the task of policymakers to create a system in which the political activity of superintendents is channeled in constructive directions. Rather than trying to depoliticize education, reformers of public schooling should seek political incentives that encourage the system leadership to focus on performance and long-term progress rather than public relations and short-term elixirs.

Ways to Discourage Symbolic Reform

What might help to stop the furious wheel spinning in urban districts? How can urban school systems become "unstuck"? Today, policymakers are inclined to move too quickly, too dramatically, and with too little attention to the actual impact of reforms on teaching and learning. The tendency to pursue symbolic reform is largely the product of institutional pressures, and these pressures cannot be combated solely by sage advice.

The problems with school reform call for institutional and political solutions. This fact has been obscured by the tendency to address educational problems with educational solutions. Redressing the problem of policy churn in urban systems requires modifying incentives so that policymakers are encouraged to emphasize substantive, consistent, long-term improvement. The professional and political interests of urban school leaders need to be hitched to the long-term performance of urban schools.

Of course, the downside of political solutions is that they inevitably involve trade-offs. American education has evolved as a patchwork of politically treacherous compromises, such as those that limit the differentiation of successful and unsuccessful students, promise a similar education to all children, and protect teachers in the urban workforce. It is not at all clear that policymakers are willing to rework those compromises simply for the sake of educational efficacy. Increasing the accountability of school districts and administrative control of what goes on in the classroom may

14. Kowalski (1995); Tyack (1974); Norton and others (1996); and Tallerico, Poole, and Burstyn (1994).

mean revisiting these compromises. Whether we are willing to do this is an open question.

Altering Institutional Constraints

Policymakers are less likely to focus on short-term inputs if they believe that they can affect outcomes and will be assessed according to the outcomes they produce. So long as urban policymakers are evaluated by their promise—rather than by their results—they will be rewarded more for the visible than for the essential. Reliance on input proxies can be lessened by increasing policymakers' accountability for outcomes, increasing administrators' leverage in the classroom to reduce core ambiguity, and altering the visibility and the public's expectations of urban school leaders.[15] Each of these ways to alter institutional constraints is discussed in this section. The most significant factor promoting symbolic reform appears to be the lack of clear outcome measures with which to assess policymakers' performance. Tackling either of the other two dimensions without first attempting to improve accountability for performance seems unlikely to reduce churn, since policymakers will continue to be judged with input proxies. However, as accountability is enhanced, attention to control over the technical core and to organizational visibility become more important.

ACCOUNTABILITY.   As accountability for outcomes becomes more interpretable and obvious, it will be easier to judge policymakers' effect on the performance of schools and students. Consequently, the relative importance of symbolic activity will decline. This accountability can be pursued in two ways: by monitoring school and student performance or by utilizing markets. A standards-based approach uses external supervision to ensure adequate school performance, while choice-based approaches rely upon parents' and students' decisions. The two approaches are not mutually exclusive.

The most effective approach to increasing the importance of outcomes and reducing the incentives to engage in symbolic reform may be the adoption of the West European–Japanese model of standard universal tests.[16]

15. This study does not explore the relative significance of these three dimensions, nor the elements comprising each one. Further research is needed to evaluate the relative impact of particular modifications.
16. Testing is not a miracle cure. The key to an effective accountability system is implementation and organizational capacity. See Newman, King, and Rigdon (1997). The Japanese and West Europeans have refined their accountability systems through decades of practice.

This kind of universal test is probably most effective if done at the national level, but the heterogeneity of the United States makes that alternative highly unlikely in the short term. An acceptable alternative may be the creation of statewide tests that otherwise abide by the tenets of the high-stakes testing model. Current tests are neither standard enough, respected enough, consequential enough, nor understood well enough to provide a legitimate outcome benchmark.

The move toward standardized state and national testing would dramatically alter the institutional incentives superintendents face. One illustration of possible changes is a 1997 Virginia law that penalizes schools where fewer than 70 percent of students achieve a threshold score. This law represents a simpler and more accessible version of the statewide testing programs that have been implemented or considered by several states in recent years. The best-known of these efforts is Kentucky's dramatic accountability plan that was instituted in 1990 as part of a court-ordered overhaul of the state's education system.

Critics have attacked Virginia's accountability measure as likely to disproportionately penalize minority students and disadvantaged students, as well as the districts in which these students are concentrated. Without a doubt, institutional remedies designed to address policy churn will have consequences unacceptable to some constituencies of urban public education. Whether Americans are willing to see disproportionate numbers of black, Hispanic, poor, and urban students fail high-stakes tests in order to increase urban school performance is an open question. It is not clear that voters and policymakers consider the goal to be worth the risk of inflaming societal and racial tensions. This indecision is both natural and healthy given the conflicting concerns of great social significance.

Like the states, the national government has gingerly moved in the direction of better testing. Under the Goals 2000 legislation enacted in 1994, the U.S. government theoretically embarked on a commitment to more uniform standards.[17] By focusing the attention of professional educators on a clear, consistent, comparable standard, rigorous cross-sectional testing discourages districts from trying to play with scores and encourages them to minimize disruptions to teaching and learning in the classroom. Authoritative national exams in Western Europe and Japan focus attention on how students actually perform on the tests. Administrators know the outcomes

17. Cohen (1996b).

by which they will be assessed, and consequently they have institutional incentives to enhance demonstrated performance.

Efforts to develop formal and measurable standards are impeded by disagreement about the purpose of schooling. This is a conflict with deep cultural and philosophical roots. Attempts by districts to clarify their mission often end up as all-encompassing mission statements out of deference to the multiple perspectives that comprise the local and professional communities. Clear expectations can be advanced only to the extent that a district and its community can agree on uniform benchmarks. In the absence of formal benchmarks, one option is to develop simple outcome proxies. For instance, a general expectation within the community that X percentage of students should graduate or go to four-year universities is a functional accountability mechanism if the members of the community agree on the benchmark. It is crucial to recognize that the introduction of standardized and comparative outcome measures tends to render obsolete disagreements about what the purpose of schooling *should* be. The new rules of the game determine what the practical measure of school quality will be.

Any high-stakes testing system, regardless of the curricular matter or the particular skills emphasized, will increase attention to outcomes and focus district administration. It is the existence of the test, and not what is on the test, that will discourage symbolic reform. Although the substance of these tests has tremendous significance for educational and societal reasons, it is relatively unimportant if one's goal is to change institutional incentives.

Testing may be used in concert with other measures. Particularly attentive to enhancing administrative focus is the "systemic reform" approach, which integrates testing with other changes that help to focus district personnel on the same bottom-line concerns.[18] Proponents of this approach advocate a cohesive and interlocking set of changes to standards, testing, curriculum, and teacher training, with the notion that each component will reinforce attention to the other components. This approach may be misinterpreted by administrators as endorsing yet another wave of reform, but it also offers the possibility of reinforcing and channeling the administrative response to high-stakes testing.

Testing is not the only means to improve accountability. An alternative accountability mechanism is provided by school choice: using the preferences of local parents and children to punish and reward schools.

18. O'Day and Smith (1991).

Choice-based systems can make it easier to judge school performance by decentralizing the task and then requiring only that families judge the quality of the schools they use. Under choice, so long as provision is made to collect and distribute information on school performance, parents and students will theoretically punish schools that do not perform adequately by taking their business elsewhere.

Of course, in the real world other factors may reduce the market discipline imposed by choice arrangements.[19] These factors include parents' imperfect information, restrictions on parental decisionmaking, reticence to change schools, and concerns with school qualities other than optimal school performance. Nonetheless, there is reason to believe that choice will help focus local policymakers on the fundamental issues of performance.

The analyses proffered by choice proponents presume that urban schools are in trouble primarily because they are public sector organizations. But many problems plague urban education: immensely troubled student populations, massive size, the loose linkages of schools to the central administrators and one another, multitiered leadership hierarchies that distance system leaders from the classrooms, constraints on administrative activity, unclear outcome expectations, and high visibility. These characteristics of urban public school systems are only partially a function of their public sector status.[20] If choice proposals are not designed to address these concerns, they will not have the desired effects on the management of schooling.

In addition to potentially increasing accountability, carefully constructed choice plans can discourage policy churn in other ways. Choice can break up the massive urban systems into smaller entities that are controlled by administrators closer to the classroom faculty. Small systems, whether a handful of schools or a single school, enhance accountability by helping local observers judge system output and trace that output to system leadership. Small systems also make it easier for leaders to exercise control over the classroom. Choice plans can increase the system leadership's le-

19. There is no guarantee that private sector schools will concentrate on outcomes. The need for schools to differentiate themselves in a competitive marketplace and to have some "sizzle" to offer potential customers could increase the rate of policy churn. In fact, reform efforts could easily become selling points under choice arrangements. If families lack solid criteria with which to judge schools, they may use the same sort of input proxies that currently encourage political school leadership.

20. This discussion is not attempting to critique the overall effect market-based remedies may have on schooling. It is solely addressing the effect these remedies will have on symbolic reform and policy churn.

verage in the schools by reducing or eliminating union contract and state-mandated restrictions. Increased control enhances the incentives for the system leadership to invest in efforts to improve core performance. Finally, choice plans foster the creation of communities with shared expectations, making it easier to measure system performance against a clear set of desired outcomes. Choice can help to reduce policy churn by making outcomes more transparent or by offering school leaders more control over teaching and learning.

A particularly popular version of choice-based reform is charter schooling, which has been adopted in more than half of the states. Charter schooling is a system of modified school choice in which competition is regulated and restricted by the requirement that school practices receive a charter from the state or from a state-designated authority. Legislative limits on the number, nature, and scope of charters have made charters relatively palatable to many policymakers. For the purpose of addressing policy churn, charter schooling conveys many of the same potential benefits and risks as less regulated choice alternatives. Charter schools operate in an environment that is easier to manage and encourages attention to outcomes, but such schools also may rely on input proxies in an attempt to attract students. Further, school districts may respond to competitive pressures by launching new initiatives or by reshuffling resources, rather than by improving their performance.[21]

Another response to the problems inherent in public sector governance is educational contracting in which private firms are hired to operate schools. Like school choice, educational contracting is a market-based approach to improving accountability.[22] This approach gives school managers the authority to hire and fire employees, set salaries, shape curricula, and determine school missions.

Competition among firms to win and retain contracts is expected to increase attention to actual outcomes. This could powerfully orient schools around real achievement. There is a danger, however, that contracting will be ineffective at curbing policy churn. Many of the existing problems with assessing and interpreting real outcomes will continue, making it likely that school boards will rely to some extent on input proxies. Community

21. On the promise of charter schooling, see Bierlein (1997) and Nathan (1996). In competing with existing public schools for students, charter schools may increase policy churn, as districts strive to attract families by launching new initiatives. See Millott and Lake (1996) on school board response to charter school competition.

22. Hill, Pierce, and Guthrie (1997) and Hill (1997).

pressure is likely to encourage urban boards to choose exciting firms promising quick results.

If contracting produces large firms that control fifty or a hundred schools in multiple cities, these firms will confront many of the current problems of urban school districts: loose coupling, extended leadership hierarchies, and constricted local control. In this environment, especially if school boards are attentive to input proxies, contracting firms are likely to use these proxies in evaluating managers. There is no assurance that contracting will create a management structure that discourages symbolic reform.

The rapid turnover of school superintendents is a massive problem, both in terms of accountability and because it prohibits superintendents from significantly affecting teaching and learning. Additionally, rapid turnover assumes a self-fulfilling quality, with superintendents consciously thinking of their position as a short-term audition for the next job. The obvious solution is to hire superintendents for a longer period of time. This could be done by dramatically extending the length of a superintendent's contract—to six or seven years, for instance. This approach would be particularly effective if superintendents were to commit to the district for much or all of the contract, agreeing to stay long enough to follow through on the job they begin. A weaker alternative approach is to make it harder for the school board to terminate a superintendent before the end of a contract. A supermajority of the board (60 percent or more) could be required to terminate an ongoing contract.[23] Particularly important is that boards renounce the temptation of repeatedly finding leaders who will "shake up" the system. In addition, to maintain continuity, promote long-term thinking, and focus attention on the performance of the entire system, school boards could adopt an explicit policy of favoring inside candidates over outsiders when searching for a new superintendent.

In large urban school districts parents lack firsthand information about school performance. Urban systems do not have to be designed that way. Large systems theoretically enjoy economies of scale, but that need not be the end of the discussion. Operational control can be shifted to more manageable and more accountable subunits, while the district continues to handle routine services that benefit from economies of scale. The questions raised by decentralization experiments in New York and Chicago suggest

---

23. The problem with this idea is that some superintendents would be in the position of attempting to manage a system while opposed by a majority of the board.

that while the promise of this approach is uncertain, it is worth further consideration. Choice advocates envision urban districts with dramatically fewer public schools. These smaller systems would coexist with large numbers of private schools. Whether a child is enrolled in the smaller urban school system or in the private schools, it will be marginally easier for the parents to assess the performance of those making the relevant policy decisions. The significance of the change would depend upon the size of the local district and the nature of choice-inspired changes. The key point is that increasing parents' firsthand information about school performance and school policymakers reduces their reliance on media cues and input proxies.

CORE AMBIGUITY   Emphasis on outcomes alone will not put an end to policy churn. Increased emphasis on outcomes, without enhancing administrative control over the mundane elements of system performance, may exacerbate the pressure on administrators to try dramatic ideas that promise to shock systems into improvement. Consequently, any attempt to remedy policy churn must include efforts to lengthen superintendents' tenure and improve their ability to shape the practices of teaching and learning.

Currently, policymakers have limited control over the behavior of urban schools. It is this mismatch between authority and accountability that helps discourage superintendents from quietly building on their predecessors' efforts. Increasing the leverage of administrators over the technical core will increase their incentives to work for significant long-term organizational improvement. Increased administrative control will make it easier to implement reforms, but it also can increase the instability of urban districts if wielded in a haphazard fashion. Enhancing administrative control without improving accountability may do little to stem policy churn. If administrators continue to rely on input proxies, they will have incentives to use their new tools to create the *promise* of improvement. Therefore, changes in administrative control must be linked to measures that will hold administrators responsible for outcomes and will encourage them to use their enhanced control to improve school performance.

Superintendents lack effective tools with which to promote change. District organizations are staffed by people the superintendent did not hire and cannot fire. Superintendents have little discretion over salaries, have few sanctions at their disposal, and are constrained by union contracts. Furthermore, the physical structure of the urban school system means that teaching and learning take place far from the superintendent. Superintendents who find themselves unable to effectively control classroom activity have that much more incentive to turn to the relatively unconstrained arena of policy initiation. As superintendents' leverage over the core is increased, the prospect of trying to change faculty behavior becomes less daunting.

There are several ways to give superintendents more control over the performance of their school district and more control over their own fate: increase their discretion on salaries or hiring, relax the laws and contract provisions governing firing and tenure, broaden the sanctions they are permitted to wield, and reconfigure the superintendency to permit superintendents to spend more time in the schools. Of course, each of these changes also makes the superintendency more powerful and creates the possibility that a superintendent can disrupt the school system, increase instability, and provoke conflict with teachers. It is necessary that any district carefully weigh the grant of increased authority, and that the authority be linked to accountability measures that will encourage organization leaders to focus on core performance.

The vast size and multiple layers of bureaucracy in urban districts make it very difficult for superintendents to penetrate to the teaching and learning core, no matter how hard they try. Given their experience with reform efforts, teachers often aggravate this problem by sealing themselves off from the larger school environment as much as possible. One approach to reducing the distance of the superintendent from the classroom is simply to shrink the size of school districts. A second approach is to go to a flatter organizational structure, reducing the layers of bureaucracy insulating the superintendent from the classrooms. A third approach is to use decentralization primarily as a way to invest principals or department chairs with a grant of authority from the superintendent, as part of a sustained effort to project leadership influence more firmly into classrooms. In other words, decentralization would be a means of extending the superintendent's reach into the schools, rather than a way to increase community input or institute site-based governance.

VISIBILITY.   In school systems that are less visible, policymakers are under less pressure to continuously demonstrate their competence and energy. However, it is clear that this is the institutional dimension least susceptible to formal remedies. The visibility of schooling is largely a product of the value the American people ascribe to education, the nature of the modern media, and the realities of contemporary urban society. Nonetheless, to the extent that the media or community leaders reduce the glare of the spotlight on the schools, become more patient, or depict a fuller picture of school system performance, they can reduce the pressure on policymakers to focus on input rather than outcomes.

Changing the Reward Structure

There is one way to tackle policy churn without formally modifying institutional arrangements: stop rewarding those who engage in it. This solution requires altering the political calculus of urban school leadership. Currently, superintendents are rewarded for being "innovative." Education reformers who design and promote reforms receive grants, win consultant contracts, gain status in the policy community, and are hailed in the media for their insights. Government agencies and foundations fund these activities and then promote themselves as "part of the solution." All of this activity continues to absorb attention and money, even though it has produced little of demonstrated value.

Changing the tenor of school policy discussions is possible. Opinion makers, in the press and in government, must stop lionizing reformers and publicizing isolated innovations that have been perceived as successful. If columnists, reporters, state and national government officials, and other observers of education viewed innovation with a more skeptical eye—and demanded to see convincing large-scale evidence before praising reformers—the incentives to engage in reform would be sharply reduced. Likewise, if short-term expectations for rapid improvement were reduced, grant-giving agencies and foundations might become more willing to fund projects that come without the glitz and glitter. Responsible outsiders are needed to discourage the pursuit of reform by changing the atmosphere in which educational problems and remedies are discussed. By becoming immune to the allures of the reform industry, outsiders can persuade professional associations and policy organizations to pay more attention to rewarding incremental progress and effective management.

Another way to change the risk-reward ratio is to modify the procedures by which school boards endorse and enact reform measures. On most Third Wave reforms, school boards reached an easy and informal consensus. In this atmosphere symbolic reform flourished. The public should compel urban boards to spell out in writing the purpose, goals, required resources, and expected outcomes of any given reform.

Of course, efforts to increase the school board's commitment to a selected course of action are highly vulnerable to the same political pressures that hamper boards in the first place. The purpose of increasing the profile and formality of the board's commitment to a specific superintendent and to a specific program is that it makes it relatively more costly for the board to change course midstream. The more clearly and visibly a board asserts that "this is our course," the more difficult it will be for board members to swerve off in a new direction.

To discourage placid acceptance of policy churn, the board should require a supermajority vote on future reform initiatives. Board elections and decisions by sitting board members in democratically governed schools will inevitably produce turmoil and sudden changes of direction. The object is to see that these reversals are not frivolous or the result of drift, but the product of a deliberate decision to commit wholeheartedly to a new course of action.

There is no magical solution to the problem of symbolic reform. Each of these institutional solutions has the potential to remedy the problems, but there are no sure things. As with everything, the design and implementation of any institutional reform will be crucial to determining the effect it has in practice.

No More Silver Bullets

The vigilant search for the right "silver bullet" reform, the one that will save urban education, is distracting and unproductive. The search for quick fixes wastes resources even as it fosters apathy, cynicism, and disillusionment among veteran teachers. These costs help to explain why the vast energies devoted to urban school reform have failed to deliver the promised results. Reducing the prevalence of symbolic reform will not "turn around" urban school systems. However, until steps are taken to address symbolic reform, urban school reform will continue to be a dead-end route to educational improvement.

Good intentions are not enough. In fact, the good intentions and big-hearted aspirations of all the players in the drama have produced the phenomenon of policy churn. It is precisely this faith in the next hero or the next silver bullet that creates the circumstances under which sustained improvement becomes an impossible task.

When your car is stuck on a muddy road, the easiest solution is the optimist's solution—stand on the gas and wait for the car to get traction. If the car catches—when the car catches—the whole affair proves the power of positive thinking. In the meantime you can always hope a tow truck will happen along. It is much more difficult and much less reaffirming to turn off your car, take off your jacket, crouch in the mud, wedge a board under the tire, and gently coax your car out of the rut. Unwavering optimism about urban school reform has left urban students in the ditch. To help them advance, policymakers and administrators must get serious about performance.

Appendix A

Conducting the Study

HOW MUCH REFORM do urban schools pursue? Which districts pursue reform, and why do they pursue it in the manner that they do? What is the general impact of extensive reform activity on the fate of reform initiatives? Studying the incidence and the location of reform requires consistent measures of reform activity that are not present in media coverage, cannot be distilled from budgets, and cannot be tallied from formal documents.[1] These questions can best be answered by interviewing people with a wide range of perspectives on urban school reform.

The community survey methodology utilized in this study is imperfect. However, for this study, the methodology used was the most efficient approach. I hope that this study will generate future research using multiple sources of data, and that the ensuing discussion may spur districts to begin keeping track of relevant data on reform. In an academic discourse increasingly dominated by easily collected and apparently "precise" data (such as test scores, expenditures, and public opinion numbers), researchers doing comparative research are increasingly opting for safe variables that appear concrete and precise. On the other hand, case studies are useful but are limited in their scope. The result has been a lack of empirical research on some of the most important issues in education policy. Attempting to partially bridge this gap, I used matched sources across each district to conduct what are essentially fifty-seven small case studies.

---

1. Newspaper coverage of urban school reform is uneven across districts. Stories do not attempt to survey the landscape but tend to focus on certain kinds of events. Moreover, newspaper coverage is a poor judge of implementation and effectiveness. Education reporters generally lack experience, expertise, and local perspective.

I conducted more than 200 hours of interviews with 325 respondents in fifty-seven school districts over a period of nine months from February 16, 1995, to October 6, 1995. The result was more than 2,000 pages of interview transcripts. Most previous studies have examined one or two reforms in fewer than ten locations, or multiple reforms in no more than two or three locations. This study examined five different types of reform in fifty-seven locations.

The possibility of systematic bias was addressed by using consistent sampling rules to obtain structurally matched sets of respondents across districts. Lack of precision—a problem in all research—merely makes us less sure of the results than we might otherwise be and does not systematically bias the findings. The sample design included a broad cross section of respondents, from inside and outside each school system, in order to ensure a diverse set of perspectives on school affairs. A large number of documents on district affairs was also collected from the respondents.

Other alternative sources of data, such as budgets, site visits, and board minutes, were considered for this study. These kinds of data can be used effectively to conduct case studies but are problematic for a large-scale comparative study such as this. With all of these approaches, it is exceedingly difficult to collect meaningful, reliable, and comparable data on the variables of interest. Another way to study these questions is through the analysis of local newspaper coverage, which is a particularly attractive way to collect data on a large number of districts. This approach was considered in the initial research design, but suffers several handicaps that the community survey methodology avoids.

The Sample Districts

Four criteria were used to select the sample of fifty-seven urban school districts throughout the United States. (See appendix B for the list of districts.) First, the sample had to be large in order to create a useful context for interpreting the results from earlier, smaller studies. Second, the sample had to be national in character and geographically dispersed. Third, several states should contain multiple districts, so the behavior of districts within a state could be compared. Finally, the sample should already exist, permitting future researchers to combine the data collected here with existent data.

The Permanent Community Sample (PCS), initiated by the National Opinion Research Center (NORC) at the University of Chicago, had all the

desired characteristics. The PCS was designed in 1960 as a sixty-city stratified sample of the 312 American cities with 50,000 or more residents. The
first PCS study examined the fifty-one smallest cities, excluding the nine
with populations over 750,000 because of concerns about access for elite
interviewing.[2] In 1970 the sixty original cities were supplemented by three
others that surpassed one million residents in the 1970 census. For this
study I took the fifty-one from the first PCS study and randomly added six
of the twelve larger cities.[3] This created a regionally balanced mix of
fifty-seven.

The PCS presented two potential problems. First, the sample was a collection of cities—not school districts. Second, the stratified sample was
constructed in the 1960s, and I was collecting data in 1995. I addressed the
first problem by determining which local school district included most of
the sample city. An examination of the cities by region and size resolved
the second problem, showing that they still constituted a cross-section of
urban America according to the 1990 census. Consequently, there was no
compelling reason to compile a new sample, which would have prohibited
future analysis from pooling this data with longitudinal data on PCS cities.

The Respondents

The sample of respondents was collected and interviewed on a rolling
basis, starting with the local education reporter for the leading circulation
local newspaper in each sample city. The local education reporter was contacted. Either that reporter was interviewed, or the reporter would steer me
to the education editor or to another local reporter. In all cases I accepted
the advice of the person being contacted, thus ensuring a constant decision
rule across the sample.

Near the conclusion of the interview with the journalist, I would obtain
five other names for the subsequent district interviews. The five names obtained were for the head of the teachers' union, the "most knowledgeable"
senior school administrator, the head of the local Chamber of Commerce or
the most influential local business group, the head of the most influential

2. Clark (1968).
3. Two of the twelve cities were not considered for inclusion. New York and Chicago have
both adopted unusual governance structures. New York has thirty-two community school boards,
the result of a 1969 reorganization. Chicago adopted a radical version of site-based management in
the late 1980s, which has essentially created more than 500 school boards. Consequently, neither
New York nor Chicago makes districtwide policy in a conventional manner. In fact, using the
methodology in this study either city could be studied as a collection of school organizations.

local minority organization, and the "most knowledgeable" school board member. If the reporter could not supply the requested name, I used directory assistance to contact the appropriate organization and then asked for a name.

At the local teachers' union I interviewed either the president or the director, depending on the journalist's recommendation. Occasionally, the suggested individual would steer me to the other. I always accepted the respondent's guidance. In a few instances I interviewed the former union president at the suggestion of the current president.

When contacting the "most knowledgeable" senior school administrator, I always started with the reporter's suggestion. If the administrator recommended that I interview a colleague instead, I always took the advice. When the journalist could not or would not suggest an administrator, I would call the school offices and ask for the superintendent's office. I would explain the nature of the interview to the superintendent's executive assistant, and schedule the interview with either the superintendent or the recommended administrator.

If the journalist suggested a local business organization or the Chamber of Commerce, I would call the organization suggested. If the journalist did not have a suggestion, I would get the number for the local chamber from directory assistance. If the journalist supplied a name, I would contact that person. If the journalist did not supply a name, I would contact the organization and ask the receptionist to connect me with whoever handled local educational affairs for the organization. If no such person existed, I would ask for the organization's president. I would explain the nature of the interview to the contact and schedule the interview with either the contact or the colleague to whom they steered me.

Contacting the "most influential minority organization for educational affairs" was quite similar to contacting the local business organization. If the journalist supplied the name of an official, I contacted that person. If the journalist supplied an organization, I would contact that organization and ask for the individual who followed local educational affairs or for the president. If the journalist could not supply an organization, I would contact the local National Association for the Advancement of Colored People (NAACP) branch. If no local NAACP chapter existed, I would contact the local Urban League chapter. When calling the organization, I requested the individual who followed local education affairs, or for the president if no one coordinated educational affairs. When steered to another individual, I interviewed the suggested respondent.

The last person interviewed in each district was a local member of the school board. The board member was interviewed last because the identity of the board respondent depended upon the recommendations of the other local respondents. Near the end of each of the first five interviews, I asked each respondent to name the school board member who was the "most knowledgeable" about local school affairs. I would contact the board member suggested most frequently. If two or more board members were recommended an equal number of times, I would randomly select a board member. In the two or three cases where I contacted a recommended board member and that member suggested a different board member to interview, I accepted the suggestion.

The mean respondent reported following local educational affairs for about seventeen years (see appendix table C-1). Five of the six types of respondents had extended frames of reference with local schooling, while the education reporters demonstrated the short job tenure suggested by previous research.[4]

Success at reaching and interviewing respondents varied by type of respondent. School board members and the business community representatives were the easiest respondents to reach and to schedule, while minority community respondents were by far the most difficult to reach and to interview. The interview success rate varied across the six types of respondents interviewed: 100 percent of journalists and board members were interviewed, 98 percent of union heads, 96 percent of business organization respondents, 93 percent of administrators, and 82 percent of minority organization respondents.

The Interviews

Interviewing the six targeted respondents in each district called for a maximum of 342 interviews; the actual percentage of interviews completed was 95 percent (325 interviews). The average interview lasted 39 minutes, yielding a total of about 211 hours of interviews.

The high completion rate for the sample was primarily the result of four factors. First, I used an exceptionally stringent twelve-call-back rule. (I did not accept nonresponse status for a targeted respondent until attempting to make contact at least twelve times.) Second, extraordinarily few respondents (only three) refused to participate in the study once they had been

---

4. Hennessey and Kowalski (1996) and Wells (1986).

contacted. Third, the emphasis on finding respondents in similar structural positions across districts gave me flexibility within any given district. Finally, I made it a point to accommodate respondents by scheduling interviews for any time they desired.

In order to increase the accuracy of information collected on close-ended answers, I followed up imprecise answers with nondirective probes.[5] Nondirective probes included such prompts as "So, using the zero-to-ten scale, what numerical value would you give it?" or "Where in that range would you say the answer probably is?" Using nondirective probes encouraged many respondents who would say "a lot" or "over a seven" to select a specific numerical value when answering a question. Once respondents had been probed a few times, they tended to increase the specificity of their answers.

A significant minority of respondents had a tendency to answer questions by saying, "That's a 6 or a 7." I would respond by asking, "Would you say that's a 6 or a 7?" Normally, respondents would cease the straddling after several prompts. For the small number of respondents who continued to straddle on some answers, I rounded down when they refused to select a specific number. This consistent decision rule affected only a small number of interviews and did not bias the analysis, which is primarily concerned with *relative* variation across districts.

Data Preparation

The interview data, once collected, were prepared for the purposes of analysis. Three issues require further explanation: district composites, nonresponses, and open-ended responses.

District Composites

Because this was primarily a study of urban school district behavior and not an attempt to measure local perceptions of schooling, the unit of analysis is the district rather than the individual. To distill an understanding of local activity, I averaged the various responses to create composite scores for each variable in each district.

The most widely used dependent variable in the study is the measure of whether or not a proposal was made in a district in each of the five reform

5. Fowler and Mangione (1990, 39–46).

areas. Respondents were asked whether a reform proposal was made in each category, so they provided five "yes-no" responses. This produced a dilemma in creating a districtwide composite. How should Seattle be scored, if four respondents said "yes," that a curriculum proposal was made, and two said "no," that one was not? In order to weight more heavily those districts where respondents were unanimous in agreeing that a proposal had or had not been made, the percentage of answering respondents who reported a proposal being made was used as the composite measure of reform activity.[6] If every respondent in Detroit reported a professional development proposal was made, Detroit's composite professional development proposal score would be 1.00. If each Detroit respondent then reported no proposal had been made on site-based management, Detroit's composite SBM score would be 0.00. Seattle, in the hypothetical case above, would have had a curriculum proposal composite of 0.67. A percentage composite for a "yes-no" question is useful because it weights the amount and the visibility of each reform along a zero-to-one continuum. The overall measure of proposal activity is simply the sum of the zero-to-one composites for each of the five reform areas. A district where it was reported that every reform was proposed would score a composite 5.00.

Nonresponses

The 95 percent response rate essentially eliminated a common concern in survey research: biased results from nonparticipation of a large part of the sample population.[7] A second problem that often arises is respondents' refusal to answer certain questions. That was not a concern in this study, probably because respondents did not feel as vulnerable as respondents do who are being asked about personal views. In fact, there was only one question that as many as 5 out of the 325 respondents refused to answer: "On the whole, how many school board members would you say are ambitious for higher office? All, most, some, or none?" A few respondents said they were not comfortable discussing the topic, and two others said that they had no way of reading the minds of school board members.[8] Even on

6. Respondents who answered "don't know" as to whether a proposal was made were excluded in making this calculation.

7. Schuman and Presser (1981).

8. One Chamber of Commerce representative declined to answer that question, saying, "That's a tricky question to ask a stranger over the phone."

that one question, however, the five represented less than 2 percent of total responses. Overall the rate of nonresponse was so low (less than 1 to 2 percent on the four questions where it occurred at all) as to be irrelevant.

When asked questions that called for familiarity with school affairs, respondents, particularly school system outsiders, sometimes said they did not know. Because of these "don't knows," the composite responses in districts were often based on the average of fewer than six responses.[9] Because the missing data points represented a lack of empirical knowledge, rather than a reticence to share personal views, there was little reason to suspect nonresponse bias. No statistical adjustments were made for "don't knows" or for missing interviews.

Open-Ended Responses

Although most of the quantitative analysis focused on the close-ended responses, two kinds of open-ended responses were coded. The first concerned the local school system agenda and the political context in which the district operated. Respondents were asked about the most prominent local issues, the leading local actors in school affairs, the role the state played locally, the system's greatest recent success, and similar questions. The second set were reform-specific questions. Respondents who indicated a "significant" reform had been proposed were asked to briefly describe the proposal. Respondents who indicated there was no proposal, or that the proposal was not enacted, were also asked to briefly state why a reform did not emerge or was not enacted, if any particular reason came to mind. The variables constructed from this second set of descriptions, on the nature of proposals and on reasons for inaction, are used cautiously for reasons discussed below.

Both kinds of open-ended responses were coded using a similar approach. After reading all of the responses to a question, I generated a set of response categories that included all of the answers respondents had offered and then coded each response. For the reform proposals, I took the additional step of coding the sketchy descriptions of the measure proposed along several dimensions: the percentage of local schools reported to be involved in the reform, what grade levels were affected, and how significant the reform appeared to be.

9. For instance, if two respondents in Houston said they did not know whether the local paper had stood on a proposal for evaluation reform, then the rating of the paper's position would be the composite of four—rather than six—responses.

Coding the responses on the nature of the reform proposals was exceedingly difficult and produced somewhat unreliable results. There were three reasons for this. First, the attempt to keep the interview to a reasonable length meant that respondents provided limited descriptions. Second, most respondents possessed imprecise knowledge of specific reforms. Third, in most districts different respondents cited more than one proposal within a given reform category. This hindered my ability to forge a composite picture of the reform. Determining the percentage of schools affected by a reform and the significance of the proposal called as heavily upon the general description of the local district as upon the respondent's explicit description. Consequently, these measures are used very sparingly in the analysis.

Possible Sources of Bias and Inefficiency

Because all of the interviews in this study were conducted by a single interviewer, the results can be analyzed without concerns about interviewer effects. Typically, large-scale studies introduce some degree of error by using a variety of interviewers.[10]

The large number of close-ended questions provided two advantages. First, it sped up the interview, permitting the collection of more information on a larger number of reforms than would otherwise have been possible. Second, numerical responses meant that researchers did not have to interpret the responses for the purpose of systematic analysis. Asking respondents to apply numbers and labels to matters that they are used to thinking about qualitatively imposes different problems, but those are offset by the opportunity to reduce the researcher's role in creating the data for analysis.

Other features could have biased the findings but presented no noticeable problems. These were the length of the study, the time when the study was conducted, and possible question-order effects. Bias can result when a systematic relationship between an explanatory variable and the dependent variable is produced by the method of data collection.[11] The interviewing process took nine months. During that extended period changes in the nation, in my interviewing, or in the phase of the school year could have systematically biased the results if I had interviewed certain types of districts at different stages in the project. However, analysis by time period shows

10. Fowler and Mangione (1990).
11. King, Keohane, and Verba (1994).

no evidence of time-induced bias.

Concerns about time-related biases were alleviated by the timing of the project. The year 1995 featured three elements that reduced the possibility that a national contagion impacted the educational scene and obscured the effects of local behavior in the sample. First, 1995 featured no national elections, reducing the chance that the education agenda would be buffeted by national politics. Second, 1995 was a year marked by the first Republican Congress in forty years, so the media focused extensively on Washington politics. Third, 1995 featured no major national reports or studies on education. Any of these might have dramatically remade the education agenda in mid-study.

Question-order bias is always a concern when conducting a survey, but previous research has shown that biases are usually significant only when questions encourage certain responses or expose explicit contradictions in responses.[12] In a survey such as this, which focused more on recollections than on opinions, those kinds of concerns are minimal.

12. Schuman and Presser (1981).

Appendix B

List of Districts Studied

School district in study[a]	Permanent community sample city
Akron City School District	Akron, Ohio
Albany City Schools	Albany, New York
Amarillo Independent School District	Amarillo, Texas
Atlanta City School District	Atlanta, Georgia
Baltimore City Public School System	Baltimore, Maryland
Berkeley Unified	Berkeley, California
Birmingham City	Birmingham, Alabama
Monroe County Community School Corporation	Bloomington, Indiana
Boston School District	Boston, Massachusetts
Buffalo City Schools	Buffalo, New York
Cambridge School District	Cambridge, Massachusetts
Mecklenburg County	Charlotte, North Carolina
Clifton City	Clifton, New Jersey
Dallas Independent School District	Dallas, Texas
Detroit City School District	Detroit, Michigan
Duluth School District	Duluth, Minnesota
Euclid City School District	Euclid, Ohio
Fort Worth Independent School District	Fort Worth, Texas
Fullerton Elementary	Fullerton, California
Gary Community School Corporation	Gary, Indiana
Hamilton County School District	Hamilton, Ohio
Hammond City Schools	Hammond, Indiana
Houston Independent School District	Houston, Texas
Indianapolis Public Schools	Indianapolis, Indiana
Irvington Township	Irvington, New Jersey
Duval County School District	Jacksonville, Florida
Long Beach Unified	Long Beach, California
Malden School District	Malden, Massachusetts
Manchester School District	Manchester, New Hampshire
Memphis City School District	Memphis, Tennessee
Milwaukee School District	Milwaukee, Wisconsin
Minneapolis Special School District	Minneapolis, Minnesota
Newark City	Newark, New Jersey

School district in study[a]	Permanent community sample city
Palo Alto Unified	Palo Alto, California
Pasadena Unified	Pasadena, California
Philadelphia City School District	Philadelphia, Pennsylvania
Phoenix Unified High School District 210	Phoenix, Arizona
Pittsburgh School District	Pittsburgh, Pennsylvania
Saint Louis City School District	Saint Louis, Missouri
Saint Paul School District	Saint Paul, Minnesota
Pinellas County School District	Saint Petersburg, Florida
Salt Lake City School District	Salt Lake City, Utah
San Antonio Independent School District	San Antonio, Texas
San Francisco City/County Unified	San Francisco, California
Santa Ana Unified	Santa Ana, California
San Jose Unified	San Jose, California
Santa Monica-Malibu Unified	Santa Monica, California
Schenectady City Schools	Schenectady, New York
Seattle	Seattle, Washington
South Bend Community School Corporation	South Bend, Indiana
Hillsborough County School District	Tampa, Florida
Tyler Independent School District	Tyler, Texas
Utica City Schools	Utica, New York
Waco Independent School District	Waco, Texas
Warren Consolidated Schools	Warren, Michigan
Waterbury School District	Waterbury, Connecticut
Waukegan County Unified School District 60	Waukegan, Illinois

a. As identified by the U.S. Department of Education (1995).

Appendix C

Summary Data on Respondents

Table C-1. Years Respondent Spent Following Local School Affairs

Type of respondent	Mean number of years	Minimum	Maximum
School administrator	20.2	2	50
School board member	19.3	3	48
Union director	23.4	3	55
Journalist	3.9	1	18
Business community respondent	13.9	1	40
Minority group respondent	20.3	5	46
Total	16.7	1	55

Table C-2. Tenure of Respondent in Current Position

Type of respondent	Mean number of years	Minimum	Maximum
School administrator	6.5	0	32
School board member	6.8	1	24
Union director	6.8	0	26
Journalist	3.8	0	23
Business community respondent	6.8	1	24
Minority group respondent	8.2	1	36
Total	6.0	0	36

Table C-3. Positions Held by Each Type of Respondent

Position of respondent	Number of respondents
School administrators	
Deputy, assistant, or area superintendent	29
Program director/coordinator	10
Superintendent	7
Other	5
Administrative assistant	2
Total	53
Board member	
Board member	27
Board president	15
Board vice president	9
Immediate past president (now member)	4
Total	55
Union director	
President	45
Executive director	7
Immediate past president	2
Assistant to president	1
Total	58
Journalist	
Education reporter	24
Staff writer	24
Editor/assistant editor	9
Total	57
Local business group respondent[a]	
President	17
Education director/chairman/vice president	11
Vice president	8
Executive director, manager, or chairman	6
Other	6
Consultant	4
Board member	3
Total	55
Local minority group respondent[b]	
President or chairman	28
Director or executive secretary	5
Education chairman	6
Other	4
Past president	2
Local preacher	2
Total	47

a. Affiliation: Chamber of Commerce, 43; local committee, 8; others 4.
b. Affiliation: NAACP, 19; Urban League, 9; other black organization, 5; Hispanic organization, 5; other, 4; school-led organization, 3; and community organization, 2.

Appendix D

OLS Regression Results for Chapter 6

Explanatory variable	Number of reform proposals	Attention to reform	Controversy over reform	Perceived district performance
Intercept	−3.60 (2.10)	−20.75 (11.36)	−31.46 (15.97)	−4.70 (3.66)
Adult high school completion rate	2.61 (1.16)	14.21 (6.29)	9.87 (8.83)	5.24 (2.03)
Poverty rate	3.80 (1.83)	−8.84 (9.93)	19.40 (13.96)	−8.22 (3.20)
Black population percentage in the district	−1.36 (0.57)	4.93 (3.09)	−6.42 (4.34)	0.27 (0.99)
Change in retail sales, 1987–92	0.73 (0.59)	11.61 (3.19)	13.03 (4.48)	0.60 (1.03)
Number of students in system	0.12 (0.02)	0.45 (0.12)	0.43 (0.17)	−0.03 (0.04)
Percentage of district students enrolled in public schools	3.19 (1.82)	28.75 (9.84)	31.55 (13.83)	8.42 (3.17)
Per pupil expenditures	0.14 (0.07)	0.21 (0.41)	0.47 (0.57)	0.04 (0.13)
Number of observations	51	51	51	51
Adjusted R^2	0.39	0.53	0.36	0.42

Note: Standard errors are presented in parentheses.

References

The Advocate (Baton Rouge). 1997. "Class Time for EBR Schools." June 3, 6B.

Aldrich, Howard, and Peter Marsden. 1988. "Environment and Organizations." In *Handbook of Sociology*, 6th ed., edited by Neil J. Smelser, 31–92. Sage.

Altshuler, Alan A. 1997. "Bureaucratic Innovation, Democratic Accountability, and Political Incentives." In *Innovation in American Government*, edited by Alan A. Altshuler and Robert D. Behn, 38–67. Brookings.

Anderson, Lorin W., and J. Robert Shirley. 1995. "High School Principals and School Reform: Lessons Learned from a Statewide Survey of Project Re: Learning." *Educational Administration Quarterly* 31: 405–23.

Ansolabehere, Stephen, Roy Behr, and Shanto Iyengar. 1993. *The Media Game*. MacMillan.

Anyon, Jean. 1997. *Ghetto Schooling: A Political Economy of Urban Educational Reform*. New York: Teachers' College Press.

Arnold, R. Douglas. 1990. *The Logic of Congressional Action*. Yale University Press.

Avenoso, Karen. 1996. "Boston Students Lag in Tests." *Boston Globe*, June 25, 1.

Bacharach, Samuel, ed. 1990. *Education Reform: Making Sense of It All*. Boston: Allyn and Bacon.

Banfield, Edward C., and James Q. Wilson. 1963. *City Politics*. Harvard University Press.

Barth, Roland S. 1980. *Run School Run*. Harvard University Press.

———. 1991. "Restructuring Schools: Some Questions for Teachers and Principals." *Phi Delta Kappan* 73: 123–28.

Baumgartner, Frank R. 1989. *Conflict and Rhetoric in French Policymaking*. University of Pittsburgh Press.

Baumgartner, Frank R., and Bryan D. Jones. 1993. *Agendas and Instability in American Politics*. University of Chicago Press.

Bennett, David. 1991. "Big-City Blues." *American School Board Journal* 178: 22–24.

Berliner, David, and Bruce Biddle. 1995. *The Manufactured Crisis: Myths, Fraud and the Attack on America's Public Schools*. Addison-Wesley.

Berman, David, and Lawrence Martin. 1992. "The New Approach to Economic Development: An Analysis of Innovativeness in the States." *Policy Studies Journal* 20: 10–21.

Berry, Frances, and William Berry. 1990. "State Lottery Adoptions as Policy Innovations: An Event History Analysis." *American Political Science Review* 84: 395–415.

———. 1992. "Tax Innovation in the States: Capitalizing on Political Opportunity." *American Journal of Political Science* 36: 715–42.

Bierlein, Louann A. 1993. *Controversial Issues in Educational Policy.* Sage.

———. 1997. "The Charter School Movement." In *New Schools for a New Century: The Redesign of Urban Education*, edited by Diane Ravitch and Joseph P. Viteritti, 37–60. Yale University Press.

Blase, Joseph, and Gary L. Anderson. 1995. *The Micropolitics of Educational Leadership: From Control to Empowerment.* Cassell.

Bourisaw, Diana, and Serena Berry. 1996. "From Dinosaurs to Decision-making." *Thrust for Educational Leadership* 25: 22–24.

Boyd, William L. 1978. "The Changing Politics of Curriculum Policy Making for American Schools." *Review of Educational Research* 48: 577–628.

Bridge, Gary. 1978. "Information Imperfections: The Achilles' Heel of Entitlement Plans." *School Review* 86: 504–29.

Brint, Steven, and Jerome Karabel. 1991. "Institutional Origins and Transformations: The Case of American Community Colleges." In *The New Institutionalism in Organizational Analysis*, edited by Walter W. Powell and Paul J. Dimaggio, 337–60. University of Chicago Press.

Brody, Richard. 1991. *Assessing the President: The Media, Elite Opinion, and Public Support.* Stanford University Press.

Brouillette, Liane. 1996. *A Geology of School Reform: The Successive Restructurings of a School District.* State University of New York Press.

Bryk, Anthony S., and others. 1993. *A View from the Elementary Schools: Reform in Chicago.* Consortium on Chicago School Research, University of Chicago.

Bryk, Anthony S., Valerie Lee, and Peter Holland. 1993. *Catholic Schools and the Common Good.* Harvard University Press.

Cannell, John. 1987. *Nationally Normed Elementary Achievement Testing in America's Public Schools:* Princeton, N.J.: Eye on Education.

Canon, Bradley, and Lawrence Blum. 1981. "Patterns of Adoption of Tort Law Innovations: An Application of Diffusion Theory to Judicial Doctrines." *American Political Science Review* 75: 975–87.

Carmines, Edward, and James Stimson. 1989. *Issue Evolution: Race and the Transformation of American Politics.* Princeton University Press.

Carter, Gene, and William Cunningham. 1997. *The American School Superintendent: Leading in an Age of Pressure.* San Francisco: Jossey-Bass.

Chase, Bob. 1996. "Do Teacher Unions Have a Positive Influence on the Educational System?" *Washington Times,* October 21, 24.

Chicago Tribune. 1997. "A State Wind in Springfield." November 18, 16.

Chrispeels, Janet H. 1997. "Educational Policy Implementation in a Shifting Political Climate: The California Experience." *American Educational Research Journal* 34: 453–81.

Chubb, John, and Terry Moe. 1990. *Politics, Markets, and America's Schools*. Brookings.

Cibulka, James G., and Frederick I. Olsen. 1993. "The Organization and Politics of the Milwaukee Public School System, 1920–1986." In *Seeds of Crisis: Public Schooling in Milwaukee since 1920*, edited by John L. Rury and Frank A. Cassell, 73–109. University of Wisconsin Press.

Clark, David L., and Terry A. Astuto. 1994. "Redirecting Reform: Challenges to Popular Assumptions about Teachers and Students." *Phi Delta Kappan* 75: 513–20.

Clark, Terry N. 1968. "Community Structure, Decision-making, Budget Expenditures, and Urban Renewal in Fifty-One American Communities." *American Sociological Review* 33: 576–93.

Clark, Terry N., and Lorna C. Ferguson. 1983. *City Money: Political Processes, Fiscal Strain, and Retrenchment*. Columbia University Press.

Clarke, John, and Russell Agne. 1997. *Interdisciplinary High School Teaching: Strategies for Integrated Learning*. Boston: Allyn and Bacon.

Clotfelter, Charles T., and Helen F. Ladd. 1996. "Recognizing and Rewarding Success in Public Schools." In *Holding Schools Accountable: Performance-Based Reform in Education*, edited by Helen F. Ladd, 23–63. Brookings.

Cohen, David K. 1996a. "Rewarding Teachers for Student Performance." In *Rewards and Reform*, edited by Susan H. Fuhrman and Jennifer A. O'Day, 60–112. San Francisco: Jossey-Bass.

———. 1996b. "Standards-Based School Reform: Policy, Practice, and Performance." In *Holding Schools Accountable: Performance-Based Reform in Education*, edited by Helen F. Ladd, 99–127. Brookings.

Cohen, Michael D., and James G. March. 1986. *Leadership and Ambiguity: The American College President*. 2d ed. Harvard Business School Press.

Coleman, James S., and others. 1966. *Equality of Educational Opportunity*. Washington, D.C.: U.S. Office of Education.

Consortium for Policy Research in Education. 1996. *Public Policy and School Reform: A Research Summary*. University of Pennsylvania, Graduate School of Education.

Council of Great City Schools. 1992. *Superintendent Characteristics*. Washington, D.C.

Crain, Robert, Elihu Katz, and Donald Rosenthal. 1969. *The Politics of Community Conflict: The Fluoridation Decision*. Indianapolis: Bobbs-Merrill.

Crains Cleveland Business. 1995. "Thankless Job." February 27, 10.

Crenson, Matthew. 1983. *Neighborhood Politics*. Harvard University Press.

Cuban, Larry. 1976. *Urban School Chiefs under Fire*. University of Chicago Press.

———. 1984. *How Teachers Taught: Constancy and Change in American Classrooms, 1890–1980*. Longman Press.

————. 1988. *The Managerial Imperative and the Practice of Leadership in Schools.* State University of New York Press.

————. 1995. "Hedgehogs and Foxes among Educational Researchers." *The Journal of Educational Research* 89: 6–12.

Danzberger, Jacqueline P. 1994. "Governing the Nation's Schools: The Case for Restructuring Local School Boards." *Phi Delta Kappan* 75: 367–73.

Danzberger, Jacqueline P., and Michael D. Usdan. 1992. "Strengthening a Grass Roots American Institution: The School Board." In *School Boards: Changing Local Control*, edited by Patricia F. First and Herbert J. Walberg, 91–124. Berkeley, Calif.: McCutchan Publishing.

Darling-Hammond, Linda. 1996. "Restructuring Schools for High Performance." In *Rewards and Reform*, edited by Susan H. Fuhrman and Jennifer A. O'Day, 144–92. San Francisco: Jossey-Bass.

David, Jane. 1989. *Restructuring in Process: Lessons from Pioneering Districts.* Washington, D.C.: National Governors' Association.

Deal, Terence E., and Kent D. Patterson. 1994. *The Leadership Paradox.* San Francisco: Jossey-Bass.

Doll, Ronald. 1996. *Curriculum Improvement: Decision Making and Process.* Boston: Allyn and Bacon.

Donnelly, James, James Gibson, and John J. Ivancevich. 1981. *Fundamentals of Management: Function, Behavior, Models.* Plano, Texas: Business Publications.

Doyle, Dennis P., and Terry Hartle. 1985. *Excellence in Education: The States Take Charge.* Washington, D.C.: American Enterprise Institute.

Doyle, Dennis P., Bruce S. Cooper, and Roberta Trachtman. 1991. *Taking Charge: State Action on School Reform in the 1980s.* Indianapolis: Hudson Institute.

Driscoll, Mary. 1996. "Book Review of the Politics of Curriculum and Testing." *The Journal of Education Finance* 21: 419–31.

Duchensne, Paul Drew. 1998. "School Board's Feuds Taking Toll, Trustees Say Tensions Blamed for Lack of Focus on Key Issues." *The Dallas Morning News*, February 1, 39A.

Eberts, Randall W., and Joe A. Stone. 1984. *Unions and Public Schools.* Lexington, Mass.: Lexington Books.

Edelman, Murray. 1972. *The Symbolic Uses of Politics.* University of Illinois Press.

Elam, Stanley, ed. 1978. *A Decade of Gallup Polls of Attitudes toward Education, 1969–1978.* Bloomington, Ind.: Phi Delta Kappa.

Elam, Stanley, Lowell Rose, and Alec Gallup. 1994. "The Twenty-Sixth Annual Phi Delta Kappa/Gallup Poll of the Public's Attitudes toward the Public Schools." *Phi Delta Kappan* 76: 41–64.

Elmore, Richard F. 1991a. "Innovation in Education Policy." Paper prepared for the Conference on Fundamental Questions of Innovation, Duke University, November 7–8.

————. 1991b. "Teaching, Learning, and Organization: School Restructuring and the Recurring Dilemmas of Reform." Paper presented at the annual meeting of the American Educational Research Association, Chicago, April 3–7.

————. 1996. "Getting to Scale with Good Educational Practice." *Harvard Educational Review* 66: 1–26.

————. 1997. "The Paradox of Innovation in Education: Cycles of Reform and the Resilience of Teaching." In *Innovation in American Government*, edited by Alan A. Altshuler and Robert D. Behn, 24–73. Brookings.

Elmore, Richard F., Penelope Peterson, and Sarah McCarthy. 1996. *Restructuring in the Classroom: Teaching, Learning, and School Organization*. San Francisco: Jossey-Bass.

Fagan, Alex. 1997. "Factions Must Unite to Upgrade City Schools." *Richmond Times Dispatch*, April 6, F-1.

Farah, Barbara, and E. Elda Vale. 1985. "Crime: A Tale of Two Cities." *Public Opinion* 8: 57–58.

Finn, Chester. 1991. *We Must Take Charge: Our Schools and Our Future*. Free Press.

————. 1992. "Reinventing Local Control." In *School Boards: Changing Local Control*, edited by Patricia F. First and Herbert J. Walberg, 21–25. Berkeley, Calif.: McCutchan Publishing.

————. 1997. "The Politics of Change." In *New Schools for a New Century: The Redesign of Urban Education*, edited by Diane Ravitch and Joseph P. Viteritti, 226–50. Yale University Press.

Firestone, William, Susan Fuhrman, and Michael W. Kirst. 1991. "State Educational Reform since 1983: Appraisal and the Future." *Educational Policy* 5: 233–50.

Fiske, Edward B. 1984. "States Gain Wider Influence on School Policy." *New York Times*, December 2, 1:1.

Fowler, Floyd, and Thomas Mangione. 1990. *Standardized Survey Interviewing: Minimizing Interviewer-Related Error*. Sage.

Freire, Paulo. 1970. "Cultural Action and Conscientization." *Harvard Educational Review* 40: 452–77.

Friedman, Milton. 1982. *Capitalism and Freedom*. University of Chicago Press.

Fullan, Michael. 1991. *The New Meaning of Educational Change*. New York: Teachers' College Press.

————. 1993. *Change Forces: Probing the Depths of Educational Reform*. London: Falber Press.

Fuhrman, Susan, William Clune, and Richard F. Elmore. 1991. "Research on Education Reform: Lessons on the Implementation of Policy." In *Educational Policy Implementation*, edited by Allan R. Odden, 197–218. State University of New York Press.

Gallegos, Gene. 1996. "Transforming America's Schools." *Thrust for Educational Leadership* 25: 26–27.

Gergen, David. 1997. "Chasing Better Schools." *U.S. News and World Report*, December 8, 100.

Ginsberg, Rick, and Robert Wimpelberg. 1987. "Educational Change by Commission: Attempting Trickle Down Reform." *Educational Evaluation and Policy Analysis* 9: 344–60.

Glasman, Naftaly, and Lynette Glasman. 1990. "Evaluation: Catalyst for or Response to Change?" In *Education Reform: Making Sense of It All*, edited by Samuel B. Bacharach, 392–99. Boston: Allyn and Bacon.

Glick, Henry. 1981. "Innovation in State Judicial Administration: Effects on Court Management and Organization." *American Politics Quarterly* 9: 49–69.

Gray, Virginia. 1973a. "Innovation in the States: A Diffusion Study." *American Political Science Review* 67: 1174–85.

————. 1973b. "Rejoinder to Comment by Jack L. Walker." *American Political Science Review* 67: 1192–93.

Greenfield, William D. 1995. "Toward a Theory of School Administration: The Centrality of Leadership." *Educational Administration Quarterly* 31: 61–85.

Gunn, Elizabeth. 1993. "The Growth of Enterprise Zones: A Policy Transformation." *Policy Studies Journal* 21: 432–49.

Gutmann, Amy. 1987. *Democratic Education*. Princeton University Press.

Hanson, Mark. 1996. *Educational Administration and Organizational Behavior*. Boston: Allyn and Bacon.

Hay Group. 1996. "Change: Everybody's Doing It, but Not Many Doing It Well." Washington, D.C. http://www.haygroup.com.

Hearn, James C., and Carolyn P. Griswold. 1994. "State Level Centralization and Policy Innovation in U.S. Postsecondary Education." *Educational Evaluation and Policy Analysis* 16 (2): 161–90.

Heclo, Hugh. 1977. *A Government of Strangers: Executive Politics in Washington*. Brookings.

————. 1978. "Issue Networks and the Executive Establishment. In *The New American Political System*, edited by Anthony King, 87–123. Washington, D.C.: American Enterprise Institute.

Hennessey, Ann, and Theodore Kowalski. 1996. "Working with the Media." In *Public Relations in Educational Organizations: Practice in an Age of Information and Reform*, edited by Theodore J. Kowalski, 210–25. Prentice-Hall.

Hersey, Paul, and Kenneth Blanchard. 1977. *Management of Organizational Behavior: Utilizing Human Resources*. Prentice-Hall.

Hertert, Linda. 1996. "Systemic School Reform in the 1980s: A Local Perspective." *Educational Policy* 10 (3): 379–98.

Hess, Frederick M. 1995. "The Effects of Social Class on Views of Schooling: Implications for School Choice." Paper presented at the American Political Association annual meeting, Chicago, August 31–September 3.

Hess, Frederick M., and Robert F. McNergney. 1998. "Electronic School: Fitting Technology to Local Educational Needs." *American School Board Journal* (March): A30–33.

Hill, Paul T. 1995. *Reinventing Public Education*. Santa Monica, Calif.: RAND Corporation Institute on Education and Training.

————. 1997. "Contracting in Public Education." In *New Schools for a New Century: The Redesign of Urban Education*, edited by Diane Ravitch and Joseph P. Viteritti, 61–85. Yale University Press.

Hill, Paul T., Gail Foster, and Tamar Gendler. 1990. *High Schools with Character*. Santa Monica, Calif.: RAND Corporation.

Hill, Paul T., Lawrence C. Pierce, and James W. Guthrie. 1997. *Reinventing Public Education: How Contracting Can Transform America's Schools.* University of Chicago Press.

Hirsch, E. D. 1987. *Cultural Literacy: What Every American Needs to Know.* Houghton Mifflin.

Holland, Holly. 1994. "Experts Tell School Leaders to Find Unified Vision, Lead Community to It." *Courier-Journal* (Louisville, Ky.), February 2, 2B.

Hoxby, Caroline M. 1996. "How Teachers' Unions Affect Education Production." *Quarterly Journal of Economics* 111: 671–718.

Iannaccone, Laurence, and Frank W. Lutz. 1995. "The Crucible of Democracy: The Local Arena." In *The Study of Educational Politics,* edited by Jay D. Scribner and Donald H. Layton, 39–52. Washington, D.C.: Falmer Press.

Institute for Educational Leadership. 1986. *School Boards: Strengthening Grass Roots Leadership.* Washington, D.C.

Johnson, Gary R., and Naftaly S. Glasman. 1983. "Evaluation Authority and Financial Control: A Study of State Mandates." *Studies in Educational Evaluation* 9 (1): 59–76.

Johnson, Margaret J., and Frank Pajares. 1996. "When Shared Decision Making Works: A Three-Year Longitudinal Study." *American Educational Research Journal* 33: 599–627.

Johnson, Susan Moore. 1996. *Leading to Change: The Challenge of the New Superintendency.* San Francisco: Jossey-Bass.

Jones, Bryan D. 1983. *Governing Urban America: A Policy Focus.* Little, Brown.

———. 1994. *Reconceiving Decision-making in Democratic Politics.* University of Chicago Press.

Kaplan, Fred. 1996. "For Bratton, A New Beat." *Boston Globe,* February 7, 3.

Katznelson, Ira, and Margaret Weir. 1985. *Schooling for All: Class, Race, and the Decline of the Democratic Ideal.* Basic Books.

Kaufhold, Jack. 1993. "What They Don't Teach Superintendents in Graduate School." *The School Administrator* 50: 40–42.

Khator, Renu. 1993. "Recycling: A Policy Dilemma for American States." *Policy Studies Journal* 21: 210–26.

King, Gary, Robert Keohane, and Sidney Verba. 1994. *Designing Social Inquiry: Scientific Inferences in Qualitative Research.* Princeton University Press.

Kingdon, John W. 1984. *Agendas, Alternatives, and Public Policies.* Glenview, Ill.: Scott Foresman.

Kirp, David L., and Cyrus E. Driver. 1995. "The Aspirations of Systemic Reform Meet the Realities of Localism." *Educational Administration Quarterly* 31: 589–612.

Kirst, Michael W. 1990. "The Crash of the First Wave." In *Education Reform: Making Sense of It All,* edited by Samuel B. Bacharach, 20–29. Boston: Allyn and Bacon.

Kirst, Michael W., and Gail Meister. 1985. "Turbulence in American Secondary Schools: What Reforms Last?" *Curriculum Inquiry* 15: 69–186.

Kirst, Michael W., and Richard Jung. 1991. "The Utility of a Longitudinal Approach in Assessing Implementation: A Thirteen-Year View of Title I, ESEA."

In *Education Policy Implementation*, edited by Allan R. Odden, 39–63. State University of New York Press.

Koretz, Daniel. 1990. "Educational Practices and Test Scores: The Search for the Missing Link." In *Education Reform: Making Sense of It All*, edited by Samuel B. Bacharach, 382–91. Boston: Allyn and Bacon.

Kowalski, Theodore J. 1995. *Keepers of the Flame: Contemporary Urban Superintendents*. Thousand Oaks, Calif.: Corwin Press.

Kritek, William, and Delbert Clear. 1993. "Teachers and Principals in the Milwaukee Public Schools." In *Seeds of Crisis: Public Schooling in Milwaukee since 1920*, edited by John L. Rury and Frank A Cassell, 145–92. University of Wisconsin Press.

Kyle, Regina M. 1993. *Transforming our Schools: Lessons from the Jefferson County Public Schools/Gheen Professional Development Academy, 1983–1991*. Louisville, Ky.: Jefferson County Public Schools.

Ladd, Helen F. 1996. "Introduction." In *Holding Schools Accountable*, edited by Helen F. Ladd, 1–19. Brookings.

Lakonishok, Josef, Andrei Shleifer, and Robert Vishny. 1992. "The Structure and Performance of the Money Management Industry." In *Brookings Papers on Economic Activity: Microeconomics*, edited by Martin N. Baily and Clifford Winston, 339–91. Brookings.

Lee, Valerie E. 1997. "Catholic Lessons for Public Schools." In *New Schools for a New Century: The Redesign of Urban Education*, edited by Diane Ravitch and Joseph P. Viteritti, 147–63. Yale University Press.

Lee, Valerie E., and Julia B. Smith. 1994. "Effects of High School Restructuring and Size on Gains in Achievement and Engagement for Early Secondary School Students." Madison, Wis.: Wisconsin Center for Education Research.

Lewis, Anne C. 1996. "Urban Middle-Grades Reform: Foundations Keep Trying." *Harvard Education Letter* 11 (4): 5–6.

Lezotte, Lawrence. 1992. "Learn from Effective Schools." *Social Policy* 22: 34–36.

Lieberman, Myron. 1993. *Public Education: An Autopsy*. Harvard University Press.

———. 1997. *The Teacher Unions: How the NEA and AFT Sabotage Reform and Hold Students, Parents, Teachers, and Taxpayers Hostage to Bureaucracy*. Free Press.

Light, Paul. 1983. *The President's Agenda: Domestic Policy Choice from Kennedy to Carter*. Johns Hopkins University Press.

Lightfoot, Sara Lawrence. 1983. *The Good High School: Portraits of Character and Culture*. Basic Books.

Los Angeles Times. 1996. "Oakland School Board Tries to Redefine Ebonics Issue." December 31, 8A.

Louis, Karen S., and Matthew B. Miles. 1991. "Toward Effective Urban High Schools: The Importance of Planning and Coping." In *Rethinking Effective Schools: Research and Practice*, edited by James R. Bliss, William A. Firestone, and Craig E. Richards, 91–111. Prentice-Hall.

Lynn, Laurence. 1981. *Managing the Public's Business*. Basic Books.

MacIver, Douglas J. 1992. "Scheduling and School Organization." In *Encyclope-*

dia of Educational Research, 6th ed., edited by Marvin Alkin and others. MacMillan.

Magat, Richard. 1995. "Unions and Foundations as Public Policy Actors." *Policy Studies Review* 14: 161–70.

Malen, Betty, Rodney T. Ogawa, and Jennifer Kranz. 1990. "What Do We Know about School-Based Management? A Case Study of the Literature—A Call for Research." In *Choice and Control in American Education.* Vol. 2: *The Practice of Choice, Decentralization, and Restructuring,* edited by William H. Clune and John F. Witte, 289–342. Washington, D.C.: Falmer Press.

March, James G., and Johan P. Olsen. 1987. *Ambiguity and Choice in Organizations.* Oslo, Norway: Universitetsforlaget.

Marsh, David D., and Allan R. Odden. 1991. "Implementation of the California Mathematics and Science Curriculum Frameworks." In *Education Policy Implementation,* edited by Allan R. Odden, 219–39. State University of New York Press.

Marsh, David D., and Patricia S. Crocker. 1991. "School Restructuring: Implementing Middle School Reform." In *Education Policy Implementation,* edited by Allan R. Odden, 259–78. State University of New York Press.

Mayhew, David. 1974. *Congress: The Electoral Connection.* Yale University Press.

McCarthy, Martha M. 1994. "The Courts and School Finance Reform." *Theory into Practice* 33 (2): 89–97.

McCrone, Donald J., and Charles F. Cnudde. 1969. "Party Competition and Welfare Policies in the American States." *American Political Science Review* 63: 858–66.

McLaughlin, Judith B., and David Reisman. 1990. *Choosing a College President: Opportunities and Constraints.* Princeton, N.J.: Carnegie Foundation for the Advancement of Teaching.

McLaughlin, Milbrey. 1991a. "Learning from Experience: Lessons from Policy Implementation." In *Education Policy Implementation,* edited by Allan R. Odden, 185–95. State University of New York Press.

———. 1991b. "The Rand Change Agent Study: Ten Years Later." In *Education Policy Implementation,* edited by Allan R. Odden, 143–55. State University of New York Press.

Medley, Donald M. 1992. "Teacher Evaluation." In *Encyclopedia of Educational Research,* 6th ed., edited by Marvin Alkin and others. MacMillan.

Meier, Kenneth J., and Joseph Stewart Jr. 1991. *The Politics of Hispanic Education.* State University of New York Press.

Menzel, Donald, and Irwin Feller. 1977. "Leadership and Interaction Patterns in the Diffusion of Innovation among the American States." *Western Politics Quarterly* 30: 528–36.

Meranto, Philip. 1970. *School Politics in the Metropolis.* Columbus, Ohio: Charles E. Merrill Publishing.

Meyer, John W., and Brian Rowan. 1991. "Institutionalized Organizations: Formal Structure as Myth and Ceremony." In *The New Institutionalism in Organizational Analysis,* edited by Walter W. Powell and Paul J. DiMaggio, 41–62. University of Chicago Press.

218   REFERENCES

Miller, Edward. 1992. "Breaking the Tyranny of the Schedule." *The Harvard Education Letter* 8: 6–8.
———. 1996. "Idealists and Cynics: The Micropolitics of Systemic School Reform." *The Harvard Education Letter* 12: 1–3.
Millott, Marc D., and Robin Lake. 1996. *So You Want to Start a Charter School?* Seattle: University of Washington Institute for Public Policy Management.
Mirel, Jeffrey. 1994. "School Reform Unplugged: The Bensensville New American School Project, 1991–93." *American Educational Research Journal* 31: 481–518.
Mitchell, Susan. 1994. "Why MPS Doesn't Work: Barriers to Reform in the Milwaukee Public Schools." Milwaukee, Wis.: Milwaukee Policy Research Institute.
Mohr, Lawrence. 1969. "Determinants of Innovation in Organizations." *American Political Science Review* 63: 111–26.
Mohrman, Susan A., and Edward E. Lawler. 1996. "Motivation for School Reform." In *Rewards and Reform*, edited by Susan H. Fuhrman and Jennifer A. O'Day, 115–43. San Francisco: Jossey-Bass.
Muncey, Donna E., and Patrick J. McQuillan. 1993. *Reform and Resistance in Schools and Classrooms: An Ethnographic View of the Coalition of Essential Schools*. Yale University Press.
Murphy, Joseph. 1991. *Restructuring Schools: Capturing and Assessing the Phenomena*. New York: Teachers' College Press.
Murphy, Joseph, and Lynn G. Beck. 1995. *School-Based Management as School Reform: Taking Stock*. Thousand Oaks, Calif.: Corwin Press.
Nakamura, Robert. 1991. "Environmental Dispute Resolution and Hazardous Waste Cleanups: A Cautionary Tale of Policy Implementation." *Journal of Policy Analysis and Management* 10: 204–21.
Nathan, Joe. 1996. *Charter Schools: Creating Hope and Opportunity for American Education*. San Francisco: Jossey-Bass.
Neustadt, Richard. 1990. *Presidential Power and the Modern Presidents: The Politics of Leadership from Roosevelt to Reagan*. Free Press.
Newmann, Fred M., M. Bruce King, and Mark Rigdon. 1997. "Accountability and School Performance: Implications from Restructuring Schools." *Harvard Educational Review* 67: 41–74.
Newmann, Fred M. 1991. "Student Engagement in Academic Work: Expanding the Perspective on Secondary School Effectiveness." In *Rethinking Effective Schools: Research and Practice*, edited by James R. Bliss, William A. Firestone, and Craig E. Richards, 58–75. Prentice-Hall.
Nieto, Sonia. 1992. *Affirming Diversity: The Sociopolitical Context of Multicultural Education*. Longman.
Norton, M. Scott, and others. 1996. *The School Superintendency: New Responsibilities, New Leadership*. Boston: Allyn and Bacon.
O'Day, Jennifer A. 1996. "Introduction: Incentives and School Improvement." In *Rewards and Reform*, edited by Susan H. Fuhrman, and Jennifer A. O'Day, 1–16. San Francisco: Jossey-Bass.
O'Day, Jennifer, and Marshall S. Smith. 1991."Systemic School Reform." In *The Politics of Curriculum and Testing: The 1990 Yearbook of the Political Educa-*

tion Association, edited by Susan H. Fuhrman and Betty Malen, 233–67. New York: Falmer Press.

Odden, Allan R. 1991a. "The Evolution of Education Policy Implementation." In *Education Policy Implementation*, edited by Allan R. Odden, 1–12. State University of New York Press.

———. 1991b. "New Patterns of Education Policy Implementation and Challenges for the 1990s." In *Education Policy Implementation*, edited by Allan R. Odden, 297–327. State University of New York Press.

Odden, Allan R., and William Clune. 1995. "Improving Education Productivity and School Finance." *Educational Researcher* 24 (9): 6–10.

OECD (Organization for Economic Cooperation and Development). 1996. *Knowledge Bases for Education Policies*. Paris, France.

Ogawa, Rodney T. 1994. "The Institutional Sources of Educational Reform: The Case of School-Based Management." *American Educational Research Journal* 31: 519–48.

Olson, Lynn, and Robert Rothman. 1993. "Roadmap to Reform." *Education Week* 12, April 21. Supp. 13–17.

Opheim, Cynthia. 1991. "Explaining the Differences in State Lobby Regulations." *Western Politics Quarterly* 44: 405–21.

Orfield, Gary, and Carole Ashkinaze. 1991. *The Closing Door: Conservative Policy and Black Opportunity*. University of Chicago Press.

Orlich, Donald. 1989. "Education Reforms: Mistakes, Misconceptions, Miscues." *Phi Delta Kappan* 70 (2): 512–17.

Ornstein, Allan, and Francis Hunkins. 1993. *Curriculum: Foundations, Principles, and Theory*. Boston: Allyn and Bacon.

Passow, A. Harry. 1990. "How It Happened, Wave by Wave." In *Education Reform: Making Sense of It All*, edited by Samuel B. Bacharach, 10–19. Boston: Allyn and Bacon.

Patterson, Thomas. 1994. *Out of Order*. Vintage Books.

Pauly, Edward. 1991. *The Classroom Crucible: What Really Works, What Doesn't, and Why*. Basic Books.

Peterson, Paul E. 1976. *School Politics Chicago Style*. University of Chicago Press.

———. 1991. "The Urban Underclass and the Poverty Paradox." In *The Urban Underclass*, edited by Christopher Jencks and Paul E. Peterson, 3–27. Brookings.

———. 1993. "Are Big City Schools Holding Their Own?" In *Seeds of Crisis: Public Schooling in Milwaukee since 1920*, edited by John L. Rury and Frank A. Cassell, 269–301. University of Wisconsin Press.

———. 1994. "The President's Dominance in Foreign Policy Making." *Political Science Quarterly* 109: 215–34.

Peterson, Paul E., Barry Rabe, and Kenneth Wong. 1991. "The Maturation of Redistributive Programs." In *Education Policy Implementation*, edited by Allan R. Odden, 65–80. State University of New York Press.

Pincus, John. 1974. "Incentives for Innovation in Public Schools." *Review of Educational Research* 44: 113–44.

Plank, David. 1988. "Why School Reform Doesn't Change Schools: Political and

Organizational Perspectives." In *The Politics of Excellence and Choice in Education*, edited by William L. Boyd and Charles T. Kerchner, 143–52. New York: Falmer Press.

Popkin, Samuel. 1991. *The Reasoning Voter: Communication and Persuasion in Presidential Campaigns*. University of Chicago Press.

Powell, Arthur, Eleanor Farrar, and David Cohen. 1985. *The Shopping Mall High School: Winners and Losers in the Educational Marketplace*. Houghton Mifflin.

Powell, Brian, and Lala Carr Steelman. 1996. "Bewitched, Bothered, and Bewildering: The Use and Misuse of State SAT and ACT Scores." *Harvard Educational Review* 66: 27–59.

Pressman, Jeffrey L., and Aaron Wildavsky. 1984. *Implementation*. University of California Press.

The Public Perspective. 1993. "U.S. Educational Performance: A Failing Grade." 5 (1): 3–14.

———. 1996. "Issues '96." 7 (6): 40–45.

Purkey, Stewart, and Marshall Smith. 1985. "School Reform: The District Policy Implications of the Effective Schools Literature." *The Elementary School Journal* 85: 353–89.

Ravitch, Diane. 1997. "Somebody's Children: Educational Opportunity for all American Children." In *New Schools for a New Century: The Redesign of Urban Education*, edited by Diane Ravitch and Joseph P. Viteritti, 251–74. Yale University Press.

Ravitch, Diane, and Joseph P. Viteritti. 1997. "The Obsolete Factory." In *New Schools for a New Century: The Redesign of Urban Education*, edited by Diane Ravitch and Joseph P. Viteritti, 17–36. Yale University Press.

Reitzug, Ulrich C., and Jennifer E. Reeves. 1992. "Miss Lincoln Doesn't Teach Here: A Descriptive Narrative and Conceptual Analysis of a Principal's Symbolic Leadership Behavior." *Educational Administration Quarterly* 28: 185–219.

Rich, Wilbur. 1996. *Black Mayors and School Politics: The Failure of Reform in Detroit, Gary, and Newark*. New York: Garland Publishing.

Ringquist, Evan. 1993. "Testing Theories of State Policy-Making: The Case of Air Quality Regulation." *American Politics Quarterly* 21: 320–42.

———. 1994. "Policy Influence and Policy Responsiveness in State Pollution Control." *Policy Studies Journal* 22: 25–43.

Roeder, Philip. 1979. "State Legislative Reform: Determinants and Policy." *American Politics Quarterly* 7: 51–70.

Rogers, David, and Norman Chung. 1983. *110 Livingston Street Revisited: Decentralization in Action*. New York University Press.

Rogers, Everett. 1962. *Diffusion of Innovations*. Free Press.

Rothman, Robert. 1988. "Teacher vs. Curriculum in Philadelphia." *Education Week* 7 (26): 20–22.

————. 1993. "Obstacle Course: Barriers to Change Thwart Reformers at Every Twist and Turn." *Education Week* 12 (20): 9–12.

Rury, John L. 1993. "The Changing Social Context of Urban Education: A National Perspective." In *Seeds of Crisis: Public Schooling in Milwaukee since 1920*, edited by John L. Rury and Frank A. Cassell, 10–41. University of Wisconsin Press.

Sabatier, Paul A. 1991. "Toward Better Theories of the Policy Process." *Political Science and Politics* 24: 147–56.

Sabatier, Paul A., and Daniel A. Mazamanian. 1981. "The Implementation of Public Policy: A Framework of Analysis." In *Effective Policy Implementation*, edited by Daniel A. Mazamanian and Paul A. Sabatier, 3–35. D. C. Heath and Co.

Sagor, Richard. 1996. *Local Control and Accountability: How to Get It, Keep It, and Improve School Performance*. Thousand Oaks, Calif.: Corwin Press.

Sanchez, Rene. 1996. "Oakland School System Recognizes 'Black English' as Second Language." *Washington Post*, December 20, A8.

————. 1997. "Mixed Returns on Gift to Education; Expectations for Record Public School Initiative Diminishing." *Washington Post*, October 13, A1.

Sarason, Seymour. 1982. *The Culture of the School and the Problem of Change*. 2nd ed. Boston: Allyn and Bacon.

————. 1991. *The Predictable Failure of Educational Reform: Can We Change Course before It's Too Late?* San Francisco: Jossey-Bass.

————. 1996. *Revisiting the Culture of School and the Problem of Change*. New York: Teachers' College Press.

Savage, Robert. 1978. "Policy Innovativeness as a Trait of American States." *Journal of Politics* 40: 212–24.

Schempp, Paul G., Andrew C. Sparkes, and Thomas J. Templin. 1993. "The Micropolitics of Teacher Education." *American Educational Research Journal* 30: 447–72.

Schuman, Howard, and Stanley Presser. 1981. *Questions and Answers in Attitude Surveys: Experiments on Question Form, Wording, and Context*. New York: Academic Press.

Scott, Hugh. 1976. "The Urban Superintendency on the Brink." *Phi Delta Kappan* 58: 347–48.

Sharkansky, Ira, and Richard Hofferbert. 1969. "Dimensions of State Politics, Economics, and Public Policy." *American Political Science Review* 63: 867–79.

Shepard, Lorrie, and Amelia Kreitzer. 1987. "The Texas Teacher Test." *Educational Researcher* 16 (6): 22–31.

Silberman, Charles. 1970. *Crisis in the Classroom*. Vintage Books.

Simon, Aaron, and David May. 1995. "Washington State Twenty-First Century School Innovations and Practical Expectations of Reform: An Analysis of the Effect of Innovative Education Policy on Student Achievement." Paper presented at the annual meeting of the American Political Science Association, Chicago, August 31–September 3.

Sizer, Theodore. 1968. "The Schools in the City." In *The Metropolitan Enigma: Inquiries into the Nature and Dimensions of America's Urban Crisis*, edited by James Q. Wilson, 87–123. Harvard University Press.

———. 1996a. *Horace's Hope: What Works for the American High School.* Houghton Mifflin.

———. 1996b. "Hard-Won Lessons from the School Reform Battle: A Conversation with Ted Sizer." *The Harvard Education Letter* 12: 3–6.

Skalaban, Andrew. 1992. "Interstate Competition and State Strategies to Deregulate Interstate Banking, 1982–1988." *The Journal of Politics* 54: 793–809.

Skocpol, Theda, and others. 1993. "Women's Associations and the Enactment of Mothers' Pensions in the United States." *American Political Science Review* 87: 686–701.

Slackman, Michael. 1997. "D'Amato Is No Teacher's Pet: Attacks Union Stance on Tenure." *Newsday*, December 18, A3.

Slavin, Robert E. 1994. "Statewide Finance Reform: Ensuring Educational Adequacy for High-Poverty Schools." *Education Policy* 8 (4): 25–34.

Smart, Tim. 1997. "No. 2's No. 1 Problem: The Ritual of Corporate Succession Is Shifting as CEO Turnover Rates Accelerate." *Washington Post*, November 9, H1.

Smith, Louis, and Pat Keith. 1971. *Anatomy of Educational Innovation: An Organizational Analysis of an Elementary School.* John Wiley and Sons.

Smith, Marshall S., and Jennifer A. O'Day. 1991. "Systemic School Reform." In *The Politics of Curriculum and Testing: The 1990 Yearbook of the Political Education Association*, edited by Susan H. Fuhrman and Betty Malen, 233–67. New York: Falmer Press.

Spady, William. 1988. "Organizing for Results: The Basis of Authentic Restructuring and Reform." *Educational Leadership* 46: 4–8.

Sparkman, William E., and Fred Hartmeister. 1995. "The Edgewood Saga Continues: The Texas School Finance System Is Constitutional—But Not out of the Woods Yet." *West's Education Law Quarterly* 4 (4): 666–86.

Stake, Robert. 1986. *Quieting Reform: Social Science and Social Action in an Urban Youth Program.* Urbana: University of Illinois.

Stephens, Scott. 1995a. "Ballot on Cleveland Schools Proposed; Bill Would Put Elected Board's Fate to Vote." *The Plain Dealer*, November 16, 1B.

———. 1995b. "More Mayors Taking Control of Schools." *The Plain Dealer*, October 29, 1B.

Stimson, James. 1990. "A Macro Theory of Information Flow." In *Information and Democratic Processes*, edited by John A. Ferejohn and James H. Kuklinski, 345–68. University of Chicago Press.

Stone, Deborah. 1988. *Policy Paradox and Political Reason.* Harper Collins.

———. 1989. "Causal Stories and the Formation of Policy Agendas." *Political Science Quarterly* 104: 281–300.

Stout, Robert T., Marilyn Tallerico, and Kent P. Scribner. 1995. "Values: The 'What?' of the Politics of Education." In *The Study of Educational Politics*, edited by Jay D. Scribner and Donald H. Layton, 5–20. Washington, D.C.: Falmer Press.

Swanstrom, Todd. 1985. *The Crisis of Growth Politics: Cleveland, Kucinich, and the Challenge of Urban Populism.* Temple University Press.

Tallerico, Marilyn, Wendy Poole, and Joan Burstyn. 1994. "Exits from Urban Superintendencies: The Intersection of Politics, Race, and Gender." *Urban Education* 28: 439–54.

Thompson, Joel. 1981. "Outputs and Outcomes of State Workmen's Compensation Laws." *Journal of Politics* 43: 1129–52.

Tittle, Diana. 1995. *Welcome to Heights High: The Crippling Politics of Restructuring America's Public Schools.* Ohio State University Press.

Toch, Thomas. 1991. *In the Name of Excellence.* New York: Oxford University Press.

Toch, Thomas, and others. 1996. "Why Teachers Don't Teach." *U.S. News and World Report*, February 26, 62.

Tyack, David B. 1974. *The One Best System: A History of American Urban Education.* Harvard University Press.

Tyack, David B., and Larry Cuban. 1995. *Tinkering toward Utopia: A Century of Public School Reform.* Harvard University Press.

Tyack, David B., and William Tobin. 1994. "The Grammar of Schooling: Why Has It Been So Hard to Change?" *American Educational Research Journal* 31: 453–79.

U.S. Department of Education. 1995. *School District Data Book.* Washington, D.C.: National Center for Education Statistics.

———. 1996. *Digest of Education Statistics 1996.* Washington, D.C.: GPO.

———. 1998. *Pursuing Excellence: A Study of U.S. Eighth-Grade Mathematics and Science Teaching, Learning, Curriculum, and Achievement in International Context, Executive Summary.* Washington, D.C.: GPO.

Vergari, Sandra. 1995. "School Finance Reform in the State of Michigan." *Journal of Education Finance* 21 (2): 254–70.

Verstegen, Deborah A. 1994. "The New Wave of School Finance Litigation." *Phi Delta Kappan* 76 (3): 243–50.

Verstegen, Deborah A., and Kent C. McGuire. 1991. "The Dialectic of Reform." *Educational Policy* 5 (4): 386–411.

Wagner, Tony. 1994. *How Schools Change: Lessons from Three Communities.* Boston: Beacon Press.

Walker, Decker. 1992. "Curriculum Policymaking." In *Encyclopedia of Educational Research,* 6th ed., edited by Marvin Alkin and others, 280–86. MacMillan.

Walker, Jack L. 1969. "The Diffusion of Innovations among the American States." *American Political Science Review* 63: 880–99.

———. 1973. "Comment: Problems in Research on the Diffusion of Policy Innovations." *American Political Science Review* 67: 1186–91.

Wallace, Richard. 1996. *From Vision to Practice: The Art of Educational Leadership.* Thousand Oaks, Calif.: Corwin Press.

Washington Post. 1995. "Engaging Teachers' Interest." January 12, A26.

Wayland, Sloan R. 1964. "Structural Features of American Education as Basic

Factors in Innovation." In *Innovation in Education*, edited by Matthew B. Miles, 587–613. New York: Teachers' College Press.

Weaver, R. Kent. 1986. "The Politics of Blame Avoidance." *Journal of Public Policy* 6: 371–98.

Wehlage, Gary, Gregory Smith, and Pauline Lipman. 1992. "Restructuring Urban Schools: The New Futures Experience." *American Educational Research Journal* 29: 51–93.

Weick, Karl. 1976. "Educational Organizations as Loosely Coupled Systems." *Administrative Science Quarterly* 21: 1–19.

Wells, Amy Stuart. 1986. *A Study of Education Reporting in American Newspapers*. Master's thesis, College of Communication, Boston University.

———. 1993. "The Sociology of School Choice: Why Some Win and Others Lose in the Educational Marketplace." In *School Choice: Examining the Evidence*, edited by Edith Rasell and Richard Rothstein, 29–48. Washington, D.C.: Economic Policy Institute.

Willis, Frances G., and Kent D. Peterson. 1992. "External Pressures for Reform and Strategy Formation at the District Level: Superintendents' Interpretations of State Demands." *Educational Evaluation and Policy Analysis* 14 (3): 241–60.

Willower, Donald J. 1992. "Educational Administration: Intellectual Trends." In *Encyclopedia of Educational Research,* 6th ed., edited by Marvin Alkin and others, 364–75. MacMillan.

Wilson, James Q. 1989. *Bureaucracy: What Government Agencies Do and Why They Do It*. Basic Books.

Wirt, Frederick M., and Michael W. Kirst. 1972. *The Political Web of American Schools*. Little, Brown.

———. 1989. *Schools in Conflict*. Berkeley, Calif.: McCutchan Publishing.

Wohlstetter, Priscilla. 1995. "Getting School-Based Management Right: What Works and What Doesn't." *Phi Delta Kappan* 77 (1): 22–26.

Wohlstetter, Priscilla, Susan A. Mohrman, and Peter J. Robertson. 1997. "Successful School-Based Management: A Lesson for Restructuring Urban Schools." In *New Schools for a New Century: The Redesign of Urban Education*, edited by Diane Ravitch and Joseph P. Viteritti, 201–25. Yale University Press.

Zeigler, L. Harmon, and M. Kent Jennings. 1974. *Governing American Schools: Political Interaction in Local School Districts*. North Scituate, Mass.: Duxbury Press.

Zeigler, L. Harmon, Ellen Kehoe, and Jane Reisman. 1985. *City Managers and School Superintendents: Response to Community Conflict*. Praeger.

Index

153–54, 193–202. *See also* Policy churn; School reforms

Tax abatement, as city political tool, 41n
Teachers' unions: effect on school productivity, 20–21; evaluation of reforms, 46, 171–72; reform role, 59–60, 77–81, 96, 113, 115–16, 147–48, 163, 169; study representation, 24, 196
Teaching practices, U.S.: administrative control issues, 37–39, 179, 181–82; evaluation difficulties, 36–38; lack of change, 10, 12n, 179; study, 8
Tennessee, 45, 166
Testing. *See* Student performance
Texas, 84, 172; Amarillo, 74; Dallas, 59; Fort Worth, 74; Houston, 200n; San Antonio, 142; Tyler, 134
Texas Teacher Test, 155
Third International Mathematics and Science Study *(1995)*, 8
Third Wave reforms, 3n, 4n, 12n, 15, 24, 29, 51, 110, 177–78; cost comparisons, 109–110; curriculum, 26, 108; minority concerns, 147; performance evaluation, 26, 108; professional development, 27, 108; public awareness, 91–92, 95; scheduling measures, 25–26, 108–13, 115–18,

120–22; school board role, 59, 190; site-based management (SBM), 27, 45, 107–11, 113–123, 133–34, 155, 167–72, 195n; state role, 60, 82–86; teachers' union role, 60, 77–81
Tinkering Towards Utopia (Tyack and Cuban), 18
Tittle, Diane, 17–18
Tobin, William, 152
Tyack, David, 3n, 9n, 18, 125, 152

Unions. *See* Teachers' unions
Urban League, 148, 196
Urban school reforms. *See* School reforms
Utah, 146

Vermont, assessment reform, 34
Virginia, statewide testing, 183

Wagner, Tony, 156
Washington (state), 84, 169
Welcome to Heights High (Tittle), 17–18
Western Europe, standardized testing, 32, 182–83
Wilson, James Q., 40
Wisconsin, 42n, 53, 74, 81, 95

Breinigsville, PA USA
21 January 2011
253858BV00002B/32/A

9 780815 736356